EMBRACING AN UNCERTAIN RETIREMENT

MAKING BETTER FINANCIAL DECISIONS
WHEN YOU DON'T KNOW WHAT WILL HAPPEN NEXT

TAYLOR STEWART

Independently published

Cover design by Avery Harrison Meginnis

ISBN Print: 979-8-6748405-7-2

Printed in the United States of America
First Printing 2021
First Edition
10 9 8 7 6 5 4 3 2 1

em•brace

em-breys

1. to take or receive gladly or eagerly; accept willingly

un•cer•tain

uhn-sur-tn

1. not definitely ascertainable or fixed, as in time of occurrence, number, dimensions, or quality.

2. not confident, assured, or free from hesitancy

3. not clearly or precisely determined; indefinite; unknown

4. subject to change; variable; capricious; unstable

5. vague; indistinct; not perfectly apprehended

6. ambiguous; unreliable; undependable

7. dependent on chance or unpredictable factors; doubtful; of unforeseeable outcome or effect

CONTENTS

Introduction   1

Part I An Overview

1   Groundwork   23
2   Framework   37
3   Forecasting   57

Part II Deep Dive

4   Longevity   89
5   Introduction to Outflows   97
6   Spending   103
7   Inflation   111
8   Insurance   119
9   Health Care   129
10   Taxes   145
11   Summary of Outflows   161
12   Introduction to Inflows   163
13   Social Security   165
14   Pensions   175
15   Introduction to Inside Sources   181
16   Risk and Return   183
17   Cash   197
18   Bonds   201
19   Stocks   209
20   Blended portfolio   227
21   Creating Income From Investments   231
22   Investing in Stocks   251
23   Annuities   273

24	Life Insurance	291
25	Real Estate	307
26	Summary of Risk and Return	311
27	Summary of Inflows	313
28	Summary of the Deep Dive	315

Part III Decision Time

29	Get Out of My (Own) Way!	319
30	Advisors	343
31	Parting Thoughts	369

Acknowledgments	377
About the Author	379
Recommended Reading	381
Notes	383

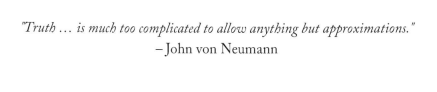

"Truth ... is much too complicated to allow anything but approximations."
– John von Neumann

INTRODUCTION

I feel for the person planning for retirement today. They suffer a special kind of torture, much like that of a sailor stranded at sea. They each know what they need (water for the sailor, advice for the retiree), and they're surrounded by plenty of it. The cruel part is, they can't trust it. Why? Because despite the appearance of being what they need, there are impurities in it that can effectively act as a poison if consumed without discretion.

Here's the good news. With the proper knowledge and tools, both the sailor and the retiree can filter these impurities and extract what they need. If you give the sailor a pot and the know-how to boil water, they can get along just fine. Similar methods exist for the retiree, and in a way, that's the goal of this book; to equip the reader with the knowledge and tools to extract what they actually need from the sea of information and advice they are forced to swim in.

The conception of this book came from trying to answer a seemingly simple question. During a training event in 2019, I was sharing with a friend and fellow advisor my questions and thoughts on the material that had just been presented. I don't remember which comment of mine prompted his response, but with a tinge of annoyance, my friend said to me, "Taylor, I hear you talk a lot about what doesn't work, but what do you believe does work?"

As I recall it, I didn't respond verbally but instead paused and turned inward. I asked myself, "What *do* I believe?" This was hardly the first time someone had grown tired of my questioning, but annoyance wasn't my point or purpose. I wanted to know *why*.

I have found "Why?" to be a powerful and surprisingly complex question. The answer is key to discovery and learning, yet it is rarely obvious despite its apparent simplicity. However, I've also found that if we continue asking "Why?" the answer will eventually reveal itself. This book is the culmination of many years' incessantly asking "Why?" as it relates to financial planning.

To understand my passion for "Why?" and why it ultimately led to me writing this book, it will be helpful to understand my life up to this point. I recognize that no one is reading this book to hear about Taylor Stewart, but I've also read quite a few books myself, and I know that the author is a human with their own views and experiences that influence the words they write, especially on topics like money. Sometimes the author's beliefs and incentives are clear; other times, you have to piece them together or guess. I imagine every author feels this way, but I'm fairly certain this book is unlike any retirement book you've ever read. Without the proper context, some of these ideas could be misconstrued. So, to help you understand the spirit of this book and the experiences that shaped my views, it's worth spending a few minutes telling you about myself.

I should start by explaining how I came to be a "financial advisor." For some, it starts with an interest in school, a persuasive recruiter, or a general passion for money and helping people. While I can relate to this last reason, my journey started even earlier. You see, my father, Owen, has been a financial advisor since the year before I was born. I quite literally grew up looking at investment portfolios and insurance illustrations, having after-dinner conversations about tax laws and interest rate moves, and tagging along to outings and client meetings.

Like many kids, I idolized (and surely, idealized) what Dad did. Around age 10, I decided that if my quest to challenge Tiger Woods on the PGA Tour didn't pan out (it didn't), then my dream was to become a financial advisor. I even figured I could become an advisor after my golf career to help all my fellow tour pros. I had it bad. I truly believed that being a financial advisor was second in nobility to being a doctor, with your financial wealth being the next most important thing to protect after your physical health.

My interest in becoming an advisor progressed into formal degrees in accounting and finance. As tends to happen for accounting majors, I was funneled into my first job as an auditor at one of the "Big 4" accounting firms. If you're less familiar with what an auditor does, there are two ways to describe it. There's the honorable definition, "protecting the integrity of the capital markets by assuring that what a company tells investors is reasonably accurate (without material misrepresentation, to be exact)." And then there's the CliffsNotes definition, "they check other people's work."

While the latter description sounds derisive, there's actually an art to it. Checking others' work is not the same as recalculating. We don't just say, "Yes, 2 + 2 does equal 4. Good job!" No, to truly know how to check people's work, you need to know how to *think* a certain way. You need to be able to put yourself in the company or individuals' shoes and understand what incentives they have. You must understand where the numbers came from, what formulas were used, what inputs are assumptions, and what are facts. From there, you verify facts and evaluate the validity of assumptions by asking how they came up with their assumptions, or better yet, *why* did they assume what they did?

On Day 1, auditors are taught the standard of *professional skepticism*, which essentially means to not blindly accept what the company tells you but to make them prove it. You must take nothing at face value and question everything.

If you're thinking this job sounds annoying, it is. While the role auditors serve is a necessary evil, I knew from that same Day 1 that my heart wasn't in it—being an auditor is not a punishment you tolerate if you have no aspirations of climbing the accounting ladder. I did, however, learn *how to think* like an auditor. I certainly didn't realize it at the time, but this way of thinking about finances (and all things, for that matter), of disaggregating then verifying, I have taken with me, and it continues to shape how I evaluate strategies, products, and decisions as an advisor to this day.

After serving my obligatory three years as an auditor, it was time to move on. Before I even began searching, I received a call from a mid-size financial planning firm in town. Financial planning wasn't on my radar at the time, but remembering the dreams of my youth, I went in for an interview. I had one prior experience interviewing with a very large financial planning firm when I was in college. That interview consisted mostly of touting how much time I could take off and required me to list 50 people I could call and estimate how much money they had. I found this to be quite strange at the time. Thinking that experience was an anomaly, I approached this new interview full of optimism. However, this optimism was short-lived as I was again asked to list 50 people I could call and estimate how much money they had. (I later realized and will explain why I was asked to do this.)

Confused and slightly concerned but having had the fire to be an advisor rekindled, I called Owen to discuss where else I should look. It was then that he floated the idea of us working together. A long hinted at, but never directly spoken about, dream for both of us became a reality.

While at first, it felt like a dream, it quickly began to feel like a nightmare. I soon realized that my affinity for the financial planning industry was not widely shared, to say the least. That's because, in my childish ignorance, I never stopped to consider how "financial advisors" were paid. All I knew was that they analyzed illustrations and reports, created financial plans, and met with people—numbers and people, two of my favorite things. In all my conversations with Owen over the years, we only discussed concepts and features, never commissions and fees.

Looking back, I now laugh (on two occasions until I've cried) at how naïve I was. With my hand on the Bible, I can say that I didn't know financial advisors "sold" anything. (Although this did explain why the previous two companies I interviewed with were so concerned with the net worth of my friends and family.) I always thought advisors gave advice like doctors gave prescriptions. I thought we were helping people, and they were grateful for it. I didn't realize that for many people, "life insurance" was a euphemism for snake oil.

I struggled mightily with this contradiction. I was never quiet about my confusion, hence why I previously said my conversation in 2019 was hardly the first time someone had grown tired of my questioning. Aside from Owen, most people's responses were a mix of "That's just the way it is" or, "You just don't understand it yet."

I was learning to co-exist with the industry until March of 2020. As we all know, the markets crashed, and fear, panic, and uncertainty abounded. The response from our industry shook me to my core, and a line in the moral sand was crossed. Rather than serving people, I saw advisors engaged in a feeding frenzy reminiscent of something you would see on the Discovery Channel that was based on fear-mongering and self-serving advice. More so than ever, I was embarrassed to call myself an advisor.

Truly disgusted, I remembered my friend's question and began to write down what I believed was wrong with the industry. Except for this time, I also began to write down what I believed we should do instead. At the time, I planned to leave the industry, but as I began to write my "goodbye letter," the scattering of thoughts I had put down began to crystallize into something of a framework. Realizing this framework could perhaps do some good for people, rather than throwing in the towel, I expanded my letter into the book you are now holding. While it may have been born out of frustration, this book was nurtured by a love for financial planning that comes from a child seeing his cherished dream job tarnished and fighting to restore its honor. While I still believe this industry can be what I thought it was, I did not write it to change the industry; I wrote it to help those who have to deal with it make better financial decisions.

So far, I've had mostly nice things to say about myself. I know advisors are supposed to paint a picture of stability and trust and whatnot, but I'm not all that interested in creating a facade. You see, I left out an important part of my journey to this point, and many of the concepts in this book won't fully make sense without understanding what I consider to be my greatest "gift."

While I can appreciate my experience as an auditor now, at the time, I hated being an auditor. Like *really* hated it. Most auditors joke about being an alcoholic; when you're regularly working 100 hours a week, you don't always cope in the healthiest of ways. The thing is, I actually am one. I know. For some, that's a turnoff. But here's the rest of the story; I'm also a *gratefully recovered* alcoholic. The word "gratefully" gets thrown around a lot, but I have a personal definition for it. I don't believe you are truly grateful for an experience until you would honestly not go back and change it if you could, which is exactly how I feel about being an alcoholic. Let me explain why.

Before sobriety, I had a world view about as wide as a pinhole. I could see two things, 1) my perspective, and 2) when others didn't share mine. I was the guy who would passionately argue why my team or opinion or worldview was right, yours was wrong, and that you should change yours because I know what's best for you, and I'm trying to help you.

You probably know that AA has 12 Steps, but my life-changing moment occurred during Steps 4 and 5. For those less familiar, Step 4 asks you to list out all your resentments, and in Step 5, you share them with someone else. I listed my petty resentments and was just a few minutes into Step 5 when the person I was sharing with quite irritably slammed his fist on the table to make me stop. He'd heard enough and proceeded to lay out what AA calls an "inventory of defects." What he said about me was mean, offensive, hurtful, and gosh dang it, every last word of it was true.

My life changed right then and there. I sat dumbfounded as if told that we breathe water and drink air, except it was true. I had been so confident, yet so wrong. I began to wonder how I could be so blind and where else the truth was hiding in plain sight.

Good for me, right? But what does this have to do with financial planning? Well, it taught me a crucial lesson: Not everything is as it seems. I quickly realized the hazard of a closed mind; so many ideas I had dismissed were completely valid. This realization also removed the fear of being wrong, or perhaps even more impactful, showed me the *value* of being proven wrong. Sure, I'd rather be right, but being proven wrong is far better than being wrong and not knowing it.

I found this new perspective incredibly liberating—it's amazing how your views (and advice) will change when you no longer have a "side" you need to protect. I began actively seeking out where else I was wrong and joyfully uncovering the fallacies and biases I was so guilty of committing. It didn't take long for me to apply this perspective to my job as an advisor. When I gazed upon my profession and the topic of financial planning with this new pair of glasses, it all started to make sense. Here's what I found.

At first, I wanted to know why the retiree must suffer the fate of a stranded sailor, why they can't trust the advice they are surrounded by. That was actually pretty easy to answer. I'll further explain in Chapter 30, but essentially, what people want from advisors and what advisors are *incentivized* to give do not align.

What do people want? All else being equal, people want more money. Duh. But when things are not equal, there are varying degrees of risk or uncertainty they're willing to accept in order to have more money. At the most basic level, people want to make sure they'll be okay and are being good stewards of their money. (Again, there are varying degrees of what "okay" means.) If they don't know how to provide that for themselves, they may seek help or advice, likely from someone trained to give advice on these topics, such as a "financial advisor."

In theory, working with such an advisor should solve their problem. But given the reputation advisors have, something must be amiss. Something is amiss because advisors are not incentivized just to give good advice. Here's what I mean.

First, let's be clear about the role of incentives. Incentives do not affect every person, but if applied to enough people or the same person for a long enough period, there will be a change in behavior. If enough individuals change their behavior, the whole group gets a reputation. So what is the advisor's incentive?

It's partially true that advisors are incentivized to give good advice, but the fact is, most advisors are not paid to give advice; they're paid to *move money*. (When you buy insurance or hire an advisor to manage your investments, you "move money.") The advisor may advise you on what to invest in or what insurance to buy, but there is no compensation unless money is moved. This is where it gets murky. Advisors still give advice, but they don't get paid unless their advice results in money being moved.

That might seem like a simple and obvious statement, but there is one obvious and one less obvious but profound takeaway from it. The obvious takeaway is that advisors' advice often involves money being moved. This is where the "they're just trying to sell me something" reputation comes from. But to identify the second takeaway, we need to think a level deeper. If they're only paid when you move money, that means for them to be paid, yes, you have to move money, but it also means that you followed their advice. At first, this might seem logical; they should only get paid for advice people follow. But we must consider what kind of advice this encourages. First, it could encourage them to tell you what you want to hear since you're more likely to follow things you already believe, which obviously may not be the best advice for you. Second, if you don't already believe it, then they must *convince* you to follow it.

Again, this may seem logical. But we must realize that convincing is a short hop from manipulating. Sometimes you need to be convinced to do things that are good for you, but sometimes you can be convinced to do things that aren't good for you but are good for the convincer. If enough people are "convinced" to do things that aren't good for them, the reputation of the people giving the advice will sour. So at the end of the day, the advisor's incentive is not just to give good advice; it's to give advice that appears good enough to convince you to move money. I believe this conflict is at the root of most of the problems people have with advisors.

This realization led me next to ask, what kind of advice is convincing? We'll talk about greed and fear in Chapter 1, but I find many people follow advice from people they "trust." Where does trust come from? There are many sources, but in this context, it usually comes from confidence in the "advice-givers" competence. Confidence and competence have a tricky circular relationship. The appearance of one can imply the existence of the other. A quick example explains.

Imagine you have to choose between two pilots who will fly you. Pilot A tells you, "I will get you there safely," and Pilot B says, "I probably will get you there safely." Based on that response, you'll likely trust Pilot A. But what about their competence? Pilot A has flown for 20 hours, and Pilot B has flown for 20,000 hours. Hmm, now you'll likely trust Pilot B.

Notice the lesson in this example. *In the absence of further information, confidence can create the illusion of competence.* I realized that advisors are incentivized to portray confidence to build trust that encourages people to follow their advice.

As we'll see, sometimes confidence can be used to manipulate. It's easy to stop there and blame the "advice-giver," but then I thought about the other side of the transaction and wondered, "Why do people follow confident advice?" There's actually a lot of psychological research that directly answers my question.

We need to think about what confidence is. Several snippets from the dictionary include words like "full trust," "certitude," and "assurance." The definition of certitude is "absolute certainty or conviction that something is the case." Essentially, if you're confident about something, it means you have a belief about or a feeling that you know what the outcome will be.

But what if you don't have confidence? If you don't have confidence, you lack certitude, and if you lack certitude, you lack absolute certainty. In other words, you are uncertain. What do you do when you lack certainty? You look for someone who has it.

And that's what the research confirms. When people don't know what is going to happen—when they lack a belief or feeling that they know what the outcome will be—they look for someone who has that belief or feeling, someone who is confident. All else equal, people will follow a confident person, whether they're right or not, over a less confident person.

So the answer to my question, "Why do people follow confident advice?" is again simple. People follow confident advice because they are uncertain. Uncertainty is an uncomfortable feeling, and people wish to get rid of uncomfortable feelings, and following confident advice does just that. We follow confidence because we want to feel confident ourselves.

I then began to focus on people's relationship with uncertainty. I found people either resisted, denied, or were held captive by it. People deny uncertainty when they try to optimize for specific outcomes, ignoring what could happen if they're wrong. They resist it when they try to outrun it, like investing money they can't afford to lose but believing they can time when to sell to avoid getting hurt. They're held captive by it when they are fearful of taking any risk whatsoever.

While I can understand where all these relationships come from, they all seemed to be missing something. I toiled with this in my mind until it started to sound familiar. All of these relationships were futile. Uncertainty is a fact of life, so denying uncertainty, like denying gravity, is just delusional. Resisting uncertainty by thinking you can outsmart it is like being Tantalus of Greek mythology;[1] it's striving for something you can never attain. And being held captive by uncertainty is like being the dog who cowers in front of the vacuum cleaner; it leads to a life of unnecessary fear. If resisting, denying, and submitting to uncertainty doesn't work, then our only other option is to accept it.

Acceptance is a funny word. We all nod along when we hear it but never like to practice it. Some think acceptance is akin to apathy or giving in. Not at all. Acceptance doesn't mean you deny how you feel; it means you acknowledge that it's okay to feel that way. You don't deny it. You don't resist it. You aren't held captive by it. No, acceptance means you work *with* it. That's how you handle uncertainty.

And that's what this book is about, embracing uncertainty. As I'll explain, when we embrace uncertainty rather than resist or deny it, we can begin to make better financial decisions when we don't know what will happen next (which just so happens to be the subtitle of this book.) That's an admittedly vague and ambitious objective, so the following will clarify what that means.

The word "financial" clearly implies that we're discussing *money*, but more specifically, we will focus on the stage of life when we *rely on our money to go to work for us*—what we call retirement.

Making "decisions" requires us to make choices, and we make choices about what to do or think. Since we don't make choices about the past, this book is necessarily about *what to do next*.

The most important concept to clarify is what a "better" decision is. If we can determine that something is better, that implies we can measure it and compare it to others. Since the word is used in the context of making decisions, this suggests we can measure or rate our decisions. But how or when do we measure our decisions? The usual practice is to evaluate in hindsight; we deem a coach's play call good or bad based on how many yards it gains, or an investment decision good or bad depending on how much money it makes. But this method is flawed and introduces a central point to this book: *we cannot determine the quality of our decisions based on the outcome.*

I can explain why with an example. Suppose you run across a busy highway and survive unscathed. Since you didn't get hit by a car, did you make a good decision? What if five of you run across, but this time, one of you gets hit. Did four of you make a good decision, and one of you make a bad decision? Clearly not. The decision wasn't good because we know if we keep running across a busy highway, eventually we'll get hit. Hopefully, none of us are running across busy highways, but many of us will likely attempt the financial equivalent, such as trying to time the market, optimizing for specific outcomes, and neglecting to protect against large threats. "Surviving" these decisions doesn't mean we made a good one.[2]

So, a good outcome does not mean a good decision was made, and consequently, a good decision does not guarantee a good outcome will occur. This also means a good decision can have a bad outcome, and a bad decision can have a good outcome.

Making this distinction matters because we often use past outcomes to make decisions about the future. If an outcome was good (not getting hit by a car), we might think the decision (running across a busy highway) was good and be inclined to repeat it—even if the decision was actually "bad." If we keep repeating bad decisions, eventually, we'll get hit by a car. Again, while it's evident in this example the decision was bad, it's less clear when evaluating financial decisions. Was investing all your money in stocks a good decision since the market didn't crash? Was not having insurance a good decision since you didn't get sick?

If we can't evaluate decisions based on the outcome, that means we must evaluate them at the beginning. So what makes a decision "good" from the beginning? We could say it is the one that gives us the highest chance of "success," but this definition is lacking on two fronts. First, what is "success?" Success could be attaining the best outcome (e.g., making the most money), or it could be avoiding a bad outcome (e.g., not losing money), in which case we could rephrase success as "minimizing the chance of failure." For now, we'll say a good decision is one that gives us the highest chance of experiencing the outcome we want.

But there is a more glaring problem with this definition. Regardless of how we define success, when we use a word like "chance," we are implying probability. Probabilities can be quantified. Sometimes we can know the probability absolutely. For example, we know a "fair" coin flip has a 50/50 chance of landing on heads or tails. Sometimes we *think* we can know the probability based on a record of what has happened in the past. For example, we think a healthy 65-year-old has a 50% chance of living to age 84 because that is when half of the healthy 65-year-olds died in the past (this is how life expectancy is calculated). When we can quantify the probability, we are dealing in the domain of risk. When we cannot quantify the probability, we enter the domain of uncertainty.[3]

How we react, i.e., make decisions (and also what determines if a decision is good or not), usually varies based on whether we are dealing in the domain of risk or uncertainty. With risk, we have the option of insuring or taking "calculated risks" because we can quantify and define all possible outcomes. In this case, we can take the "poker player" approach—not expecting to win every hand but making the decisions that stack the odds in our favor over the course of many hands. With uncertainty, we cannot calculate the odds and thus cannot insure and cannot calculate the risk we are taking. In this case, the wisest response is to minimize the chance of disaster, or as Leonard "Jimmie" Savage called it: "minimax regret," i.e., minimize the maximum regret.

Regret itself is a feeling and quite subjective. Regret comes from wishing the outcome was different than it is, and we usually wish for better outcomes. This means regret is felt when we wish the outcome was better than it was. A better outcome may mean that we lost less or gained more, and lead to comments like, "I wish I had bought ABC," or "I wish I had sold XYZ." But here's the thing, we have to evaluate regret now, when making the decision, not after. We have to look at what outcome we'd regret standing here today.

For example, assume you have two choices. With Choice A, you could make $1 million, but you could also lose $1 million. Choice B eliminates the chance of losing $1 million and also eliminates the chance of making $1 million. You'd probably regret losing $1 million more than making $1 million, so you make the decision that minimizes the chance of losing $1 million (Choice B). By doing so, you had to give up the potential upside of making $1 million.

Here's the crucial takeaway. The decision that minimizes regret now may not be the optimal choice in hindsight, but it is the optimal choice in the moment with incomplete and imperfect information. This again means the best decision may not have the best outcome. If the bad outcome doesn't happen and you later find out you could have instead made $1 million if you'd chosen Choice A, yes, you might regret that, but you regret it less than the alternative.

While there is a formal difference between risk and uncertainty, they share an important commonality—we don't know for sure what the outcome will be. For this reason, I will use them interchangeably throughout the book. We can also link the definitions of risk and regret. Risk is a dynamic word with multiple definitions. There is the quantifiable definition, such as "volatility." There is the more eloquent definition, "more things can happen than will happen." A spinoff of this definition that I think captures the spirit of what risk is to people is "the possibility that bad stuff can happen." Of course, the word "bad" is subjective, so more precisely, risk is "the possibility that stuff we don't want to happen happens." When stuff we don't want to happen happens, it leads to regret. So, when making decisions, we want to minimize the possibility that stuff we don't want to happen happens.

We can now give this book a comically long description and say that it is about *making choices of what to do with the money that is going to work for you that minimizes the possibility that stuff we don't want to happen happens when you don't know what will happen next.*

To show how to do this, the book will oscillate between the conceptual and technical. Much of its length comes from building each concept from the ground up—sometimes, the easiest way to explain the number three is first to describe the numbers one and two. Despite its length, it is not exhaustive. There are too many intricacies to retirement planning, and it is impossible to cover every caveat and exception, leaving nothing in this book beyond reproach.

We begin in Part I by laying the groundwork, understanding what money is, what retirement is, what our fears are, why we plan, and what retirement planning really means. We will then see a framework for evaluating these decisions both quantitatively and qualitatively and discuss the intrinsic challenges of prediction. Part II looks closer at each of the assumptions made when we plan and examines the different tools at our disposal. Part III reviews how we get in our own way, touring the thriving field of behavioral economics, before ending with a jarring look at the industry that deals in financial advice.

It is easy to believe that information is the most important ingredient to making good decisions, but information is just part of the recipe. Equally important is *how you think*. This book is not light on information, but the true goal of this book, which doubles as my goal as an advisor, is not to tell you *what* to think; it is to help you understand *how* to think about the decisions you must make when planning for retirement.

How to think in the face of uncertainty doesn't come naturally to us. Our natural tendency is to react or intervene because doing something makes us feel better—it makes us feel in control. But there is too much in life that we cannot control for this to be productive. The key is to determine what we can and cannot control. For the things we can control, we do what we can. For the things we cannot, we accept it. That means determining what we can and cannot control is of the utmost importance. (Yes, I just rephrased the famous Serenity Prayer.)[4] That's what this book does. It helps you determine what you can and cannot control, shows you what to do about the things you can, and how to best position yourself for the things you cannot.

I recognize that this way of approaching finances is different. We're so used to optimizing, maximizing, striving for efficiency, etc., but we need to change the way we approach financial decision-making. Despite the plethora of data and advances in computing power, there is still an inherent limitation to our ability to predict. Most prediction relies on analyzing the past to divine the future, but there is a difference between understanding how things came to be and knowing how things *will* be.

When we evaluate things in hindsight, it's easy to declare a winner and loser, who was right and wrong, and what decision was good and bad, so we get used to this way of thinking.[5] But in the present, financial decisions are not that cut and dry. There are too many variables and differences amongst the people making the decisions. Thus, the best (and most frustrating) answer to what makes a good decision is usually, "it depends." I use the following three principles to remind myself of this ambiguity and guide how I think.

First, we must recognize that truth itself is often subjective. This idea again goes against our natural wiring and preference for the binary. We prefer matters to be concrete and absolute, not abstract and contingent. To understand what I mean, look at the figure below.

6

What is this figure? If you laid this book down flat, you'd confidently tell me "six." However, if someone were standing across from you, they'd tell me "nine." Neither of you is wrong; it's just a matter of perspective.

The subjective nature of truth can hide the second paradoxical lesson: despite there being multiple "right" answers, there can also be definitively "wrong" answers. For example, there is no perspective of the above figure that would make "seven" a correct answer.

The third and final lesson is that how we experience life is relative. We see this in the physical world with time, temperature, and distance. Is 6 miles a long way? It depends if you're walking or riding in a car. Is 6 minutes a long time? It depends if you're warmly snuggled up in bed, hitting the snooze button, or at the gym sweating out a plank. Would you walk across the street to save $6? It depends if you're buying a cup of coffee or a new car.

And so it is with financial planning. There can simultaneously be multiple right ways and definitively wrong ways to manage our money. The same advice can be both good and bad depending on who it is given to, and it ultimately depends on each person's circumstances and values. This means we must remain open to multiple right answers yet not be afraid to declare something wrong when it is. This is different than the confident, absolutist, and dogmatic advice we are accustomed to hearing. But remember, while confident and dogmatic advice may be convincing, what is convincing may not be good for you. If advice isn't good for you, it can lead to bad decisions, and bad decisions can lead to getting hit by a car.

The subjective and relative nature of truth explains why, compared to its peers in the genre, this book lacks case studies—vignettes designed to apply the material into a "real-life" example. While case studies can be helpful in explaining concepts, they also usually lead to conclusions. I initially planned for Part III to be a collection of case studies but became troubled upon writing them. By designing the case studies, I am in complete control and must determine the outcome of every variable. Depending on the outcomes I select, certain tools (i.e., places to put your money, like stocks or insurance) and strategies will appear better or worse, which favors some over others. This presents a trio of problems. First, choosing favorites is not the purpose of this book. Second (and most importantly), no tool is best in every situation; it depends on multiple factors, which leads to the third problem. Illuminating every possible factor is too large a task. Instead, I attempt to identify when a tool is best by identifying the most important variables and outcomes that swing the analysis, taking care to point out what we can and cannot control.

The dilemma faced when designing case studies is a microcosm of the broader advice giver/receiver relationship. There are too many scenarios to cover, so we must sample only a few. We can derive a very different interpretation of the same story depending on which scenarios we cover. Which scenarios the "advice-giver" chooses to cover likely depends on the outcome they hope to generate. As we now know, when the best outcome for the advice-giver differs from the best outcome for the advice-receiver, we have a problem.

I bring this introduction to a close by clarifying what embracing uncertainty really means and explaining why it can actually lead to a better life in general. To embrace means to accept completely. As I said, acceptance isn't apathy. It doesn't mean pretending you don't feel the way you do, and it's not akin to giving up. It's far from it, and in fact, it makes life easier.

It's not a coincidence that grief isn't complete, and sobriety can't begin until there's acceptance because only then are you dealing in reality. You must deal with reality to bring your expectations in line with reality, and when your expectations are in line with reality, you can improve your decisions and prevent the costly ones. Here's what I mean.

How we interpret an experience (i.e., the emotions we feel) is determined by the gap between reality and our expectations. For example, if someone hands you a $100 bill, what do you feel? If it's a stranger in line at the store, you're thrilled. If it's your boss giving you your Christmas bonus, you're "not thrilled." Either way, it is not the receiving of $100 that crafts your interpretation; it is receiving the $100 compared to your expectations of what would happen.

We can learn two things from the gap. First, the direction of the gap determines the type of emotion—a positive gap leads to positive emotions (happy, excited), and a negative gap leads to negative emotions (disappointed, upset). Second, the size of the gap determines the intensity of emotion—a big gap is shocking while a small gap is mildly surprising. Here's why this is important. When people are surprised, they tend to (over) react, and these reactions can lead to "bad" decisions that often prove costly, like selling all of your investments because their values dropped more than expected. So not only do better expectations lead to better experiences, but it also helps prevent bad decisions.

Where does uncertainty fit into this? Uncertainty itself is a feeling and comes from not knowing what to expect. So uncertainty bites us before the gap even appears. Since we want to eliminate this feeling, many people will prefer a bad expectation to no expectation and will jump to the expectation that makes the most sense (or was presented most confidently) and make decisions accordingly. Conversely, if you embrace uncertainty, you realize the limit of your expectations, prepare for multiple outcomes, and subsequently are less surprised by the results and don't overreact. Here's an example.

Consider the question, "What is the market going to do?" If someone expects it to go down, they'll likely sell. If it goes up, they're upset (because the gap between reality and their expectation was negative), and to remedy this feeling, they might soon buy right before the market falls. If the market did go down and they were right, they likely feel emboldened and might double down (a result of overconfidence). The exact opposite will occur if someone initially expects the market to go up and it instead goes down.

How about the person that embraces uncertainty? They say, "I don't know what the market's going to do. It will probably go up in the long run, but it might go down in the short-run, so I'm only going to invest money I can afford to lose in the short run." Whether the market goes up or down, this person is unaffected and thus has a cool head to reassess and won't be prone to emotional overreactions.

The person who resists uncertainty, expecting to control and predict the future, is set up for disappointment. The harder they try to control, the bigger the gap and the more frustrated they will be when they can't. This type of person is easy to spot. They try to model every detail on a spreadsheet and check their accounts daily as if somehow the market cares how much they care. They worry and second guess as if they somehow "should have (or could have) known" what to do at all times. Like Tantalus, they'll never reach their goal.

Admittedly, very few truly accept uncertainty, but if you can, you may even begin to smile at your new friend when it rears its head. For it is the unpredictability of life that makes it the beautiful journey that it is. Yes, getting blindsided isn't fun, but if you're honest with yourself, after a while, a frictionless life where all goes as planned will soon lose its flavor. You can't enjoy your highs if you're always high. If your favorite sports team won every game they played, you'd eventually stop watching. Blowouts are less stressful, but it's the nail-biters we all remember. Risk only exists when we don't know for sure what will happen, and without risk, nothing changes. It is uncertainty that makes us get up in the morning, work hard, and try to be our best selves. Just as a movie is ruined when you know the ending, consider how your life would change if you knew how and when you die. We all know we will, but the lack of specifics keeps us pushing forward.

To tame any opponent, you must first learn what gives it life. You must understand its qualities, what it likes and dislikes, what causes it to thrive, and what causes it to retreat. You must also study yourself. When faced with uncertainty, what do you feel, how do you react? Doubtless, uncertainty has burned us all, but not all that hurts us is evil. Pain is perhaps the greatest teacher of all.

We will never eradicate uncertainty, but we can, like a river, harness it and use it to our advantage. The way to harness a river is not to fight it but to accept what it does and work with it. The same goes for uncertainty. So, let's stop fighting it and start embracing it.

PART I
AN OVERVIEW

1

GROUNDWORK

Money is fascinating. It's a tool and a drug, a cure and a cause, a blessing and a curse. We spend the better part of our lives working for and worrying about it, and our moods and livelihoods swing based on its presence or absence. Why? A quick review of human history and nature will tell us.

Every species has two basic instincts, 1) to survive and 2) to pass on their genes. Don't worry; this book isn't about the second one. However, we can learn something from the first, the need to survive.

What do humans need to survive? Physically, our basic needs are food, water, and warmth. Psychologically, we have a need to feel safe. Our needs can expand and move up the hierarchy, but there is no survival without meeting these basic needs.

How do we meet these needs? As hunter-gatherers, we tracked them down. We followed the animals, plants, and weather that gave us food, water, and warmth. After the invention of farming, we no longer needed to follow our food and could settle and build permanent structures. We were also no longer limited to only owning what we could carry with us, which meant we could begin accumulating things. When we accumulated things, we needed a place to store them. To have room to store them, we needed to expand our structures, and our expanded structures needed to be furnished and maintained. So, as we accumulated things, our "needs" increased (funny how that works). As our material needs increased, so did our need to trade.

For simple things, we could barter. If I had a chicken and needed firewood, and you had firewood and needed a chicken, we could trade. But finding this *coincidence of wants* was difficult, so we created a standardized *medium of exchange*. Now, I could trade this medium with you, and you could trade the medium I gave you with someone else for something else in the future.

This medium of exchange is *money*. At first, money was something useful, like a sack of rice. Then it became something we desired, like gold coins. Then it became paper certificates backed by something we desired (called a currency), and then paper backed by nothing (fiat currency), and now, numbers on a screen, mostly backed by nothing. In the history of humankind, money has been and can be nearly anything—sticks, stones, cigarettes (in prisons), toilet paper (in pandemics). The only thing that makes modern money worth anything is confidence—the confidence that other people think it is valuable too. You accept a $20 bill from me for your services because you trust you can trade that $20 bill with someone else for something else in the future.

So, money is a tool that multiple people agree to use to exchange things. It stores the power to buy goods and services, but most importantly, it is a tool to acquire our needs, which means, to meet our needs, we need money.[1]

How do we acquire money if we don't already have some? The easiest way is to be given some, and a quick way is to steal from others. But one of these requires good fortune, and the other is frowned upon and comes with consequences if caught. So instead, we opt to trade our time for money and go to work. With that, the cycle begins.

When we work, money comes in, and to meet our needs, money goes out. This simple trade allows us to meet our physical needs.

But remember our psychological need, security. Security comes from knowing that our physical needs are met—and *will be* met. This means we think of not only the present but also the future. Since the future is unknown, to prepare for the unknown (provide security), we want to make sure we'll have money available to meet our needs. Since we have money today and aren't sure we will tomorrow, we spend less today to set aside some for tomorrow. We call this saving.*

Time really is money

We've all heard time is money, and it's true. Not only do most of us trade our time for it, but when we have money, it gives us control of our time. Typically, the more time something saves or, the more time something takes to create, the more money it costs.

Think of this with transportation. Walking is free. A bike is faster than walking (saves time), but it costs money. A car is faster than a bike (saves more time), but it costs more money. A plane is fastest, but it also cost the most money.[2]

Think of this with services. We can all clean a house, mow a yard, and cook a meal, but we can save time by trading money for someone else to spend their time doing it. Advice, whether it is medical, legal, or financial, is also a trade for time. We could learn the subject ourselves, but learning takes time, so we pay someone else who has already traded their time to learn it.

This is also true with the *quality* of goods and services. "Custom" often costs more than standard. Why? Custom takes more time. Expertise can be a proxy for quality, and experts cost more than novices (e.g., lawyers, plumbers, accountants), and most expertise is gained with time.

You might be thinking that prices are set by supply and demand, which they absolutely are. But supply is very often a function of time. Journeyman plumbers cost more because there is a lower supply of them, but there is a lower supply of them because it takes so much time to become one. If a freeze kills all the oranges, the price of orange juice jumps

---

* Morgan Housel, in his book *The Psychology of Money*, gives my favorite definition of saving: "the gap between your ego and your income."

because the supply is down, but the supply is down because it takes time to replenish the supply.

One area this concept is not always true is with intangibles. Putting a crocodile on a shirt or an "LV" on a purse can drastically increase the price. Part of this is social, but another part is a result of time—time spent gaining a reputation.

What does all of this mean? The more money we have, the more security we have, but also, the more control of our time we have. We can call how much control of our time we have, our *lifestyle*, which we will revisit shortly.

How much money should we save? Everyone's exact answer varies based on values and circumstances, but the general answer is "more." Remember, money gives us security and control of our time, so it's logical to believe more is better.

How do we get more money? We only have so much time we can trade, so another way is for the money we've already saved to earn money (grow). We can do this by investing, which is like sending our money to work. When we send money to work, it can come back with more money. But the more money it *can* come back with, the higher the risk that it comes back with less money (losses), or doesn't come back at all, which captures the relationship between risk and return.

All through life, this process continues—money comes in, it goes out, and in between, it either grows or shrinks. We continue to accumulate until one day we determine that we have enough money (or will have enough money coming in from other sources) that we can reverse the trade and exchange the money we've accumulated for our time. When we stop trading our time for money, we are retired.

We all have different aspirations for retirement. Some of us want to spend as much as we can while we're alive, some want to pass on as much as we can when we die, and others are somewhere in between.

While we may want different things, we usually fear the same thing—that our money won't provide for our needs, meaning that we "fall short" or "run out." If we fall short, that means too little is coming in or too much is going out, which means the way to fix the problem is to have more coming in or less going out. To have more coming in would require us to either 1) trade our time again, which may not be feasible at this stage of life, or 2) take more risk when investing, which could backfire and make things worse. If neither of these is palatable or plausible, we control what we can—what is going out—and begin to "cut back." When we cut back, we reverse what we can of the time trade— start mowing the yard, cleaning the house, or eating at home again. We may also downsize the house or car. Since very few people run out of money in the literal sense, depleting their accounts to $0, our fear of running out of money is really the fear that we will have to negatively change our lifestyle (i.e., have less control of our time).

Whenever we don't want something to happen, we plan. One of the greatest determinants of happiness and well-being is a sense of control over our lives, and planning is a way of exerting that control. When we plan, we chart out a path to avoid the unwanted outcome— if we don't want to gain weight, we create an exercise plan; if we don't want to fail a test, we create a study plan; if we don't want to run out of money…we create a financial plan. Like checking the traffic before work or the weather before a vacation, when we plan, we create or update our assumption of what we expect the future to be like.

Retirement planning is no different. We don't want to run out of money, so we plan how we'll use our money by making assumptions, forecasts, predictions, projections, judgments, estimates, and guesses about the future. What assumptions do we make? Retirement is like any other stage of our financial life: money comes in, money goes out, and in between, it either grows or shrinks. Our life still consists of inflows and outflows, which means retirement planning is simply the practice of projecting our inflows and outflows and what will happen in between over an unknown length of time. When working, we start with nothing and grow it into something. In retirement, we start with something and try not to end up with nothing.

Sometimes, despite our efforts to plan, we still run out of money (have to cut back on our lifestyle). *How* this happens is simple: more money goes out than comes in. More specifically, it can happen because the price of the things we buy increases (inflation was higher), the government takes more of what we earn (taxes increased), our investments lose money, we lived a long time, our health fails, we experience unexpected expenses (e.g., long-term care), etc. All of these are different *ways* to run out of money.

But *why* do we run out of money? (Some people truly just do not have any money, but most readers of this book are not in this dire of a situation.) As mentioned, when we plan, we create expectations, and to run out, more money went out than came in. So, we run out because more money went out or less came in *than expected*. In other words, reality differs from our expectations.

Why does reality differ from our expectations? Some of the variables we project are fundamentally unpredictable, like our health, longevity, and investment performance. Unexpected or "outlier" events like 9/11 or a pandemic can happen with negative consequences that were unforeseeable.

Some of the variables, however, we have more control over, and our projections are just plain wrong. Our expectations can be wrong as a result of ignorance; we may not know what bad things can happen, how certain financial tools work, or that our money can't do what we're asking of it. Our expectations can also be wrong because of arrogance; we know what bad things can happen but don't think they will. Arrogance is a cousin of overconfidence, and overconfidence can lead us to believe we can do it all ourselves or cause us to take more risk because we think we can time when to avoid the bad things. (Ironically, overconfidence and arrogance can also cause ignorance.)

So reality differs from our expectations because either we can't know what will happen (unpredictable), don't know what will happen (ignorance), or don't care what could happen (arrogance). Clearly, our expectations play an important role in how our retirement unfolds, as they directly affect how we make decisions and assumptions.

Making decisions require us to make choices, and choices between two or more things require tradeoffs. When trading one thing affects our ability to have another, it creates a balancing act. Figure 1-1 shows the most common balancing acts related to financial planning.

FIGURE 1-1: A List of Balancing Acts

We balance our needs with our wants, our future with our present, and risk with return. All of these affect our chances of running out of money. For example, we need a house, but how big of a house? We should save for tomorrow, but how many tomorrows? We want our money to grow, but how much are we willing to lose? The more 1) we spend today, 2) tomorrows we plan for, and 3) risk we take, the higher the chance that "bad stuff" happens and the harder it will be for our money to last.

How do we strike these balances? Previously, I said a basic instinct is to survive. In a financial context, surviving means *not* running out of money. Consider the alternative to running out of money—dying with more than intended. One outcome, running out of money while alive, is considerably worse than the other, dying with more money than intended. This difference is an example of an *asymmetric outcome*.

Asymmetric outcomes are fundamental to how we experience life; losses hurt us more than gains help us.[3] For example, a weightlifter has more to lose by letting the weight fall on his chest than he does to gain by pushing it up, and the retiree has more to lose if her account is cut in half than she does to gain if she doubles her money.

Our natural response to this asymmetry is called *loss aversion*. The lesson of loss aversion is simple, profound, and explains much of our decision-making: we are risk-averse when it comes to locking in gains and risk-seeking when it comes to avoiding losses.

Loss Aversion

Imagine you are offered the choice of either accepting or declining a coin flip. If the coin lands on heads, you win $200, and if it lands on tails, you win nothing. If you decline the coin flip, you win $100.

Research finds that most people will decline the coin flip (showing an aversion to risk) and accept a sure gain of $100 rather than risk not gaining anything at all.

Now imagine you are offered another coin flip. This time, if the coin lands on heads, you lose $200, and if it lands on tails, you lose nothing. If you decline the flip, you lose $100.

Here, the research found that most people will accept the coin flip (a risk-seeking behavior), risking the bigger $200 loss with the hope of not losing any money.

Figure 1-2 illustrates the asymmetry in how we experience gains and losses. The x-axis shows the gain or loss, and the y-axis shows our experience. [4]

This graphic raises an important point; our experiences are not *linear*. Equal amounts of "more" do not provide equal increases in utility or satisfaction. For example, if you're hungry, the first piece of pizza has more utility than the eighth. Likewise, your first million dollars is more satisfying than the 50th (so I'm told). This is known as *diminishing marginal utility* and begins to explain why thinking "more" is always better can be a trap. (It also helps explain why we are loss averse and why it can be best to "minimax regret.")

The idea that losses hurt more than gains help or that "bad is stronger than good" is also true mathematically. As shown in Table 1.1, if you lose 10%, you need more than a 10% gain to break even. If your account is cut in half (50% loss), it must double (100% gain) to get back to its starting point.

FIGURE 1-2: Graph of Prospect Theory

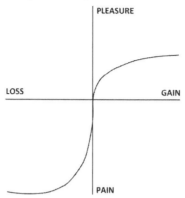

TABLE 1.1: Gain Required to Break Even After a Loss

Loss	Gain
10%	11%
20%	25%
25%	33%
33%	50%
50%	100%

Loss aversion is rooted in evolution, as avoiding threats increases our chance of survival more than pursuing and capturing opportunities. This is why we save money and don't bet all our money on black at the roulette table—some things just aren't worth the risk. But sometimes, we ignore our instincts. If we don't see or recognize a threat (perhaps because we're arrogant or ignorant), we may end up risking what we have and need for what we don't have and don't need. Why? Because there's a fourth balancing act that we are forgetting—the balance between greed and fear.

Psychologists contend that driving the decisions we make is the pursuit of pleasure and the avoidance of pain. Since many people equate money with pleasure (and therefore, believe more money is better), this balance between pleasure and pain is a proxy for greed and fear. Greed is the desire for more, and fear is the worry of having less. To be clear, both are healthy in moderation but destructive in excess. There is nothing wrong with wanting to better yourself and stay alive. But we get in trouble when we get out of balance—when we risk pain we can't afford to attain pleasure we don't need—and it is usually when we tip the scale a little too much towards greed that we can run out of money. (We can also run out if we're too fearful and our money fails to keep pace, but this is easier to fix.)

Why? There's actually a very clear and direct reason. Remember, balancing acts have a give and take relationship—more of one decreases the other. When we desire more money, we may also increase our chances of running out of money.

More specifically, we increase our chances of running out of money when we want more money to spend on things that give us pleasure (e.g., toys and vacations). If you want more money to spend on things that give you pleasure, there are two ways to do so: 1) have more money coming in, and 2) have less money going out on things that don't give pleasure.

The way to have more money coming in (assuming you are retired and not working) is for your money to grow. For your money to grow, you must take risk. If you want it to grow more, you must risk more. The more you risk, the more you increase the chance that "bad stuff" can happen, and when the bad stuff happens, you can run out.

The second way to have more money is to reduce outflows on the things that don't provide pleasure, for example, taxes, insurance, maintenance, and saving. Some of these non-fun things we have no choice over (called non-discretionary), like taxes (e.g., property and income) and certain kinds of insurance (e.g., health and homeowner's). While we cannot eliminate these expenses, we can minimize them. We can minimize them by eliminating waste, such as having too low of a deductible or paying more for the same coverage that you could get from a different company. This kind of waste elimination is healthy. (We'll discuss unhealthy waste elimination in Chapter 3.)

Some of our outflows, we have a little more say (discretion) over such as maintenance, saving, and certain kinds of insurance (e.g., life, disability, long-term care). These, we can minimize or eliminate altogether. But notice what these outflows all have in common; they prepare for and protect against the "bad stuff"—getting sick, things breaking, rainy days. So once again, the way to have more money is to take more risk—if we define risk as the chance that "bad stuff" happens. We can save less and protect less, which leaves us less prepared when the bad stuff happens.

Our definition of greed, the desire for more money, relies on the assumption that more money is better and provides more pleasure. This assumption is true, to a point. (There's also a stark difference between momentary and lasting pleasure.) Obviously, if you can't meet your basic needs, more money will increase pleasure. Offloading unpleasant tasks, like cooking and cleaning, is another way to derive pleasure from money. But above a certain threshold, the pleasure utility of money diminishes. Like the examples we saw when discussing diminishing marginal utility, each additional dollar you receive provides a little less pleasure.

We also have to consider where the pleasure is coming from. It's fairly well documented that "things" don't provide much lasting pleasure. If the pleasure you derive from buying something comes from it being "new," well, new things get old.

We must also remember the power of our expectations. We humans have an incredible ability to adapt (adjust our expectations) to our circumstances. The first time you fly Coach on an airplane is exciting, and so is the first time you fly First Class. But once you're accustomed to First Class, it's no longer exciting, and more troubling, Coach is a letdown. Like the addict building their tolerance, our desires can always expand for higher quality and quantity, and what once gave us pleasure no longer does the trick. We call this the *hedonic treadmill*, and it can run longer than any of us can stay on.[5]

If we're honest, a significant reason we want more money is that we're social beings who care about our status in the herd. Money is the scorecard society judges us by, so having more money (or at least the outward appearance of more money) elevates our standing. Pleasure that comes from impressing others rarely lasts because, well, someone will always have more or better things. (What's better than having a Bentley? Having two Bentley's!)

Comparison is not only the thief of joy, but it can also affect our decision-making. When people say, "I want to be okay," what they really mean is, "I want to be okay relative to those around me." The difference in those two statements introduces the distinction between *relative and absolute wealth*. Multiple studies have looked at this phenomenon.

A variation of these studies goes like this. Participants are asked, "Would you rather make $100,000 while everyone around you makes $120,000, or make $80,000 while everyone around you makes $60,000?" Incredibly, but not surprisingly, most people choose the latter. They would rather be worse off on an *absolute* scale (making $80,000 instead of $100,000) if it means they will be better off on a *relative* scale (everyone else makes $60,000 rather than $120,000).

The last few pages may suggest I'm some sort of advocate for asceticism who rebukes material possessions. Au contraire. Having or wanting more money is not bad. I'm simply saying we need to consider why we want more money and what we are willing to do to obtain it. We can all afford the upside, but we must make sure we can afford the downside. We also must remember the asymmetry of money. Having 10% more probably won't change your life very much, but having 10% less might. On the other hand, 100% more will likely change your life, but consider what kind of risk you have to take to earn that kind of return in a meaningful time frame.

Saving and preparing for the future will always be a challenge for two primary reasons. First, we aren't guaranteed tomorrow, so the temptation to live it up while we can is real and sometimes even valid. Second, there's another cruel asymmetry of life that says most of the things that are pleasurable in the short-term usually come back to bite us in the long term, and the things that are good for us in the long term aren't a lot of fun in the moment. We all know the examples, exercising versus lounging, eating healthy versus binging, saving versus spending. Saving for a rainy day, especially when you're not sure it will ever rain, will never be easy (or pleasurable).

So, planning for retirement requires us to make decisions, choices, tradeoffs, and balancing acts. How we balance it all will determine what "tools" we use. In the context of financial planning, tools are simply places to put our money, like, cash, stocks, bonds, real estate, and insurance. Some tools are used to grow our money. Some of these tools, such as stocks, have a wider range of outcomes than others, such as cash. The wider the range, the less predictable they are, and the less predictable they are, the higher the risk that reality differs from our expectations and we run out of money.

Other tools are used to limit the range of outcomes, such as insurance. Think of homeowners insurance. If you own a house worth $500,000 and it burns down, you lose the value of your home ($500,000). You could instead insure your home, paying a small amount each year, and if your house burns down, the insurance company pays for it. Rather than a $500,000 range of outcomes, you limit the range of outcomes to the size of your premiums (plus deductible).

FIGURE 1-3: Range of Outcomes With and Without Insurance

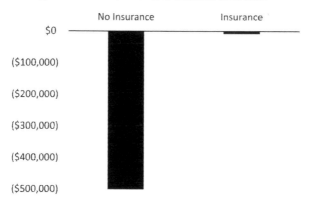

Just like any tool you use around the house, e.g., a hammer or saw, each financial tool will perform a particular job and do certain things in certain situations. A hammer doesn't do what a saw does, and stocks don't do what insurance does. There is nothing inherently "bad" about any of these tools. It is only "bad" when you use the wrong tool for the job, like trying to tighten a screw with a hammer or putting your money in the stock market to keep it safe.

With that, the groundwork has been laid. Money is a tool used to meet our needs. To acquire money, we trade our time for it. Our financial lives consist of money coming in and going out and growing and shrinking over time. When we retire, we stop trading our time for money. Our biggest fear is that we'll run out of money, which again means having to cut back on our lifestyle, and when we don't want something to happen, we plan. When we plan, we make assumptions about the future. When we make assumptions, we balance both internal and external factors. How we strike these balances determines what tools we use (where we put our money).

To keep track of all this, we need a framework, which we'll build next.

2

FRAMEWORK

If you've ever used Google maps, or any other navigation system, then you have a template for most planning processes. Before Google can give you directions, they need to know two pieces of information, 1) where you are and 2) where you are going.

FIGURE 2-1: GPS Navigation (example of Google Maps)

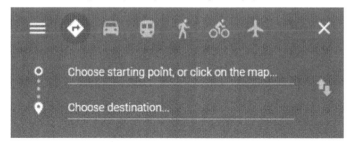

The process for retirement planning is very much the same. Your current location represents your assets (e.g., savings and retirement accounts) and sources of income (e.g., Social Security and pensions). Your destination is what you want retirement to look like (e.g., how long you will live, how much you want to spend). Once you define these coordinates, you can decide how to get there, which in this context means where to put your money (e.g., cash, stocks, insurance).

Let's think about what Google is doing on an elementary level. To solve how long your trip will take, Google determines the distance between the two points and assumes the speed you will travel. This means there are three variables: 1) distance, 2) speed, and 3) time.

Financial planning also uses a form of basic algebra. In Chapter 1, we saw that our financial lives consist of money coming in, going out, and doing something in between over some length of time. From this, we can identify five variables.

1. **Beginning Balance** – How much money you start with
2. **Spending** – How much money is coming in or out
This variable "nets" inflows and outflows. When working, this number is usually positive, and when retired, it is often negative. For simplicity, I label this net outflow "spending."
3. **Rate of Return** – What your money does
4. **Longevity** – How long you will live
5. **Ending Balance**[*] – How much money you will have left

Identifying these variables allows us to establish a basic formula.

Beginning Balance ± Spending ± Return = Ending Balance

Let's remember what algebra teaches us and allows us to do. First, these variables are connected. If we change one, it can affect the others. If A + B = C, and we increase A without changing B, then C must increase. For Google, if they increase distance without increasing speed, time increases. For financial planning, if we increase spending without increasing return, then we decrease our ending balance.

Second, algebra allows us to *solve* for an unknown variable given the value (or assumed value) of other variables. If we know A and C, we can solve for B. If Google knows distance and speed, they can determine time. If we know beginning balance, spending, return, and time, we can solve for our ending balance.

Financial planning is essentially choosing what variable to solve for and filling in the others with what you know or what you assume (think) will happen. What you need to know and what you need to assume depends on what variable you are solving for. What variable you solve for depends on what your goal is.

---

[*] Most people call this "legacy" or "inheritance." Author Cindy Arledge makes the following distinction, "To the person passing on the money, it is a legacy. To the person receiving the money, it's an inheritance."

Generally speaking, there are three types of goals people have. 1) Spend a certain amount. 2) Earn (return) a certain amount. 3) Leave a certain amount behind. In terms of variables, this means there are three we can solve for: spending, return, and ending balance.

There is an important takeaway here—there are two variables we usually do not solve for, beginning balance and time. Here's why.

For the person retiring today, beginning balance is usually a fact; they know what they have, so it is not something they "solve" for. One exception is if a person a few years from retirement does know how much they'll spend, what return they'll earn, how much they want to leave, and how long they'll live, then they can solve for what beginning balance they need to retire. This is the math behind the always popular "How much money do I need to retire?" articles. Two thoughts. First, these are usually guidelines or rough estimates to get you in the right frame of thinking that will be further refined once retirement is reached. Second, do you really know all four of those variables? We'll touch on some ways to estimate beginning balance in Part II, but unless noted otherwise, we'll assume beginning balance is a fact.

Solving for time is solving for how long you want your money to last. While that itself isn't a problem, we must consider what time is in the context of retirement planning. Since time represents how long retirement lasts, and retirement ends at death, then time is an estimate of how long we will live. Here's the problem. Usually, when we solve for a variable, we do so with the intent of targeting, controlling or manipulating it. For example, if we solve for spending, we can spend more or less, or if we solve for return, we can take more or less risk. But what control do we have over how long we live? If it looks like we're going to run out of money, time is not a variable we take into our own hands.

This concept of control raises another point. Of the five variables, only two we can actually control, spending and return. We just discussed the issues with beginning balance and time, and ending balance is just a function of the other four (Beginning ± Return ± Spending = Ending) and can only be changed by changing spending and return.

So no matter what your goal, the majority of your planning efforts will be spent determining how much you spend and how much you earn (return). With these two variables, there are two "directions" we can solve for. We can assume spending to solve for return or assume return to solve for spending. Which direction we choose also affects how we decide where to put our money.

This last point makes more sense when we put it conversationally. Suppose Person A says, "Here's how much I want/need to spend, what rate of return do I need to earn to provide this spending?" Person A assumes spending to solve for the return they need (which then tells them how much risk to take and where to put their money). Person B says, "Here's where I'm putting my money (or, here's how much risk I'm willing to take), how much can I spend?" Person B assumes a return amount (estimated based on where they are putting their money) to solve for how much they can spend.

(Understand, "How much risk I'm willing to take" and "Where I put my money" are used interchangeably since they are just different ways of phrasing the same thing.)

We can now revisit and label the three planning goals.

The person who knows how much they want to spend uses the *spending-based* approach (they "base" their plan on their spending). They assume how much they want to spend, know their beginning balance, estimate how long they'll live, and determine how much they want to have left. From there, they solve for what rate of return they need, which they can then use to determine where to put their money.

We can solve in the opposite direction, using the *risk-based* approach. This person starts with where they will put their money (which is the same as determining how much risk they'll take), which allows them to estimate their return. From there, they know their beginning balance, estimate how long they'll live, determine how much they want to have left, and then solve for how much they can spend.

Of course, we can also target a certain amount to leave behind, using what we will call the *legacy-based* approach. The person using the legacy-based approach starts by determining how much they want to have left, knows their beginning balance, and estimates how long they will live. They must then decide how to handle spending and return. Does return determine spending or spending determine return?

Yes, I know. In theory, it all sounds so simple, populate four variables and solve for the fifth, but reality is not so literal. However, these examples are not as unrealistic as you may think. They capture the two prevailing attitudes people have, "I'm investing in this, how much can I spend?" versus, "Here's what I need to spend, how do I produce it?"

There is tremendous variation amongst these approaches. Some people may assume a very conservative return; others an aggressive return. Some want to simply meet their needs; others want to maximize their spending. Some may want to leave a large cushion; others want to die with their last dollar. It's all a matter of preference and values.

What is constant is that when we plan, we must make assumptions, and slight changes in our assumptions can have drastic effects on the results. That's why it is so important to understand the sensitivity of our assumptions, which is what we'll now look at.

To explain these sensitivities, we are going to have to look at some numbers. If you're less interested in numbers, bear with me these next few pages. The rest of the book is not this way, and the following sets up the discussion in Part II.

We are going to look simultaneously at the three approaches we just covered. We must start by establishing a "base case."

Let's assume that all three approaches start with $1,000,000 (beginning balance) and estimate a 30-year retirement (time). Now let's see how the approaches differ.

The spending-based approach aims to spend $50,000 per year. The last variable they must assume is their ending balance. For simplicity, we will assume $0. The spending-based planner is all set. They now ask, "What rate of return do I need to earn to be able to spend $50,000 per year of my $1,000,000 over the next 30 years?" The answer is 3.08%. The spending-based planner will then evaluate their investment options and target a return of 3.08%.

The risk-based planner also plans to deplete their accounts. They must next determine how much risk they'll take. Let's say they are comfortable with a "moderate" level of risk, which computes to an estimated return of 6% per year. They then say, "Based on my risk preference that I estimate will allow me to earn 6% per year, how much of my $1,000,000 can I spend every year over the next 30 years?" The answer is $68,537.

It gets a little too cumbersome to add a true legacy-based approach to our example. This person would target an ending balance and adjust spending and return accordingly. Instead, we will use a third case that blends the spending and risk-based approaches, what we'll conveniently call the "mixed approach." This person targets the same $50,000 spending and 6% return, which leaves them with a legacy of $1,553,407.

The summary of our three approaches is shown in Table 2.1. Each column represents a separate plan. The gray shaded box represents what each approach "solved" for, and the unshaded boxes represent what we assumed. The purpose of this exercise is to see, 1) what return is required to meet a specified spending need (spending-based approach), 2) what is the most you can spend with a given return (risk-based approach), and 3) how much is left over with a specified spending need and given return (mixed-approach). We will also see show how the answer changes when we tweak the underlying assumptions.

TABLE 2.1: Base Case Results

	Spending-Based	Mixed	Risk-Based
Main Objective (Solve For)	*Minimum Return*	*Remaining Balance*	*Maximum Spending*
Initial Savings	$1,000,000	$1,000,000	$1,000,000
Longevity	30 years	30 years	30 years
Spending	$50,000	$50,000	$68,537
Rate of Return	3.08%	6%	6%
Ending Balance	$0	$1,553,407	$0

Before we start tweaking assumptions, we can finally introduce the framework to keep track of all this. Table 2.2 shows a full projection of the mixed approach.

TABLE 2.2 Framework Built Using the Mixed Approach

Year	Beginning	Spending	Return	Gains	Ending
1	$1,000,000	($50,000)	6%	$57,000	$1,007,000
2	$1,007,000	($50,000)	6%	$57,420	$1,014,420
3	$1,014,420	($50,000)	6%	$57,865	$1,022,285
4	$1,022,285	($50,000)	6%	$58,337	$1,030,622
5	$1,030,622	($50,000)	6%	$58,837	$1,039,460
6	$1,039,460	($50,000)	6%	$59,368	$1,048,827
7	$1,048,827	($50,000)	6%	$59,930	$1,058,757
8	$1,058,757	($50,000)	6%	$60,525	$1,069,282
9	$1,069,282	($50,000)	6%	$61,157	$1,080,439
10	$1,080,439	($50,000)	6%	$61,826	$1,092,266
11	$1,092,266	($50,000)	6%	$62,536	$1,104,801
12	$1,104,801	($50,000)	6%	$63,288	$1,118,090
13	$1,118,090	($50,000)	6%	$64,085	$1,132,175
14	$1,132,175	($50,000)	6%	$64,930	$1,147,105
15	$1,147,105	($50,000)	6%	$65,826	$1,162,932
16	$1,162,932	($50,000)	6%	$66,776	$1,179,708
17	$1,179,708	($50,000)	6%	$67,782	$1,197,490
18	$1,197,490	($50,000)	6%	$68,849	$1,216,340
19	$1,216,340	($50,000)	6%	$69,980	$1,236,320
20	$1,236,320	($50,000)	6%	$71,179	$1,257,499
21	$1,257,499	($50,000)	6%	$72,450	$1,279,949
22	$1,279,949	($50,000)	6%	$73,797	$1,303,746
23	$1,303,746	($50,000)	6%	$75,225	$1,328,971
24	$1,328,971	($50,000)	6%	$76,738	$1,355,709
25	$1,355,709	($50,000)	6%	$78,343	$1,384,052
26	$1,384,052	($50,000)	6%	$80,043	$1,414,095
27	$1,414,095	($50,000)	6%	$81,846	$1,445,940
28	$1,445,940	($50,000)	6%	$83,756	$1,479,697
29	$1,479,697	($50,000)	6%	$85,782	$1,515,479
30	$1,515,479	($50,000)	6%	$87,929	$1,553,407

Yep, the "framework" I've been touting looks a lot like the basic spreadsheet you build at home. While this framework is oversimplified, it is only oversimplified in complexity, not structure. What I mean is, this basic table of columns and rows captures your financial life (and is also the type of calculation behind nearly every financial planning software). We see how much money we start with, how much goes in or out (netted in the spending column), how much it grows or shrinks, how long it lasts, and how much is left. The only reason it is oversimplified is that it assumes a single rate of return and a single outflow per year. If we wanted to "add complexity," we would simply add columns to account for additional investments with different rates of return and add rows to attempt to account for more precise timing of inflows and outflows.

One type of complexity that is both valuable and reasonable to add is to disaggregate several of these variables. So far, we've looked at three high-level assumptions, 1) Longevity, 2) Spending, and 3) Return. There isn't much to add to longevity as it is relatively straightforward. The other two, however, are made up of several components. Let's look at spending first.

While we should have a good idea of what we spend today, there are many things that can affect our spending tomorrow. Taxes can change, inflation can occur, and we may face unexpected expenses. All of these can be considered.

As for our return, when we assume a fixed rate of return (the same return every year) as we have in our examples so far, we are also assuming the order or sequence of returns. As we'll see shortly, the exact sequence of our returns can drastically impact our plan if we are withdrawing or depositing money.

So, even in our simplified model, we make seven assumptions.

Longevity
1. How long we will live *(Longevity)*

Spending
2. How much we need to spend *(Base Spending)*
3. What inflation will be *(Inflation)*
4. If we will face any unexpected expenses *(Spending Shocks)*
5. What our tax rate will be *(Taxes)*

Rate of Return
6. What our rate of return will be *(Rate of Return)*
7. What order (sequence) returns will be in *(Sequence of Returns)*

Okay. We have built a base case, detailed in Table 2.1, and have established the seven basic assumptions that we make. It's now time to evaluate the sensitivity of each approach by looking at each assumption individually and adjusting it slightly upward and downward.

Assumption #1: How long we will live (*Longevity*)

Table 2.3 shows how each plan changes with different longevities. *Note: the "base case," which was detailed in Table 2.1, is shaded in gray.*

For the spending-based approach, living longer will require a higher rate of return. For example, instead of a 3.08% return if they live for 30 years, they will need a 3.77% return if they live 35 years. For the risk-based approach, living longer will lower maximum spending. Maximum spending drops from $68,537 to $65,069 when we change the longevity assumption from 30 to 35 years. We can also see how the ending balance for the mixed approach is affected when reality is different than expectations. Under the original assumption, the mixed approach was going to be left with $1,553,407 but living five years longer leaves $1,780,043. (Notice that for the mixed approach, living longer was actually beneficial. We'll look at why this is in a moment.)

TABLE 2.3: Sensitivity of Each Approach Based on Different Lifespans

Longevity	Spending-Based (Minimum Return)	Mixed (Remaining Balance)	Risk-Based (Maximum Spending)
20 years	0.00%	$1,257,499	$82,850
25 years	1.96%	$1,384,052	$73,968
30 years	3.08%	$1,553,407	$68,537
35 years	3.77%	$1,780,043	$65,069
40 years	4.21%	$2,083,334	$62,700

Assumption #2: How much we need to spend (*Base spending*)

Spending more will require the spending-based approach to earn a higher return and reduce how much money the mixed approach has left. This change does not affect the risk-based approach, as spending is based on the rate of return assumption, not spending needs.

TABLE 2.4: Sensitivity of Each Approach Based on Different Spending Needs

Spending Need	Spending-Based (Minimum Return)	Mixed (Remaining Balance)
$40,000	1.31%	$2,391,424
$50,000	3.08%	$1,553,407
$60,000	4.70%	$715,391

Assumption #3: What inflation will be (*Inflation*)

Does a gallon of milk cost the same today as it did 20 years ago? Of course not. The reason is inflation—the increase in the price of goods and services and the decrease in a dollar's purchasing power.

If we have to increase our spending to keep up with inflation, we'll run into the same problems as increasing our spending in Assumption #2 did. To avoid running out of money, the spending-based approach will need to earn a higher return, and the risk-based approach will have to lower their spending. Inflation also lowers the remaining balance of the mixed approach.

TABLE 2.5: Sensitivity of Each Approach Based on Different Inflation Rates

Inflation	Spending-Based (Minimum Return)	Mixed (Remaining Balance)	Risk-Based (Maximum Spending)
0%	3.08%	$1,553,407	$68,537
1%	4.11%	$1,084,110	$61,634
2%	5.14%	$533,419	$55,119
3%	6.17%	$0 (runs out)	$49,017

Assumption #4: If we will face any unexpected expenses (*Spending Shocks*)

Have you ever had to buy something you hadn't planned on—possibly something quite expensive, like a car, a new roof, or braces for your child? Unfortunately, unexpected expenses don't go away in retirement. If we build a plan based on a set of expected expenses and are forced to spend money on something unanticipated, our chances of running out of money will increase. We call these surprise expenses "spending shocks." The greatest source of spending shocks for retirees is related to health care and, in particular, long-term care. This care can be very expensive and last several years. (We will discuss long-term care in Chapter 9.) Let's look at an example of experiencing $60,000 worth of spending shocks for three years, beginning in the 20th year.

Since spending shocks represent an increase in spending, we will see the same effects of increased spending we saw in Assumption #2.

TABLE 2.6: Experiencing $60,000 Spending Shock In Years 20-22

Scenario	Spending-Based (Minimum Return)	Mixed (Remaining Balance)	Risk-Based (Maximum Spending)
Base Case	3.08%	$1,553,407	$68,537
$60,000 Spending Shock in years 20-22	3.84%	$1,230,690	$64,685

Of course, there is no way to correctly predict how much spending shocks will be or when they will occur. This is because spending shocks are, by definition, "shocks" and are therefore unknown.

This example is our first chance to introduce the importance of timing and show the impact timing of expenses has on each plan's outcome. Look at how the outcome changes if the spending shock starts in the 10th year rather than the 20th year. The expenses are of the same "magnitude" but occur 10 years earlier.

TABLE 2.7: Experiencing $60,000 Spending Shock In Years 10-12

Scenario	Spending-Based (Minimum Return)	Mixed (Remaining Balance)	Risk-Based (Maximum Spending)
Base Case	3.08%	$1,553,407	$68,537
$60,000 of Spending Shock in years 10-12	4.15%	$975,469	$61,640

Assumption #5: What our tax rate will be (*Taxes*)

We can be sure of at least one thing when planning for taxes: tax rates will change. An increase in rates reduces how much money you keep. We can view this as a reduction of income or an increase in expenses. Either way, the net effect is the same, and since it has the same effect as an increase in expenses, we will expect similar results: higher required rate of return for the spending-based approach, lower maximum spending for the risk-based approach, and lower remaining balance for the mixed-approach.

TABLE 2.8: Sensitivity of Each Approach Based on Different Tax Rates

Change in Tax Rate	Spending-Based (Minimum Return)	Mixed (Remaining Balance)	Risk-Based (Maximum Spending)
Base Case	3.08%	$1,553,407	$68,537
5% Higher	3.52%	$1,332,877	$65,109
10% Higher	3.99%	$1,087,842	$61,683
20% Higher	5.08%	$505,866	$54,829

Assumption #6: What our rate of return will be (*Rate of Return*)

There is an apocryphal story of a professional golfer and his caddy having a conversation before hitting a shot. The caddy tells the pro that the hole is 166 or 167 yards away. The pro turns to his caddy and asks, "Which one is it?" While you might think that level of precision is unnecessary on a golf course, it is that important when it comes to investing and rates of return. (It also creates a very easy way to manipulate outcomes when presenting to clients, something we'll see throughout Part II.)

As we've seen, a lower rate of return will lower maximum spending for the risk-based approach and lower the remaining balance for the mixed approach. This change does not affect the spending-based approach, as return is based on the spending assumption.

TABLE 2.9: Sensitivity of Each Approach Based on Different Rates of Return

Rate of Return	Mixed (Remaining Balance)	Risk-Based (Maximum Spending)
4%	$326,981	$55,606
5%	$833,903	$61,954
6%	$1,553,407	$68,537
7%	$2,558,603	$75,314
8%	$3,945,363	$82,248

How do we know what rate of return to use in our plan? We will answer that question in depth in Part II of the book, but while we're on the topic of rate of return, we need to discuss the last assumption we made—the order of returns.

Assumption #7: What order returns will be in (*Sequence of Returns*)

So far, we've been assuming that we earn a fixed (the same) rate of return every single year. When an investment earns the same return every year, returns are "linear." If we plot the returns sequentially, it will make a straight line, like the dashed line in Figure 2-2.

FIGURE 2-2: Linear vs. Variable Returns

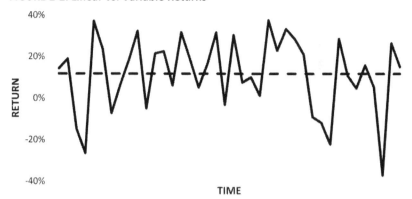

Do investments return the same amount every year? No, the returns vary from year to year; they are "variable," like the solid line in Figure 2-2. Why does this matter? When we are depositing or withdrawing money from an account, the order in which the returns happen will alter the outcome. We call this effect *sequence of returns risk*, and the following discussion will explain how it works.

Let's assume we have the option of selecting one of three different portfolios, shown in Table 2.10.

Portfolio A returns 13.3% in the first year and earns 0.5% less every year after for 30 years, meaning in the 30th year, it returns -1.2%. Portfolio B receives a linear return of 6% every single year. Portfolio C is the reverse of Portfolio A, starting with a -1.2% return in the first year and increasing 0.5% every year for 30 years until it earns 13.3% in the 30th year. *This example is hypothetical and only used to illustrate a mathematical concept, and does not imply real investment performance.*

TABLE 2.10: Three Different Return Sequences

Year	A Decreasing Returns	B Fixed Returns	C Increasing Returns
1	13.3%	6.0%	-1.2%
2	12.8%	6.0%	-0.7%
3	12.3%	6.0%	-0.2%
4	11.8%	6.0%	0.3%
5	11.3%	6.0%	0.8%
6	10.8%	6.0%	1.3%
7	10.3%	6.0%	1.8%
8	9.8%	6.0%	2.3%
9	9.3%	6.0%	2.8%
10	8.8%	6.0%	3.3%
11	8.3%	6.0%	3.8%
12	7.8%	6.0%	4.3%
13	7.3%	6.0%	4.8%
14	6.8%	6.0%	5.3%
15	6.3%	6.0%	5.8%
16	5.8%	6.0%	6.3%
17	5.3%	6.0%	6.8%
18	4.8%	6.0%	7.3%
19	4.3%	6.0%	7.8%
20	3.8%	6.0%	8.3%
21	3.3%	6.0%	8.8%
22	2.8%	6.0%	9.3%
23	2.3%	6.0%	9.8%
24	1.8%	6.0%	10.3%
25	1.3%	6.0%	10.8%
26	0.8%	6.0%	11.3%
27	0.3%	6.0%	11.8%
28	-0.2%	6.0%	12.3%
29	-0.7%	6.0%	12.8%
30	-1.2%	6.0%	13.3%
Annualized	**6%**	**6%**	**6%**

All three portfolios average a 6% annualized return. So, which portfolio is best? To answer that question, we first must determine why we are investing our money. Are we:

1. Investing a lump sum and holding it?
2. Making deposits to our account?
3. Taking withdrawals from our account?

Let's look at each scenario.

Scenario #1: Investing a lump sum

In the first example, we will invest $1,000,000 and let it grow for 30 years. Which portfolio is best?

TABLE 2.11: Results of Lump Sum Investment

Portfolio	Ending Balance
A (Decreasing Returns)	$5,743,425
B (Fixed Returns)	$5,743,425
C (Increasing Returns)	$5,743,425

FIGURE 2-3: Sequence of Returns – Lump Sum

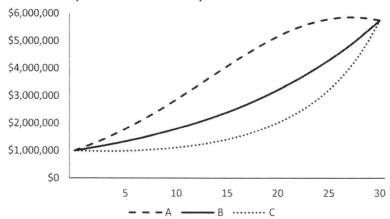

The answer may surprise you. All three portfolios end up with the same amount. Why is that? Remember, all three portfolios average an annualized 6% return. When you are not making withdrawals or deposits, the order (sequence) of the returns does *not* matter. Since they all average the same return, they all have the same ending balance.

Scenario #2: Making deposits

What if we begin with an account balance of zero and deposit $50,000 at the beginning of each year. Which portfolio is best?

TABLE 2.12: Results of Making Deposits

Portfolio	Ending Balance
A (Decreasing Returns)	$3,071,233
B (Fixed Returns)	$4,190,084
C (Increasing Returns)	$5,900,728

FIGURE 2-4: Sequence of Returns – Making Deposits

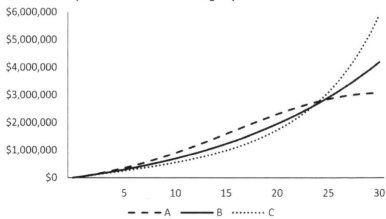

Here, Portfolio C ends up over 40% higher than Portfolio B and nearly doubles Portfolio A. When you are making deposits, the order (sequence) of returns *does* matter. More specifically, losses in the *later years* will drastically affect the outcome of your plan.

The reasoning is straightforward. The returns that occur when there is more money in the account will have a greater effect on the outcome—a 10% loss when you have a million dollars is more painful than a 10% loss when you have $100,000. When you are depositing money, you expect to have more money in the later years. Thus, the returns in the later years will have a greater impact on your plan. Portfolio C experienced the losses early, when there was not much money in the account, so the effects of the losses were less pronounced. Portfolio A suffered the reverse, positive returns when there was not much money in the account and losses when there was more money.

Scenario #3: Taking withdrawals

Finally, let's look at the example most applicable to retirement planning: beginning with a chunk of money and taking withdrawals. In this scenario, we start with $1,000,000, and instead of making deposits, we will withdraw $50,000 at the beginning of each year. Which portfolio is best?

TABLE 2.13: Results of Making Withdrawals

Portfolio	Ending Balance
A (Decreasing Returns)	$2,672,191
B (Fixed Returns)	$1,553,407
C (Increasing Returns)	$0

FIGURE 2-5: Sequence of Returns – Making Withdrawals

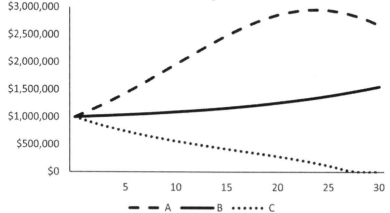

The results are both surprising and startling. Portfolio C, the portfolio with the highest ending balance in both previous examples, is not only the worst performing portfolio but actually runs out of money when we are taking withdrawals. What's going on here?

The reasoning is the same as before, the more money you have in your account, the more you will be affected by positive or negative returns. When you have more money at the beginning, losses in the *early years* will drastically affect the outcome of your plan. In this example, even though all three portfolios received the average return we expected, the results are wildly different thanks to the sequence of returns. One portfolio is fine (B), one is thriving (A), and one is devastated (C). When depositing or withdrawing money, we cannot rely on an average rate of return in our projections.

To summarize, if an investment doesn't return the same amount every year (returns are *variable*), and we don't know what the returns will be (returns are *random*), then we can't rely on projections made using a linear return. The sequence of returns must be considered.

Sequence of returns risk is one of the most important (and least understood) risks in all financial planning. Aside from unknown longevity, it is the thing that makes retirement planning so challenging. Because of sequence of returns risk, all of the examples we have previously shown, and likely all of the spreadsheet examples people create at home, are borderline worthless. Knowing the average return isn't enough; we need to know the order of returns. If correctly predicting an investment's rate of return is hard, then correctly predicting the order of returns is impossible. Since there are countless possible combinations of return sequences, we must prepare for a range of possible outcomes. We'll address how to project random variable returns in Part II.

SUMMARY

When we changed each assumption individually, some changes may not have appeared to have much of an impact. That's fine because the point of the exercise was to communicate the directional effects of changing each variable (e.g., higher spending requires a higher return, a lower return requires lower spending, etc.). A more realistic exercise would be to change multiple assumptions at the same time. Let's look at a final example to see how the outcome changes if we alter more than one assumption.

In this example, we will again begin with $1,000,000 but will expect to live two years longer and find that we need to spend $2,500 more per year. In addition, taxes increase by 5%, inflation is 1% higher, our investments return is 0.5% lower, and in year 15, we need an additional $25,000. While all of these changes have a negative impact, they are hardly unrealistic.

The effect of these changes on the outcome of the plans, shown in Table 2.15, is much more pronounced. The minimum return leaps from 3.08% to 5.38%. The remaining balance moves from a comfortable $1,553,407 to now just barely squeaking across the finish line with $72,558, and maximum income drops from $68,537 to $53,205.

TABLE 2.14: Base Case vs. Revised Case Assumptions

Assumption	Base Case	Revised Example
Initial Savings	$1,000,000	$1,000,000
Longevity	30 years	32 years
After-Tax Spending Needs	$50,000	$52,500
Inflation	0%	1%
Tax Rate	0%	5%
Rate of Return	6%	5.5%
Spending Shocks	None	$25,000 in Year 15

TABLE 2.15: Effect on Base Case Under Revised Assumptions

Main Objective	Spending-Based (Minimum Return)	Mixed (Remaining Balance)	Risk-Based (Maximum Spending)
Base Case Result	3.08%	$1,553,407	$68,537
Results Under Revised Example	5.38%	$72,558	$53,205

There's obviously a slew of oversimplifications in these examples. First, keep in mind how conservative this example was. We assumed a linear rate of return, which means we did not include any years with negative returns and did not consider sequence of returns risk. We also had only a single spending shock of $25,000. If the shock were greater, lasted longer, or happened earlier, the results would be even worse.

Second, all of the assumptions were static, meaning they never changed after we set them. Obviously, this isn't how the world works. Taxes, inflation, spending, and returns all fluctuate. If we update our model to consider ranges, it will look something like Table 2.16:

TABLE 2.16: Model Showing Range of Outcomes

Years	Beginning Balance	Spending	Tax Rate	Inflation	Return	Ending Balance
1-40	1,000,000	$40K -$60K	0%-30%	(2%) -10%	(19%) -30%	$

But even that is too precise. More realistically, our model looks like this:

TABLE 2.17: Model Showing Uncertain Range of Outcomes

Years	Beginning Balance	Spending	Tax Rate	Inflation	Return	Ending Balance
1-?	1,000,000	(?-?)	0%-?%	?-?%	?-?%	?

Clearly, there are countless scenarios we could have looked at, but as I mentioned in the introduction, we're not going to take the time or space to go through all of them. The point of this exercise is to see the directional effects of changing each assumption (spending more requires a higher return, a lower return requires lower spending, etc.) and to realize how fragile many of the "plans" people put together really are. Sure, most people understand that if their spending needs double or if they suffer terrible losses in the market that their plans will be affected, but many miss that even small, seemingly insignificant changes, like a return that is 0.50% lower, can have a massive impact on the success of their plan.

A final simplification in these examples is that we didn't change anything after the initial plan. Obviously, if things aren't going well, we can adjust. It is important to note, though, that depending on when and how bad things get, we may be limited in our options to recover. This emphasizes the importance of our expectations (which are assumptions.)

Much of the discussion in this chapter was hypothetical. I recognize the wording and numbers may have been slightly confusing. The purpose was to establish the seven basic variables, the general approaches to planning, the relationships and sensitivities between the variables, the fact that there are really only two variables we can control, and that there are two directions we can solve for, spending to return or return to spending. There are two important takeaways from this discussion. 1) Small changes in assumptions can drastically change the design of your plan. 2) Small differences between reality and expectations can drastically change the outcome of your plan.

Both of these takeaways emphasize the importance of our expectations when planning. While Part II of this book will discuss in detail how to populate these variables, we first need to get a better grasp on the process and limitations of prediction.

3

FORECASTING

O ur ability to imagine the future is truly incredible. Consider what all has to happen: we have an experience, store a memory of it, recall it, synthesize what was important, and project it to a new set of circumstances. No other species has this ability.

Now, let's talk about the ramifications of that ability. Planning is about anticipating and projecting the future. We usually plan because we want to avoid or attain a particular outcome. Interestingly, our *desire* to plan comes from our *ability* to plan. If we couldn't imagine the future, we couldn't imagine the outcomes we want to avoid or attain.

The ability to imagine the future plays an important role in how we experience life. Imagining an experience can trigger the same sensations that "actually" experiencing something can, which means we can derive pleasure or pain from imagining events just as we can from living them.[1] As a result, anticipation can have an amplifying effect on an experience, both good and bad, by extending it. For example, daydreaming about a vacation prolongs the enjoyment, but conversely, dreading a doctor's appointment drags out the suffering.

Anticipation can also muffle an experience by allowing us to adjust our expectations. Remember how our interpretation of an experience is usually determined by the gap between reality and our expectations. Anticipation lowers or raises our expectations which tighten the gap. For example, a vacation you highly anticipate (and thus have high expectations of) may not seem as great once you're on it since your expectations were already so high.

Not only do expectations affect how we perceive an experience, but they also affect how we make decisions, which is what we care about in this book. Chapter 2 showed us the quantitative importance of our expectations, and this brief discussion highlights the qualitative importance. The balance of this chapter will take a step back from the minutiae of financial planning and discuss the process and challenge of setting expectations, which is a form of prediction.

We should start by understanding what prediction is. Prediction is a broad term with many aliases, such as forecasting, estimating, judging, and guessing. In reality, all of these terms are unique, with very different meanings.[2] However, for the purposes of this book, I'm going to commit a semantic sin and use these terms interchangeably. I will give them a shared definition: *any supposition that affects how we make decisions.* In other words, any thought about the future that we'll factor into deciding what to do next.

While our predictions usually affect our decisions, there's an important distinction between the two. The outcome can determine the quality of a prediction but not of a decision. Let's say that we predict a 100% chance of success doing "something" (what "something" is does not matter for this example) and decide to go for it. Based on this prediction, we made a good decision—we minimized the chance of failure (or regret). Now let's suppose we end up failing. Our prediction was clearly bad—we predicted a 100% chance of success and were wrong. But, since the outcome doesn't determine the quality of a decision, even though the outcome was bad, our decision was still good based on what we predicted. The breakdown wasn't with our decision; it was with our prediction. Thus, making good predictions is important. We'll see later how important it is to evaluate the effect, not just the frequency, of our incorrect predictions.

Understandably then, most of us want to make "good" predictions. But what makes a prediction good? When we can eventually know the "right" answer, for example, what the market will do this year, we can say that a good prediction is one close to the actual outcome. But what if the answer cannot be known? Or what if the answer relies on probability? For example, let's say you predict a 50% chance you will need long-term care. Like a weather forecast, if you could evaluate all people you applied this prediction to, you could determine how accurate you were. But in your situation with a single outcome, you either will (100%) or won't (0%) need care. There's no way to know whether 50% was a good prediction or not. In this case, "we can only evaluate the quality of the thought process used."[3]

So, what thought process do we use to make predictions? In short, we base our predictions on our "knowledge." Our knowledge can come from our own experience, the experience of others around us, or the recorded experience of others before us (history).

But what is knowledge? Author and scientist David Deutsch says knowledge is explanation.[4] (More specifically, good explanations that are hard to vary.) If we can explain something, we usually think we understand it. When we say that we "understand something," that usually implies that we know what caused it. So we are constantly in *causal thinking* mode, searching for patterns of cause and effect that we use as explanations, and therefore call knowledge.[5]

We build knowledge by establishing cause and effect, and we establish cause and effect by observing what happens in the world. (We'll see shortly how our observations can be misleading.) For example, we feel warm when the sun comes out; therefore, we believe the sun causes warmth. When we find a cause to explain an effect, likely by fitting the facts into a coherent story, we say it "makes sense." When we can't find a coherent story, we say we are "surprised." The more that things make sense, the more confident we are in our explanation, and as a result, the more confident we are in our prediction.

Sometimes the direction of the explanation (cause and effect) is obvious—warmth does not cause the sun to come out. But two things happening together is a correlation, and correlation can sometimes hide the cause. Being tired and hungry often correlate, but which causes which? Are you tired because you're hungry, or hungry because you're tired? It's a very "chicken and egg" type problem.

Since the world is essentially an infinite sequence of cause and effects, prediction is the process of predicting cause and effects. When multiple cause-and-effect relationships affect each other, they create a system. The weather, the economy, and your body are all systems. The more relationships there are, the more complex the system is. The more complex the system, the harder it is to identify what causes what, and the more that errors in our understanding of the relationships will affect the accuracy of our predictions.

When these relationships are well understood, we can predict the outcome of incredibly intricate systems. Just look at the mind-boggling feats of NASA for proof of this. But when the relationships are less predictable, like when a cause can have multiple effects, then prediction is much harder.[6] The behavior of humans, if you believe in free will, fits this definition of less predictable. If we are perfectly predictable, then we don't have free will.

So, domains like physics and rocketry are predictable because the behavior of the individual parts follows predictable rules. But in domains such as economics, politics, and financial markets, the behavior of the individual parts (which are people) are less predictable.

Unfortunately, the variables the retiree must forecast belong to these less predictable domains. Consider again what the retiree must predict—longevity, spending, taxes, inflation, health, and investment returns. Returns are derived from market prices, which reflect human behavior. Taxes are set by governments, which are run by people. Spending is a reflection of our tastes and preferences, which vary and change with time and circumstance. Health relates to our body, which, contrary to what we like to think, still largely remains a mystery.

Are we any good at predicting these things? Well, mountains of evidence tell us no, but there are two reasons you might be tempted to think that we are.

The first is that we see people make correct predictions all the time. People predict sports scores, market returns, weather events, etc.

Given this, how could we say that we aren't good at prediction?

Essayist and risk-taker Nassim Taleb explains it this way, *the world moves forward, but we view history backward.*[7] In other words, we make decisions at the starting line but often evaluate them from the finish line. This distortion in how we see the world is where many of our struggles with prediction start. No matter what we are predicting, if enough people try, someone is bound to get it right (or close enough). But standing at the finish line with evidence of a correct prediction is not proof of our skills. We must go back to the beginning.

Imagine you hear of someone who correctly predicted ten coin flips in a row. You'll probably think, "Wow! What are the odds of that?! Clearly, they have a skill!" Well, the odds are about 1 out of 1,000 (1,024 to be exact). Standing here today looking backward, that is undoubtedly impressive. However, we must consider how many people were predicting in the first place. If I told you this person was part of a coin flip guessing competition with 10,000 other contestants, only one person correctly guessing ten in a row is far less than what we would expect. At those odds (1 out of 1,000 with 10,000 participants), we should expect ten people to guess ten coin flips in a row correctly. From the finish line, a person guessing ten flips in a row is not impressive; it's a mere statistical expectation.

This example can be expanded. Imagine five people correctly guessed ten flips in a row. Standing at the finish line, we might think that one person got lucky, but there's no way that five could. We would then point to multiple people guessing correctly as stronger evidence that we can predict, even though five is still less than expected.

Rather than recognizing these correct predictions are nothing more than statistics at work, the world will treat these oracles quite differently. Biographers and journalists will clamor for interviews, and their faces will be plastered on magazines and TV screens. Their lives will be closely examined, studies will be done on their sleep and nutrition habits, and their childhood will be scoured for early signs of clairvoyance. As word of their gift spreads, something called the *illusory truth effect* will take over—the more we hear things, the more we think it is true. All of this attention will be taken as proof that we can predict, and we will continue to do so.

If you think this is example is far-fetched, replace "coin flips" with "beating (or predicting) the market."

The Baltimore Stock Picker

The story of the Baltimore Stock Picker has many variations. A shortened version is given below.[8]

Imagine you receive a letter from a stock picker in Baltimore predicting that a stock will go up in the next week, and the stock goes up. The next week you receive another letter saying a stock will go down, and it goes down. This process continues for 10 consecutive weeks. In the 11th week, you are offered the opportunity to invest. Do you?

Based on your experience, this mystery investor has correctly predicted 10 moves in a row. You must have found a gem! But here's how the picker is doing it. The first week, the picker sends 1,024 letters, 512 predict the stock will go up, and 512 predict the stock will go down. He no longer sends letters to those he sent the incorrect predictions to, but he'll send a second round to those who received the correct prediction. Of those 512, he sends 256 predicting the stock will go down, 256 predicting it will go up. This process continues until after 10 weeks, 10 people have received 10 letters correctly predicting 10 moves in a row.

You may think this is just a harmless statistical fable until you learn about mutual fund incubation. Mutual funds do not release funds to the public right away. They often "incubate" them internally, testing their ideas. Some fail, and some succeed, and the ones that succeed can open with a "proven" track record of performance that they can advertise.[9]

The second reason we think we can predict is also related to time-line distortion. In hindsight, we can usually explain almost anything, and being able to explain the past makes us think we can predict the future. Understand this; the past will always look less random than it was for the very reason that it happened, which causes *hindsight bias*. The ability to produce coherent stories linking cause and effect is why we view the world as far more predictable than it really is. This coherence may even give us the feeling that what happened was inevitable. But this feeling of inevitability can cause us to lose sight of how easily things could have been different.[10]

You see, history plays tricks on us—it is valuable in what it tells us but dangerous in what it doesn't. History shows us the outcome that did happen but hides what could have happened. Something that may happen only 1 out of 100 (or million, or billion) times happens, and since it did, we think that is normal and to be expected.

Relying on history to predict is relying on what has been seen to determine what will be seen, which relies on the future resembling the past. Taleb calls this the *problem of induction* and uses the example of a turkey living its life for the first 1,000 days. Every day, the turkey wakes up, is fed, and goes about its turkey business. Based on history, the turkey believes it has nothing to worry about. On day 1,001, however, the butcher comes and, well, you know the rest.

Two points must be taken away from this turkey example.

First, we must consider the aggregate *effect* of our predictions, not just the *frequency* with which we predict correctly. For the turkey, it correctly predicted 999 times that it had nothing to worry about. It was only wrong once, but the effect of being wrong was catastrophic. If we can't predict the big and consequential outcomes, it doesn't really matter if we can predict the small and inconsequential. Even in Russian roulette, you "win" more often than you "lose."

The second takeaway is the power of negative evidence. It doesn't matter how many additional observations the turkey made confirming its belief it had nothing to worry about; additional observations do nothing to alert it to what is coming. It took only one observation to the contrary to invalidate its prediction based on the other 999. This is the value of negative evidence—you cannot prove anything by additional observation, but you can disprove.

These points are important and counter to how our minds work. We love to confirm our existing views, and our brains are biologically more receptive to facts that do so.[11] It is thus understandable that we surround ourselves with like-minded people or consume like-minded material. Like the turkey looking at other surviving turkeys and using them as proof of its theory, anecdotal and corroborative evidence does nothing to prove our beliefs. Instead, we should desperately try to disprove ourselves. If I try and fail 50 times to disprove a belief, I can feel more confident than if I find 50 examples confirming my belief.[12]

The power of negative evidence is the lesson behind the familiar story of black swans. As the story goes, in the Old World, people had only seen swans that were white, which led to the belief that all swans were white. One day, the people saw a swan that was black, which was impossible based on their previous observations. No amount of confirmation could prove that all swans were white. One observation proved it was not true.

The other Black Swan

The story of black swans inspired the now-ubiquitous concept of Black Swan events. Promulgated by Nassim Taleb, a Black Swan event must meet three criteria:

1. Be an *outlier*—outside the realm of regular expectations
2. Have an *extreme* impact
3. An explanation can be made *after* it happens

It's popular to label any unanticipated event a Black Swan, but this is wrong. Taleb explains the true significance of Black Swans is to illustrate a "severe limitation to our learning from observations or experience and the fragility of our knowledge," which leads to two other points regarding Black Swans. 1) A highly likely event *not* happening can also be a Black Swan. 2) An event may be a Black Swan for some people but not others. He references how 9/11 was a Black Swan for the victims but not for the perpetrators of the acts.[13]

The story of black swans introduces one of the most pervasive mistakes people make, *confusing the absence of evidence for evidence of absence*. People of the Old World made this mistake when they thought that no evidence of black swans meant evidence that there were no black swans. Our turkey made this mistake when thinking no evidence of harm meant no risk of harm. We see this frequently in retirement planning. We believe that no evidence of market risk means there's no risk in the market, or no evidence of needing long-term care suggests there is no risk of needing long-term care. But not finding evidence of harm does nothing to change the existence and probability of harm.

So things that have never happened happen all the time, but we extend the mistake by believing that the best or worst of what has happened is somehow the best or worst of what will happen (again, think market returns). We see this when investment strategies are "stress-tested" by simulating them against the worst returns in history. But all that these tests tell us is the strategy *would have* worked, not that it *will* work. Remember, what is currently the worst in history had to replace something else that was previously the worst in history.

Another problem with relying on what has happened to predict what will happen is that the "cemetery of history is a quiet place"— those that didn't make it don't get to tell their stories.[14] This creates a *survivorship bias*, which is our tendency to focus only on those that "made it." Studies are done of those who were successful without considering those that weren't. This omission creates the problem of *silent evidence* and is explained with a few examples.

In his book *The Black Swan*, Taleb points to the ancient Roman story of Cicero showing Diagoras a portrait of religious worshippers praying after surviving a shipwreck. The implication is that praying saved them from perishing. Diagoras responded, "Where is the portrait of those who prayed, then drowned?"[15]

Taleb also points to the book *The Millionaire Next Door*, a bestseller that attempted to identify traits of successful people. Among those traits were courage and risk-taking. Taleb explains that those who failed also showed courage and took risks, so it is not these traits alone that lead to success.[16] (Spoiler alert: randomness plays an enormous role in the outcome of our lives.)

Alarmingly, survivorship bias can affect how we evaluate investment returns. Let's say you want to calculate the 10-year performance of companies in a small-cap index. You start by identifying the companies in the index today and calculating their average return over the last 10 years, which we'll say is 12%. The problem is, the list of companies around today doesn't include the companies that were around 10 years ago and failed. These failed companies won't be included in your calculation. If you go back to the beginning and include the funds that are no longer around, you find the performance is actually 9%.[17] In this case, if you rely on past results to predict future performance, your expectations of small-cap stocks may be overstated.

Seeing how we can misattribute what leads to success has a parallel in the investing world. Many of the people or investors we consider "successful" are quite wealthy. We believe they are wealthy because they are "good with money." This may be true, but they are wealthy because they made money. There are plenty of ways to make money, and being "good with money" is not a requirement.

Wealth often creates what is called a *halo effect*—the tendency to let positive impressions in one area influence our impressions in another. We think people who are wealthy because of expertise in one area will be successful or give good advice in another. (For example, we think a successful businessperson will make a good politician.)

I've met many people who follow financial advice given to them by a "wealthy" doctor, engineer, or entrepreneur that they know or heard about. They listen to their advice or copy their decisions because they equate being smart or wealthy with being "good with money." While it seems logical that a "smart" or "wealthy" person would also be good with money, the link is far from guaranteed.

Interestingly, this mistake seems to go only in one direction. We know that being wealthy doesn't make you a good doctor—no one is asking Warren Buffett to remove their appendix—but we aren't so clear when we reverse the direction of advice.

The suggestion that randomness or luck plays an important role in our lives doesn't sit well with people for two reasons. First, luck is hard to identify and quantify and doesn't provide the satisfying coherent narrative of explanation that we all crave. Second, implying someone's success is due to luck makes you look rude, petty, jealous, and mean (not to mention it is demoralizing when we use that explanation on ourselves). Instead, we often attribute our winners to skill and intellect and our losers to bad luck. While there is no reason for luck to only apply to the downside, it is polite and protects our self-esteem to behave as if that is so. (I like how the entertainer Penn Gillette put it, "Luck is statistics taken personally.")

The preceding introduced the limits of using "evidence" to make predictions. We base our predictions on our knowledge and what we call knowledge is explanations of cause and effects, and we establish cause and effects based on the evidence that we observe. For there to be evidence, something happened. That which didn't or hasn't happened doesn't leave evidence. The more "evidence" we think we have, the more our explanations make sense, and the more confident we feel. In the 21st century, we have more evidence and coherent narratives than ever before, and as a result, more confidence in our ability to predict the future. This inflated confidence causes us to ignore what history is telling us.

An objective view of human history shows one big string of surprises. Our takeaway should be that the world is surprising, but instead, because we can explain past surprises, we now think we can predict future ones. We believe that even though our ancestors were all surprised, "had they known what we know now," they wouldn't have been. In a sense, we believe we are at the apex of knowledge.

Every generation thinks they are at the apex of knowledge. Most "new" ideas and explanations are ridiculed until they are accepted as commonplace (and then usually deemed to be "obvious"). An incredible example of this is the scientific battle that took place over whether smoking was bad for your health. While it seems "obvious" now, some of the greatest minds in health and science were divided on the topic.

The belief that we are at the apex of knowledge also affects our ability to imagine the future. If we can picture change, it's usually just a variation of what already exists (e.g., a faster horse and buggy) rather than an innovation (e.g., an automobile). It's not easy to conceive of innovations due to the *law of iterated expectations*—if today you expect something to happen at some point in the future, then you already expect that something today. Taleb uses the wheel as an example. "If you can prophesy the wheel, you already know what the wheel looks like, and thus you already know how to build a wheel."[18]

So, rather than thinking that the world is predictable because we can explain what happened, the proper lesson is that the world is surprising and will continue to be so. Knowledge of how things came to be is not the same as knowledge of how things will change or what things will become.[19] The best and worst of history will continue to change. Unexpected things will continue to happen, and because they are unexpected, they will be impactful. We should also remember that history (what happened) is just one of an infinite number of outcomes that could have happened. Thus, relying on this limited set of outcomes to project all future ones is misguided at best. From a planning perspective, we must simmer the confidence in our predictions and embrace this uncertainty by preparing for a range of outcomes.

A standard way to digest the past and project the future (i.e., populate the assumptions in our models) is to use statistics. Statistics are powerful, but they are not the panacea some believe them to be, as they suffer the same limitations of history we have discussed so far. Consider what statistics are. Statistics are simply a description of data, and data is a record of what happened, also known as…history.

Early in school, we are taught the three most basic descriptive statistics, the mean (average), the median (middle number), and the mode (most frequent number). These are valuable, as they allow us to summarize a range of data into one concise number. But this conciseness can disguise the true uncertainty. Statistics can put our focus on precise numbers when we should be focusing on the range of possible outcomes. It can be easier to understand this point visually.

Let's look at life expectancy. As we'll discuss further in Chapter 4, most life expectancy measures are calculated using historical data and simply represent the mid-point when we expect a group of similarly aged people to die (meaning half are alive and half are dead).

Figure 3-1 shows an example of a distribution of when people die. If you're asked, "When do you expect someone to die?" how do you answer? Do you look at the average age? The most common age? The middle age? In this example, the numbers are all pretty close, but as we saw in Chapter 2, small differences in assumptions lead to extreme differences in outcomes, and many die long before and after.

FIGURE 3-1: Distribution of Deaths

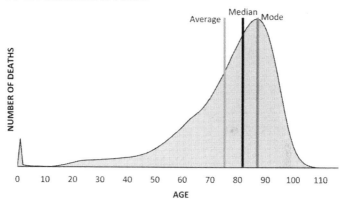

How about investment returns? Figure 3-2 shows the annual returns in the S&P 500 since 1928, as well as the average. What return will you receive next year? The average? It rarely happens.

FIGURE 3-2: Yearly and Average Historical Returns since 1928

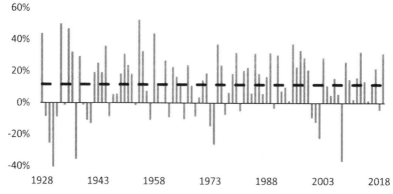

How about long-term care costs? Figure 3-3 shows the distribution of costs for those who need care. Most need a little care, others a significant amount of care, but few need average amounts of care.

FIGURE 3-3: Distribution of Lifetime Long-Term Care Costs

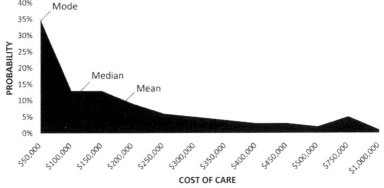

We can make the same point the preceding visuals made by asking, "Would you walk across a river that is an average of three feet deep?" Likely, the answer is no. The average may be three feet, but there are deeper sections of the river, and you'll drown if you try to walk across. What's missing in our discussion is the variability around the average. The most popular measure for variability is standard deviation. Standard deviation combined with the theory of normal distribution can prove useful in projecting future outcomes, which we'll discuss in Chapter 16.

Here's why statistics, particularly averages, are not the panacea of financial planning (aside from suffering the same limitations of history). Statistics summarize the experience of everyone, but when planning, you're concerned about what *you* will experience. Averages, for example, are useful when applied to large groups or multiple attempts at something—think of casinos, insurance companies, or baseball players throughout a season. But when applied to individuals or limited attempts at something, averages can be misleading. The law of large numbers explains.

The law of large numbers tells us, the larger the sample size, the closer the average of the sample will be to the average of the population. (The population is the entire data set, e.g., all people, and a sample is a single data point, e.g., a person.) In other words, the more things you sample, the more your sample will resemble the whole group.

Picture a roomful of 100 people. You don't know this, but the average height of everyone in the room (the population) is 6 feet. The shortest person in the room is 5 feet, and the tallest is 7 feet. You are then asked to determine the average height of the population. Rather than measuring the entire population (all 100 people), you instead "sample" the room. You start by selecting one person. The height of the individual you select could be anywhere from 5 to 7 feet tall, meaning your sample's average could be very far from the true average of the room. The more people you measure, the larger your sample size becomes, and the closer the average of your sample will be to the average of the population. (If you sample everyone in the room, your sample average will equal the average of the population.)

In the context of retirement planning, we can think of the sample as your experience and the population as everyone's experience. With this view, we see how averages can be problematic when planning. You may know the average age people die, the average amount people spend, or the average return of an investment, but since your life is a sample size of one, your experience could be very different from the average. (i.e., you might be 5 feet tall in a roomful of people with an average height of 6 feet.)

Casinos and insurance companies exist and thrive because of the law of large numbers. We can use slot machines to demonstrate. On any single spin, the casino could lose a large amount of money if the player hits the jackpot. But since there are multiple players and multiple spins, they have a large enough sample size to rely on the law of large numbers (that their experience will resemble the long-term averages). While casino games are helpful for explaining concepts, they are not a fair comparison to reality. In casinos, the odds are completely known and controlled. In the "real world," probabilities and outcomes are not clearly defined.

But there is a limit to the value of the law of large numbers that explains the predicament the retiree finds themselves in. There is a difference between predicting *how many* and predicting *which ones*. While casinos may be able to predict how many players will hit the jackpot and life insurers how many policyholders will die, they cannot predict which players or policyholders will. When it comes to predicting a single spin or policyholder, casinos and insurers are just like us; they must rely on the general odds.

So in life, we usually only get "one spin," meaning our sample size is too small to rely on the averages of the group to apply to our situation. Instead, there's a wide range of outcomes we can experience.

We can see the consequences of building a plan using averages with a small sample size when discussing life expectancy. Remember, life expectancy is when we expect 50% of the population to be dead and 50% alive. If you plan to deplete your accounts at life expectancy, you're giving yourself a 50% chance of running out of money while you're alive. In reality, you could die tomorrow or live to 120.

Using words like "50% chance" introduces probability. Probabilities can be (assuming they are accurate) extremely useful but can again be misleading when used to determine our *expected* experience. As the saying goes, "Expected value is not the value you expect."[20]

Consider a coin flip where if you flip heads, you win $100, and if you flip tails, you lose $100. Half the time, you expect to win $100, and the other half, you expect to lose $100. This means the average (expected) outcome is $0. The issue is, $0 is not a possible outcome; you'll either be better or worse off than the average (you either win or lose $100). If you flip the coin 100 times, you'll come out close to even ($0), but if you flip only once, which is how we usually experience life, you must prepare for the full range of outcomes (win or lose $100).

To apply this to retirement, replace the coin flip with long-term care. Imagine you have a 50% chance of needing long-term care, which will cost $150,000 if you do, and a 50% chance of not needing long-term care, which will cost you nothing. The average outcome is $75,000 (50% x $150,000 + 50% x $0). Once again, there isn't a scenario where you spend $75,000. You either need care ($150,000), or you do not ($0). If you save $75,000 to prepare for the average long-term care experience, and you do need care, you will still be $75,000 short. If you do not need care, you will have over saved by $75,000.

The point is, we don't experience the world in averages. There may be a 50% chance of something happening, but your experience will be either 100% or 0%. Again, averages are useful when applied to multiple people or over longer periods but are of little help in single instances. A final example is a baseball player with a .300 batting average going to the plate. (Batting average = hits ÷ total at-bats. A .300 batting average is equivalent to getting a hit 30% of the time.) Over the entire season with hundreds of at-bats, we expect he'll get a hit 30% of the time, but in any given at-bat, he will either get a hit (100%), get out (0%), or walk. He will not get 30% of a hit.

Probabilities are supposed to establish the likelihood of something happening. We seem to be pretty good at comprehending 0%, 50%, and 100% probabilities, but we struggle with those in between. For example, if there is a 20% chance of rain, it wouldn't be unusual to mentally round down to a 0% chance. If it then rains, we are furious. We must remember that if the forecast is accurate, it *should* rain 20% of the time. In a more serious application, many retirement strategies will establish a "probability of success." We see a 90% or 95% chance that we don't run out of money and fail to recognize that 1 out of 10 or 1 out of 20 times, we will run out of money.

Once again, we need to focus not just on the frequency but on the aggregate outcome. We may be right 95% of the time, but if the 5% is disastrous, we need to prepare for it. An extreme example is Russian roulette. Let's say you have a 90% chance of success (living). The 10% outcome (not living) is pretty terrible, so it's probably not worth taking that bet. This applies to other areas of our planning. You may have only a 25% chance of needing long-term care for a long time, but it can sink your retirement if you do. People wouldn't take a 10% (certainly not a 25%) chance of playing Russian roulette, yet they'll walk around taking similar or higher chances of blowing up financially.

Because of our familiarity with averages, they often feel intuitive. However, when the data is not symmetrical, we can mistake their message. The following shows several ways this can happen.

The first such way is when data is *aggregated* (known as Simpson's Paradox). Consider the following example from Sam Savage's book, *The Flaw of Averages*.[21] Table 3.1 shows the batting averages of two baseball players, David Justice and Derek Jeter, from 1995-1997.

TABLE 3.1: Batting Average From 1995-1997

	1995	1996	1997
David Justice	**.253**	**.321**	**.329**
Derek Jeter	.250	.314	.291

Looking at the table, who do you think had the highest batting average over the three years? Shockingly, the answer is Derek Jeter. If you were to average the batting averages shown, you would calculate that Justice averaged .301, and Jeter averaged .285. But this number is their "average batting average." If we want to know what their batting average was, meaning how many hits they got per at-bat over three years, we need to look at the numbers behind the average, which are shown in Table 3.2.

TABLE 3.2: Batting Average Including Total At Bats from 1995-1997

	1995	1996	1997	Total	Average
David Justice	104/411	45/140	163/495	312/1,046	.298
Derek Jeter	12/48	183/582	190/654	385/1,284	**.300**

Averages are also skewed by *outliers*. A classic example is the fictional story of nine plumbers sitting at the bar having a beer. All nine plumbers make $100,000 per year, giving them an average income of $100,000. Bill Gates, who made $1 billion last year, walks in and takes a seat at the bar. What is the average income of the ten of them now? $100,090,000. Not only is this a misleading description of the group, but once again, no one at the bar makes the "average" income.

It is common to be fooled by the effect of aggregation and outliers on investment returns. If I told you that over the last five years, Fund A averaged an 8.2% return, and Fund B averaged a 7.6% return, which fund would you rather invest in going forward? Before answering, see the yearly returns shown in Table 3.3.

TABLE 3.3: Hypothetical Performance of Mutual Fund and Stock Market

	Year 1	Year 2	Year 3	Year 4	Year 5	Average
Fund A	5%	-10%	**50%**	-5%	10%	**8.2%**
Fund B	10%	-5%	20%	0%	15%	7.6%

Although Fund A underperformed four out of five years, one exceptional year made up for the other lackluster years. Understanding that Fund A's outperformance was due to one great year, the question becomes, how confident are you that Fund A will be able to repeat this success in the future? Since there is no prolonged record of beating Fund B, will Fund A have another great year, or are you more likely to have more lackluster years?

Empirical and anecdotal evidence shows that the most common criterion investors use to select investments is past performance. While historical performance is worth considering, you must give some thought to what caused the returns, how consistent they are, and how likely they are to continue going forward. If you expect an investment to return its historical average in the future, your expectations may be too high if the historical average includes a great year that won't be repeated. The phrase "past performance is not a guarantee of future results" is disclosed on every investment statement for a reason.

Speaking of investment returns, there are multiple ways we can calculate them, which the following will illuminate.

At its simplest, an investment's "return" is the difference between what you put in and what you get out. However, there are three common ways to state returns. Look at the return sequence shown in Table 3.4. What is your return? Table 3.5 gives the three common answers.

TABLE 3.4: Hypothetical Return Sequence

	Year 1	Year 2	Year 3
Return	50%	(25%)	20%
Value of $100	$150	$112.50	$135

TABLE 3.5: Different Types of Return

Type of Return	Return
Total Return	35.0%
Compound Return	10.5%
Simple Average Return	15.0%

Total return is the simple difference between what you put in and what you got out. In this example, we put in $100 and got out $135 for a total return of 35%. Total return is helpful, but we like to think of things in terms of time, so to put returns in terms of time, we calculate an average yearly return. There are two popular ways to do this.

The easiest is to calculate the simple average, which is the average of each year's return. In this example, the simple average return is 15%. (50% - 25% + 20%) ÷ 3 years.

We can also calculate the annualized or compound return, which is the return you would have to earn each year to go from your beginning balance ($100) to your ending balance ($135) over a number of years (3). In this example, the compound return is 10.5%.

It's crucial to grasp the difference between compound and simple average returns. If someone asked you what your average return was, there is a big difference between 10.5% and 15%. It's also crucial since we often use average returns to project future returns. There is an appropriate time to use the simple average and compound average to project future returns.

We can think of the simple average as the average of all one-year returns and the compound average as the average return over a length of time. If you are projecting how your investment might perform *next year* (one year), using the simple average is appropriate since it is the average of all one-year returns. If you are projecting how your investment might perform over a *number* of years, using the compound average is appropriate since it tells us the average return over a length of time. The following example quantifies why it's important to understand the difference.

The simple average return of the S&P 500 since 1928 has been 11.64%, and the compound average return has been 9.79%.[22] Assume you are trying to project how much your $1,000 investment will grow over the next 30 years. Table 3.6 shows us the results of using the simple and compound average.

TABLE 3.6: Ending Value of $1,000 Investment After 30 years

	Return	Ending Value
Simple Average	11.64%	$27,202
Compound Average	9.79%	$16,477

The difference is huge. Projecting returns using the simple average can grossly overstate your performance. Whenever you discuss an investment's average performance, be sure you understand which average is being used.

Show me the money (weighted return)

We just saw how to calculate total, simple average, and compound average returns. These all assume that the amount of your investment is constant. But what if you buy and sell? In this case, these averages will not tell the full story. Let's use a simple example to explain.

Investment ABC increases 50% in the first 6 months of the year and then decreases 25% in the second 6 months, for a 12.5% return on the year.

Person A is pretty simple. They invest $100 for the year and do not make any changes. Person B also invests $100 at the beginning of the year. Liking the performance in the first 6 months, they invest an additional $100. What were the returns on their money?

Table 3.7 shows us the results. Person A earns the return of the investment, 12.5%. Person B, however, actually loses 6.25%. The reason is, they invested more money before the investment lost 25%. So they had more money invested for the bad period than the good.

This example begins to illustrate the effect of sequence of returns risk. If the sequence were flipped, losing 25% in the first 6 months and gaining 50% in the second 6 months, Person A would still earn 12.5%, but Person B would have earned 31.25% on the year. Remember, the returns that occur when there is more money in the account will have a greater effect on the outcome.

TABLE 3.7: Money-Weighted Returns

	Person A	Person B
Initial Invested Capital	$100	$100
Return first 6 months	50%	50%
Value after 6 months	$150	$150
Additional Investment of Capital	$0	$100
Value after Additional Investment	$150	$250
Return last 6 months	(25%)	(25%)
Ending Value after 12 months	$112.50	$187.50
Total Invested Capital	$100	$200
Gain/(Loss)	$12.50	($12.50)
Total Return on Invested Capital	12.5%	(6.25%)

So we often use statistics like averages to project the future, But before we do, we must make sure a few criteria are met. First, the sample must be representative of the population, meaning our situation is relevant to that of the average. For example, if I'm a non-smoking 65-year-old female, I wouldn't want to look at the life expectancy of 65-year-old males that smoke.

Second, we must be sure the conditions that existed at the time the average was calculated still do. As a guideline, if the conditions that existed when the historical data was captured will continue to exist in the future, then historical data can be useful. If we expect conditions in the future to change, then historical data may not be helpful. We can again use baseball as an example.

Assume a baseball player averages 20 home runs per year using a wooden bat. If a new rule allows the player to use an aluminum bat (which makes the ball go much further), how many home runs should you expect the player to hit next year? Do you still use the player's historical average? The player will likely hit more home runs with an aluminum bat than he did in the past with a wooden bat. Conditions changed, and using the historical average may not be appropriate.

We frequently see this mistake when people use historical investment returns. Bonds at the time of this writing provide a perfect example. (A tutorial of bonds is provided in Chapter 18). Historically bonds have returned roughly 6% per year.[23] When bond yields are around 1% to 2%, as they were at the time of writing, that makes it very unlikely they will continue to return their historical average of 6%. Conditions changed, and because of this, a plan built using historical bond averages will likely overstate future returns.

Averages are a generalization of a group's experience. When planning, knowing the average is not enough as our experience is likely to differ from the average. Planning based on averages may feel prudent (it may also feel "smarter" the more complex the calculation is since we often equate complexity with intelligence and value), but it can be naïve and can leave you exposed. For example, if you build your retirement plan using averages, it may seem logical to expect to live for 20 years and return 10% per year. However, it is possible to end up living for 25 years and only return 8%, in which case, the outcome of your plan will be significantly worse than you had expected.

Instead of planning for averages, we need to identify and plan for the range of possible outcomes. One of legendary investor Howard Marks' most prescient quotes is, *"...the future should be viewed not as a fixed outcome that's destined to happen and capable of being predicted, but as a range of possibilities..."* Since there are multiple possible outcomes, we should plan for multiple possible outcomes. In the examples so far, we could die tomorrow or at 120, long-term care could cost $0 or $150,000, and investment returns could be above or below the average. The wider the range of outcomes, the more risk there is to your plan. Not knowing the outcome introduces uncertainty, and the level of uncertainty depends on how wide the range is. Averages can serve as a "best guess" or the number that helps us be "less wrong," but since we only get one shot at retirement, planning for a range is more appropriate than planning for a fixed outcome.

Let's just accept it. We're suckers for a forecast. While we may be bad at it, predicting and planning is fun and part of our nature. It gives us a sense of security, helps us rekindle control, and makes us feel like we are getting ahead of the unknown, but there are a few other reasons we continue to plan and predict despite our lack of ability to do so.

One reason is that forecasts give us confidence, and confidence feels good. Since we like things that make us feel good, we'll continue to forecast, regardless of how bad we are at it. The problem is, forecasts can make us too confident, to the point that we take more risk than we should. Amazingly, studies have shown this to be true even when participants knew the forecasts were completely random.[24]

We also plan because we think that's what successful people do. This is known as the *teleological fallacy*. We see successful businesspeople, investors, inventors, etc., and think they are successful because they had a plan. While sometimes this is true, very often it is not. Of course, in hindsight, we can craft a story of how everything was intentional, but in the moment, many of them are simply improvising.[25]

There is a final explanation for our love affair with prediction that is both a reason that we plan and a reason that our plans often fail: *efficiency*.

Efficiency, and its close relatives *maximizing* and *optimizing*, are the darlings of the business and investing world today, to the point that being labeled "inefficient" is shameful. This pursuit of financial efficiency is rooted in the belief that more money is always better. If we didn't think more was better, we wouldn't try to maximize it.

There are many ways we pursue efficiency. We use leverage to maximize our returns (because we think tomorrow will always be better). We build elaborate models and spreadsheets to consider every variable and squeeze every last ounce of upside out of it. We monitor the markets to find exactly the right time to buy and sell.

It's understandable why we love efficiency. Much of the progress of the world has come from increases in efficiency through the elimination of "waste." These gains in efficiency rarely "just happen" and often are the result of thoughtful planning. Since we too strive for efficiency, we take the time to plan for it.

Here's the deal with efficiency. Efficiency tries to maximize certain outcomes. To maximize, we need to know specifics. If we're trying to maximize the fuel efficiency of a plane, we need to know how much weight we'll carry and how far we're going. To maximize our spending in retirement, we need to know how long we will live and what rate of return we will earn. When we know these things, we can maximize. But in areas of uncertainty, when we don't know these things, planning for efficiency is dangerous.

You see, efficiency increases the size of our failures. Efficiency eliminates redundancies which takes us to higher highs, but when we fail, *redundancies* are what keep us from reaching the lowest lows. Bringing extra fuel on a flight or spending less than possible in retirement is "inefficient," but if things don't go according to plan, they can literally save your life.

Redundancies, despite the negative connotations, are a natural defense in life. If you need a 75 to pass a test, you probably study to get a little higher score, just in case. If a bridge says it has a 2,000-pound weight limit, you probably don't cross with a load of 1,999 pounds, just in case. Nature is the king of redundancy, yet humans dismiss it. If an efficiency-minded person were to design the human body, they would not include a second kidney as it is inefficient and a waste of space and energy. *But by removing redundancy in the name of efficiency, we bring into play catastrophe.*

Recall Elroy Dimson's definition of risk, "when more things can happen than will happen." When you don't know what will happen, there are two more helpful ways you can respond. The first is to spread your bets, known as *diversification*. When you diversify, if one bet struggles, the others pick up the slack—the person who diversifies sacrifices maximum upside in exchange for a higher downside.

The other way to respond to multiple possible outcomes is to stay flexible, maintaining *optionality*. Optionality gives you the choice to change course as you see fit. The more unpredictable things are, the more valuable optionality is.

Optionality can come in many forms. It can come from literal financial options, like the call options discussed below, that give you the right but not the obligation to buy an asset. Optionality can come from renting or leasing instead of purchasing. Even insurance is a form of optionality. Like redundancy and diversification, optionality sacrifices a little bit of upside in exchange for far less downside.

The choice is yours

The concept of optionality goes far beyond financial options, although they provide a textbook way to explain them. The following describes how a simple call option works.

A *call option* gives you the right, but not the obligation, to buy an underlying asset at a future date.

Assume shares of XYZ stock are trading for $100. You think the stock will rise but know it could also drop. For $5, you can buy an option to buy the stock for $100 one year from now. If the stock rises to $120, you can exercise your option. When you do, you will buy the stock for $100 and sell it for $120 for a gain of $20. This gives you a profit of $15 ($20 - $5 option.) If the stock were to drop to $80, you would not exercise your option. You will have a $5 loss, which equals the price of the option.

Compare this to if you bought the shares outright. If you owned the shares and the price rose, you would have a gain of $20, $5 more than when you bought the option. But if the stock had dropped, you would have lost $20, $15 more than if you bought the option.

Since call options still offer "unlimited" upside (minus the cost of the option) but cap and limit your downside, they present an asymmetric return, shown in Figure 3-4. Yes, it takes a little off the top from the best outcome, but when you don't know what the outcome will be, this tradeoff can be worth it.

Two factors make options valuable, 1) volatility and 2) time. In other words, the crazier things are, and the longer you have to decide whether or not to use your option, the more valuable the option is.

In an uncertain world, generating better options is more important than making perfect decisions.

FIGURE 3-4: Call Option Payoff

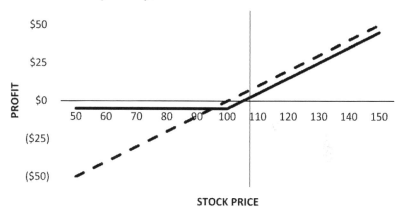

Here is the keystone of this book. *Having backups, spreading our bets, and remaining flexible is how we embrace uncertainty.*

While these all sound well and good, there are three main reasons we reject these antidotes to uncertainty.

First, redundancies, diversification, and optionality all lessen the best outcome, which we deem "inefficient." But we must understand the following principle.

If you know what will happen, going "all-in" will give you the best outcome. If you know what will happen, you don't need to diversify, build redundancies, or stay flexible. If you know what stock will be the highest performer, you'll put all of your money in that stock. If you know whether or not you will need long-term care, what taxes will do, how long you will live, and what market returns will be, you'll know whether or not you need insurance, what to invest in, and how long to plan for. But, when you don't know what will happen, you have to prepare for multiple outcomes. Doing so may require you to make sacrifices, take some off the top, spend a little less, or save a little more.

The second reason we resist these antidotes is that more *frequently,* they work against us than for us. In financial markets, there have been more good years than bad years. It may be that 9 out of 10 years, an all-in strategy would be best; thus, 9 out of 10 years, we wish we would have gone all-in. But we must remember two things, 1) losses hurt us more than gains help us—staying alive is more important than hitting it big, and 2) we can't and won't know which of the 10 years will be bad. This is why we don't play Russian roulette, even though we win more than we lose. It's better to take frequent small losses if it means avoiding a single devastating loss. This leads to the final reason we resist the antidote.

We do not comprehend the abstract. We understand what is seen but not what is not seen. We rarely celebrate the person who prevents the disaster because we usually don't know it was prevented (because it didn't happen!). The same goes for these antidotes. A diversified plan may avoid a disaster that we don't even know we would have experienced. Instead, we often just see missed upside. As the authors of the book *Noise* put it, "preventing the assault of an invisible enemy can yield only an invisible victory."[26]

So, embracing uncertainty works against us more frequently than for us and prevents disasters we may not know would have happened. Combine that with our desire to compare ourselves to others, the pressure to maximize, and a financial services industry clamoring for your business with promises to give you that upside, and you can see how and why we get out of balance.

We must be careful not to fall victim to timeline distortion. In the short run, all-in strategies may win. These are the big wins and lucky bets you see and hear about on the news. But these news stories don't usually tell the after story or show you the others who went all-in and failed. It's entirely possible to predict the future—someone always wins the lottery—but it's next to impossible to do it consistently—which is why no one wins the lottery twice. In the long run, unless your life goes perfectly according to plan, embracing uncertainty and staying alive by diversifying, building redundancies, and keeping your options open will prevail.

However, what often happens is we see the winners and fall for the 20/20 vision of hindsight. What we "should have done" seems obvious. Articles are published showing how much money you would have "if you would have done" this or that. All this does is create unrealistic expectations and resentment for not knowing what you couldn't have known. We think because we can explain what did happen, we can now predict what will happen.[27] The next time we have a choice, we don't embrace uncertainty and go all-in. When things go our way, we prosper, but when things don't go our way, we suffer.

Whether or not you choose to embrace uncertainty is decided by how you answer this question: *Do you want to maximize the outcome if you're right, or make sure you're okay if you're wrong?*

To be clear, I'm not saying you should have all of your money in cash and buy insurance for everything. Far from it. The goal in life isn't to avoid risk; it's to avoid the risk of ruin. In Chapter 8, we'll discuss how dosage matters (dropping a one-pound weight on your foot ten times hurts a lot less than dropping a ten-pound weight on your foot once)[28] and that we should protect against the catastrophic blowups, not the frequent stings. Don't protect against the thing that barely hurts you, only to ignore the thing that will destroy you simply because one happens more frequently. That's like insuring your microwave and not your house because the microwave breaks more often.

We can now bring Part I to a close. We understand that retirement is the stage of life when our money is going to work for us. We prefer not to run out of money and thus plan by making assumptions about the future. The outcome of our plan is sensitive to the outcomes of different variables. Part II will take a closer look at these variables.

Part II
Deep Dive

In Part I, we laid the groundwork of what retirement is, why we run out of money, and showed the framework for evaluating your financial life. We saw that retirement consists of inflows and outflows, and the goal of retirement planning is to ensure you have enough money to support your lifestyle without running out of money.

The discussion in Part I was general in nature, with the goal being to understand the "directional effects" of each outcome (e.g., increased spending requires a higher minimum rate of return).

In Part II, we will dive deeper into each topic to quantify these ranges of outcomes. Admittedly these discussions will, at times, be fairly detailed. This is done in the spirit of understanding. Some of these topics require a grasp of the inner workings to understand how they will change in the future.

The order of topics will be slightly reshuffled. First, we will attempt to answer the question of "How long should I plan for?" We will then evaluate the question, "How much will I need to spend each year?" by discussing common spending changes that occur in retirement. A more detailed discussion about inflation and spending shocks will tie into the spending discussion. Finally, we will look at income sources, different options for investing your money, and how those decisions affect your expected rate of return.

4

LONGEVITY

I f psychics really could see the future, and they took appointments
from retirement planners, the number one question asked of them
would be, "How long are we planning for?" That's because of all the
assumptions we make, how long we live is by far the most impactful.
Why is it so impactful?

Recall the variables of financial planning we discussed in Chapter
2. How long we live affects how much we can spend, what rate of
return we need to earn, and how much is left. This means our longevity can affect our lifestyle, investment strategy, and legacy. More than
any other variable, getting the longevity assumption wrong is the biggest reason our plans don't go according to plan, meaning we have to
cut back or leave more money on the table than intended.

How do we estimate our longevity? Like most things, we start
with what has happened before. The most common measure is known
as *life expectancy*. Life expectancy is a measure of when a group of people of a similar age is *expected* to die. These figures can be powerful but
also misleading if used inappropriately. Understanding how they are
created will illuminate both sides.

Let's revisit the example from Chapter 3. Imagine that you could
track when every person born in the year 1900 died. If you plotted how
many people died at each age, you would see Figure 4-1. If someone
asked you, "When do you expect someone born in 1900 to die?" how
would you answer them?

FIGURE 4-1: Distribution of Deaths

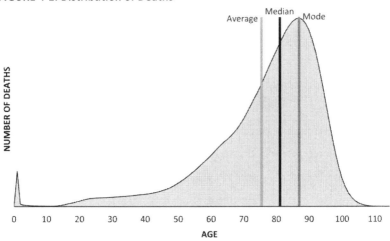

You could answer with an average (76.5). You could answer with the midpoint when half are dead and half are still alive (81). Or you could answer with the most common age people died (87).

All three measures are valid but notice two things. First, there is a significant difference between them. In Chapter 2, we saw how sensitive our plans are to small changes in longevity. Second, a lot of people live well past these ages. Most measures of life expectancy use the midpoint, which means half are still expected to be alive. If you use your life expectancy to determine when to deplete your accounts, this means you have a 50% chance of still being alive when your money is gone.

While this method gives us a starting point, there is more that we need to consider. Remember the two conditions that must exist for statistics to be useful. First, the sample must be representative of the population. Second, conditions that existed when the data was captured must still exist.

Both points can be made using vehicles as an example. If I want to know how long my 2020 Toyota Camry will last, looking at how long Ford F-150's or Chevy Suburban's last won't help much. They're both vehicles, but there are significant differences. It also won't be very helpful to look at Camry's built in 1985. A lot has changed.

Just as vehicles change with time and vary by make and model, humans do too. In Chapter 3, I used the example of a 65-year-old non-smoking female and how it does her no good to look at the life expectancy of 65-year-old smoking males, but there are other differences that affect our life expectancy. Some of these differences are more obvious than others, but the most common are shown below.

I must make two comments. First, remember that statistics are a way to summarize and describe data. There are always individual exceptions to the factors we will discuss. Second, the purpose of this section is not to comment on why these factors affect life expectancy, nor is it to quantify the exact effects. The purpose is to understand the existence and direction of the effects.

1. Gender
Females tend to live longer than males.

2. Marital status
Married individuals tend to live longer than single individuals.

3. Current health
A "less healthy" person will likely have a shorter life expectancy than an otherwise healthy person. Certain habits, such as exercise or drug use, also lead to a longer or shorter life expectancy.

4. Family history
Do all the women in your family celebrate their 100th birthday? Do all the men seem to have a heart issue in their 60s? While family history is helpful information and worth considering, there is no guarantee you will live a long or short time just because your parents or grandparents did.

5. Geography
It would surprise no one if I told you that life expectancy varied between people who live in Australia, South America, Africa, Europe, Asia, or North America. This same variation occurs with those living within different parts of the United States; however, the effect is much less pronounced when narrowed down by country.

6. Wealth

Wealthier people tend to have a longer life expectancy. The rationalization is that with affluence comes access to better medical care, cleaner living environments, possibly lower stress lifestyles, etc.

A study performed by the Health Inequality Project looked at life expectancy by percentile of income, and the results, shown in Table 4.1, are startling. Their research showed that compared to the bottom 1%, life expectancy for the top 1% was 14.6 years higher for men and 10.1 years higher for women.[1]

TABLE 4.1: Different Life Expectancies of Top and Bottom 1% Percentile of Income

	Men	Women
Top 1%	87.3	88.9
Bottom 1%	72.7	78.8

7. Education

Higher education also leads to a longer life expectancy, as it typically correlates with higher earning potential and leads to many of the same benefits associated with higher wealth. In addition, highly educated individuals are thought to be more aware of health risks and better able to avoid them.

All of the measures discussed thus far have been at birth. But what if you are 50 years old? How long are you expected to live? The answer is not your life expectancy at birth minus your current age. (This would eventually lead to "negative life expectancy" for some.) Your total life expectancy increases as you age. Not understanding this is one of the biggest reasons people underestimate their life expectancy.

Why does your life expectancy increase with age? Remember what life expectancy is effectively measuring—when half the people of a certain age are expected to die. If you're 50 years old, you've already outlived quite a few people. Including the previously deceased in your current life expectancy will understate it. You want to know, of the people currently 50 years old, how long are we expected to live? Figure 4-2 shows how life expectancy changes with age.

FIGURE 4-2: Total Life Expectancy by Current Age

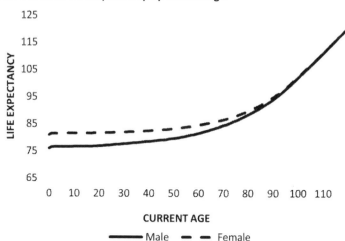

Couples have another intricacy to deal with. Since most people use life expectancy to estimate how long retirement will last, couples may want to know how long *at least one* of them is expected to live. This is called *joint life expectancy*.

Joint life expectancy is longer than the average of two individuals life expectancy. For example, if the life expectancy for a 65-year-old male is 84 years, and for a female is 87 years, how long can you expect at least one of them to be alive? You may be tempted to answer 85.5 (the average of the two), but in fact, the answer is 89 (according to the Social Security Administration's 2016 Period Life Table). The exact reason this happens is part of a longer discussion of math and statistics that we will not be having here. Figure 4-3 provides a helpful visual of the differences between individual and joint life expectancies.[2] (This *graph was adapted from Michael Kitces's blog at kitces.com.*)

This graph shows the probability of a 65-year-old male (dotted line) or female (dashed line) being alive a number of years later. It also shows the probability of at least one of them being alive (solid black line). The gray line at 50% probability marks what we consider to be life expectancy, the point at which half are alive and half are dead. You can see there is a much higher probability that at least one of them is alive at a given age than individually.

FIGURE 4-3: Individual vs. Joint Life Expectancy (at Age 65)

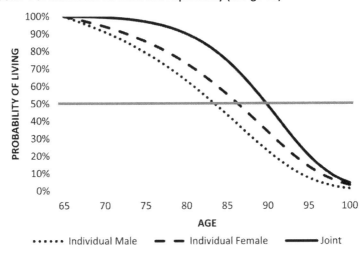

What about the fact that people change with time? I have only briefly mentioned the effect that improvements in technology and medicine have on life expectancy. The Society of Actuaries provides life expectancy projections using what they call the "Mortality Improvement Scale," which includes adjustments for such factors. Table 4.2 shows these results.[3]

TABLE 4.2: Projected Life Expectancies of Individuals and Couples

	65-year-old Male	65-year-old Female	65-year-old Couple
50% chance to live to	87	89	93
25% chance to live to	93	95	98

Notice that this table also breaks out the 25% probability. While life expectancy is normally published at the point of 50% probability, we can see how much longer 25% of us are expected to live.

Let's summarize what we've just covered:

- Life expectancy figures are the midpoint at which half of a group of people of the same age are expected to be dead, and half are expected to be alive.
- Most published figures show life expectancy at birth.
- As you age, your total life expectancy will increase.

- Specific demographic factors may adjust your life expectancy upwards or downwards, and improvements in technology and medicine have led to an overall increase in life expectancy.
- For couples, their joint life expectancy is longer than the average of each individual's life expectancy.

How should you factor all of this into your plan? Start by having an honest look at your own situation. Consider your family history, your current health, wealth, education, race, etc. Do your facts increase or decrease your life expectancy? If you go through this exercise and determine your life expectancy is now 90, remember that means there is a 50% chance you will still be alive at that age. Some people balk when they hear they may need to plan for a 30-year retirement, but the reality is, this is quickly becoming the norm (and 40-year retirements are becoming increasingly common as well).

People balk because longevity directly affects how much they can spend. Generally speaking, there are two approaches you can take when factoring longevity into your plan to generate income, 1) targeted and 2) open-ended. A targeted approach will target a specific age to deplete your accounts. An open-ended approach plans to generate income no matter how long you live. Which approach you take will affect which tools you use in your plan.

If you take the targeted approach, planning for longer longevity will reduce how much you can spend. Many people obviously don't like this. But if you plan for shorter longevity in an effort to maximize spending, then you introduce the chance of catastrophe if you guess wrong. The mental cycle goes something like this. "I don't want to run out of money; I should plan to live for a while. But! I probably will die before then, so I should plan for shorter longevity and spend more. But! I could possibly run out if I live longer, so I should plan for longer longevity." And on and on the cycle goes.

The truth is, you're not going to guess right. Obviously, there is some limit to how long you should plan for; we can't all plan to live to 110. That means there is inherently some level of risk and uncertainty we must accept. It would be great if we all died with the last dollar we wanted to spend in our pocket, but that's just not going to happen. We'll either run out or leave money unspent. Granted, there are tools like annuities that alleviate this problem, but we will all have to walk this tightrope in some capacity. This is where we must consider which outcome is worse. For most, it's running out of money.

Let's use an example to think about this from a decision-quality perspective. Refer back to Table 4.2, and this time we'll pick on couples. The table tells us that 1 out of 4 couples will have a member alive at age 98. Imagine you and three other couples are 65 years old, trying to plan how much to spend and when to deplete your accounts. Since it's a balancing act between spending more money and running out of money, you first must choose which one you're most concerned with.

Let's assume your main concern is running out of money and that all four of you plan to deplete your accounts at age 98, giving each a 25% chance of running out of money (because 1 of 4 will still be alive). Fast forward 33 years, and we'll find that three of you died before age 98, not running out of money but instead leaving money on the table, while the fourth will be out of money and still alive. Did three of you make a good decision since you didn't run out, and one a bad decision? The outcome does not tell us. Whether the decision was good or not depends on what your goal was and whether the decision you made gave you an acceptable chance of the outcome you don't want to happen happening. Think about it. You all took a 25% chance of running out of money. The fact that three of you were successful and one was not does not mean three made a good decision and one made a bad decision. The decisive factor is whether taking a 25% chance of running out of money is a good decision. For some it is; for some it's not.

Estimating longevity makes retirement planning hard. The longer we live, the more exposed to inflation, tax changes, market losses, etc., we become. That being said, on the whole, living longer is usually a gift and preferable to dying young. The truth is, you're likely not going to guess right, and you could be off by quite a few years. Embrace it by building a plan built to work no matter how long you live.

5

INTRODUCTION TO OUTFLOWS

There are many ways for money to flow out of your financial plan, some intentional and some not. Outflows can come in the form of living expenses, taxes, even donations or gifts. Some outflows we may be able to recoup or access at least a portion of in the future, like principal payments on a mortgage, and others we do not expect to see again, like money spent on a candy bar or vacation. These permanent outflows that we do not expect to see again we will call "spending." (Money we do expect to see again can be called "investing.")

As we saw in Chapter 2, how much we expect to spend impacts every other part of our plan. Yet again, this presents us with a balancing act—between the desire to spend money now and the fear of jeopardizing our future. All our lives, we are taught to save for the "long-run," but in the words of John Maynard Keynes, "In the long run, we are all dead." Eventually, we're meant to spend the money we've saved.

There are two ways to determine how much to spend: base it on how much you need or on how much you can. This is the difference between the spending-based and risk-based approaches discussed in Chapter 2, and projecting them are two very different exercises. The risk-based approach is a function of rate of return and will be discussed in later chapters. The following will discuss the spending-based approach.

To understand how challenging the task of projecting your spending in retirement is, attempt the following exercise. Imagine where you were 30 years ago. Go back to that time in your mind, and remember your life then. Imagine yourself 30 years ago trying to picture where you would be today. Where did you think you would be living? Who did you think you would be with? What did you think you would be doing? What did you think you would be spending money on? Now come back to reality. How accurate were you? Did you get it exactly right, or has life not played out quite as you thought? Most likely, there was a lot you didn't see coming. This exercise is what you are attempting to do when planning for retirement. We can attempt to picture what life will be like over the next 30 to 40 years, but we're going to get a lot wrong.

However impossible the task may be, there are steps we can take to be more accurate. Let's start with the most common way people project their spending.

Most people determine a base spending amount (often, what they are currently spending) and project an inflation rate of 1-3% into the future, resulting in Figure 5-1.

FIGURE 5-1: Inflation-Adjusted Spending

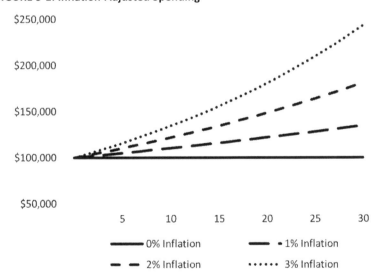

However, this method is likely to overestimate our spending needs, as it only considers the change in *price*. When planning, we are concerned with our *total spending*, which is a function of both price and *quantity*. Only focusing on changes in price ignores changes in quantity. For example, if you usually buy two gallons of milk for $2 each, you spend $4. If the next time you go to the grocery store, the price of milk has doubled to $4 per gallon, but you only need to buy one gallon, did you spend more or less? You spent the same. The increase in price was offset by the decrease in quantity.

Total Spending = Quantity x Price

Figure 5-2 helps us visualize this effect. Imagine that the quantity increases and the price decreases by the same amount each year. The net effect on your total spending is zero. *This example is for illustration purposes only and is not meant to suggest that prices and quantities will always offset.*

FIGURE 5-2: Comparing Total Spending When Quantity and Price Change

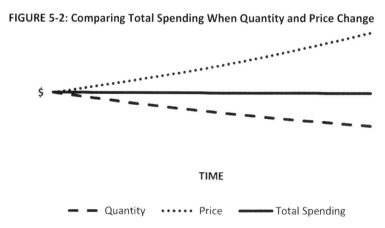

While changes in quantity and price will not always offset, we can be confident that our consumption habits, both in terms of what and how much we purchase, will change. This shouldn't come as a surprise as we change our consumption throughout our lives. We do not spend our money on the same things when we are 60, as we did when we were 30, 40, or 50, and it would be unrealistic to assume we stop changing our consumption just because we are retired.

Where did my raise go?

A phenomenon known as lifestyle inflation is an example of changing consumption habits. The concept is simple: as your income increases, so do the things you spend money on; your house gets bigger, your car gets nicer, you join that country club down the street, and the restaurants you visit now take reservations rather than your order at the counter. These are all examples of lifestyle inflation. Human beings adapt quickly, and a higher-class lifestyle can be tough to give up.

Rather than the exponentially increasing lines that we saw in Figure 5-2, a popular way to visualize retirement spending is as a "smile."[1] The retirement spending smile, shown in Figure 5-3, depicts the idea that a retiree spends more early on while exploring and enjoying their newfound freedom, begins spending less as they slow down physically, and finally spends more near the end of life due to increased health and long-term care costs.

FIGURE 5-3: Retirement Spending Smile

SPENDING

RETIREMENT YEARS

While the retirement spending smile provides a tidy visual, it is oversimplified, and we can consult the data to refine our estimates.

Ty Bernicke, in the *2005 Journal of Financial Planning*, found that the average 75-year-old spends roughly 50% less than the average 45-year-old.[2] In the February 1999 *Journal of Financial Planning*, Kenn Tacchino and Cynthia Saltzman noted that the average 65-year-old spends 26.5% more than the average 75-year-old.[3] JPMorgan, in their Guide to Retirement 2020 Edition, showed that the average 75-year-old spends roughly 40% less than the average 45 to 54-year-old.[4]

While that's a lot of numbers and citations, the overall message is the same: we spend less as we age.

The U.S. Bureau of Labor Statistics (BLS) provides perhaps the most detailed spending data when they publish the Consumer Expenditure Survey. Table 5.1 shows the average spending of different age groups, according to the 2018 Survey.[5]

A few notes about these kinds of studies. The exact numbers are meaningless. There are too many variations in the data. Just like life expectancy, your experience is likely to differ from that of the population, and we need to consider geography, gender, marital status, education, wealth, etc.

We must also understand the way averages are calculated and how they hide the variability in the data. Consider the following example. Assume the cost of a medical procedure is $100,000, and only 5% of all people will need this procedure. This means the average cost per person is $5,000. If you plan for the average ($5,000) and end up needing the procedure ($100,000), you'll be massively underprepared.

The point of these studies is to understand the "big picture" directional changes in spending.

TABLE 5.1: Average Spending by Age Group

Age Group	Average Spending Today	Percentage Decrease
45 – 54	$86,720	-
55 – 64	$78,660	(9.3%)
65 – 74	$68,140	(14.6%)
75+	$54,180	(19.3%)

These statistics again confirm that our spending decreases, but the important takeaway is that the decline appears to accelerate as we age.

So, while prices may increase, the quantity of what we purchase may decrease. To see again why it's important to consider the two together, let's look at a hypothetical example.

Assume that you are 65 years old, and you spend $100,000 per year. If you were to project your spending inflating 3% every year, you would see your expenses rise to the levels shown in Table 5.2 after 10, 20, and 30 years.

TABLE 5.2: Total Spending No Quantity Adjustment, 3% inflation

Age	Total Spending No Quantity Adjustment
65	$100,000
75	$134,392
85	$180,611
95	$242,726

What if you integrate the research and decrease the quantity of purchases by 1% per year? Keeping the same 3% inflation rate, your projections will change to the amounts shown in Table 5.3.

TABLE 5.3: Total Spending – (1%) Quantity Adjustment, 3% Inflation

Age	Total Spending Quantity Adjusted	Compared to Non-Quantity Adjusted
65	$100,000	$0
75	$121,541	($12,851)
85	$147,723	($32,888)
95	$179,545	($63,181)

Notice the enormous difference between quantity adjusted and non-quantity adjusted spending in the second column. At age 75, the difference is just under $13,000 per year, but by age 85, the difference is nearly $33,000 per year, and by age 95 is $63,000 *per year*. The cumulative difference over 30 years is more than $782,000. A retirement plan built to create $242,726 per year will look far different from one designed to generate $179,545 per year.

While this example is simple, the concepts it teaches are sound. We need to consider changes in both the quantity and price of what we purchase. Decreases in quantity may partially offset price increases. In the next chapter, we will discuss in-depth how the quantity of our spending changes and how to plan for it. Following that chapter will be a discussion of changes in price, i.e., inflation, to better understand its effects and how to plan for it as well.

6

SPENDING

In the last chapter, we established that total spending is a function of quantity and price. We will now zoom in on the quantity portion of the calculation. While it is helpful to understand that our spending will change over time, knowing *what* will change and how much it will change requires a deeper look.

Before we evaluate this empirically, we can think about it conceptually and how it makes sense that we spend less as we age. What areas do we spend less? Our spending can be separated into two categories, discretionary and non-discretionary, or "nice-to-haves" and "must-haves." Non-discretionary expenses, the must-haves, are the things you can't do without, such as housing, food, and clothing. The existence of these expenses is not likely to change much. (While they may change eventually, they do not change quickly.) Discretionary expenses, the nice-to-haves, such as travel, country clubs, and concerts, are likely to change more frequently. As we age and slow down, so do many of our discretionary expenses. Those with more discretionary expenses are likely to see their spending decrease more than those without as much "wiggle room."

Now, what about the empirical data? The previously mentioned Consumer Expenditure Survey also breaks down spending by category or sector. Figure 6-1 shows how the average spending changes by sector or category.

FIGURE 6-1: Average Household Spending By Age and Sector

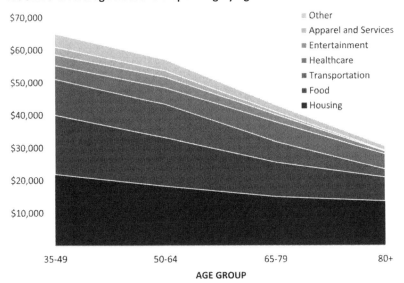

Just as I mentioned last chapter, the exact numbers are meaningless. The lesson here is that spending usually decreases, and some categories decrease more so than others.

This process of breaking down our spending into categories is one we can expand on. Since our spending is wide-ranging, consisting of costs of living, taxes, gifts, etc., trying to predict how spending as a whole will change is very difficult. However, disaggregating our spending makes it much easier to understand how the individual parts will change.

This disaggregation helps us determine what I call our "Retirement Adjusted Spending Amount" or RASA. To calculate our RASA, we can answer the questions laid out in the following steps:

Step 1: *Where do I currently spend money?*

Let's assume you've kept a record of how you spend your money, and Table 6.1 shows your personal income statement.

TABLE 6.1: Example of Personal Income Statement

Category	Amount
Income	$100,000
Taxes	($10,000)
After-Tax Income	$90,000
Housing	$25,000
Food	$15,000
Cars	$10,000
Health Insurance	$12,000
Medical	$5,000
Utilities	$2,000
Entertainment	$6,000
Travel	$3,000
Total Expenses	$78,000
Excess (Shortfall)	$12,000

Step 2: *What do I know will change?*

Some expenses we know for sure will change. Housing is one of the most common ones. If you own a home, your costs usually consist of mortgage principal and interest, as well as property tax, insurance, and maintenance. If your mortgage will be paid off when you retire, you will no longer be paying principal and interest, representing a significant increase in cash flow. (Property tax, insurance, and maintenance will not go away.) If you plan on downsizing your home, this, too, could translate into an increase in cash flow.

Health care costs are likely to change as well. Medicare is the primary source of health insurance for retirees. Depending on your health insurance during your working years, Medicare premiums may represent an increase in cost or a welcome reprieve.

Another thing to consider is what work-related expenses may go away. Whether it is clothing, business lunches, travel, commuting costs, etc., you may find some savings from eliminating these work-related expenses.

This process of evaluating what you know will change can be done for all of the lines in your income statement.

Step 3: *What would I like to change?*

Here we can account for voluntary changes in lifestyle, which may lead to an increase or a decrease in spending. If you'd like to start traveling more or purchase a vacation home, then you can build in an increase for those costs. Or perhaps you'd like to slow down, in which case, you may recognize some savings.

People often have a hard time imagining how their spending will be different in retirement. I find the following exercise to be helpful:

Let's assume during your career you worked a standard 40-hour week, Monday through Friday. For simplicity, we won't factor in your prep time and commute. When you are at work, you typically are not spending money. Now that you're retired, you have 40 extra hours a week of opportunities to spend money. How will you fill that time? Are you going to be spending money during it? Your answers will vary, but this exercise allows you to visualize what life will be like and where you may or may not be spending money. Maybe you'll hang around the house or work in the yard. Or maybe you'll travel, go golfing, or do another activity that isn't "free" during your free time. This is where we usually see an increase in "discretionary" spending.

Step 4: *What unexpected things could happen?*

This question is a bit of an oxymoron; if we can anticipate and plan for something, it's not unexpected. This exercise is easier said than done. For retirees, the most significant "unexpected" (i.e., not budgeted for) expenses come from health care, particularly those related to long-term care. Long-term care will receive an in-depth discussion in Chapter 9.

Contemplating unexpected expenses introduces the concept of *defined* and *undefined* risks. With defined risks, we know how much the potential exposure is. For example, if you need a new roof on your house, you have a pretty good idea of how much that will cost. Undefined risks, such as long-term care, are less obvious. Your future costs could be a few thousand dollars or several hundred thousand dollars. This is very difficult from a planning perspective. As I've mentioned and will expand on in Chapter 8, insurance can be used to narrow the range of outcomes of undefined risks. Insurance makes the planning process easier as you simply include insurance premiums in your RASA. If you choose not to insure or insurance is not an option, you must set aside or save money to protect against these unexpected expenses.

Now that we've adjusted for what we know will change, what we would like to change, and prepared for what might happen, we've arrived at our Retirement Adjusted Spending Amount (RASA), shown in Table 6.2. *It should go without saying that your exact amounts will vary. The RASA is more of a conceptual exercise than a literal one.*

TABLE 6.2: Retirement Adjusted Spending Amount (RASA) Example

Category	Amount	RASA
Housing	$25,000	$10,000
Food	$15,000	$20,000
Cars	$10,000	$5,000
Health Insurance	$12,000	$10,000
Medical	$5,000	$2,000
Utilities	$2,000	$2,000
Entertainment	$6,000	$11,000
Travel	$3,000	$10,000
Total Expenses	$78,000	$70,000

There are all kinds of ways we can sort and slice our RASA. For example, we could separate it into discretionary and non-discretionary. We can also use the RASA concept throughout the retirement planning process. It can help us evaluate where we are exposed to inflation, plan how much income we need, and decide the split between guaranteed and non-guaranteed income sources. (Many people like to have their non-discretionary needs met by guaranteed sources.)

"80%" Replacement Rule

A commonly used rule of thumb when calculating your income need in retirement is to plan for "80% of your pre-retirement income." As with any rule of thumb, this is simply a guideline and should not be taken literally in all contexts.

This "rule" can, at first, appear quite restrictive. It can be used as a battle cry for advisors looking to differentiate themselves: "Why take a pay cut in retirement! Work with me, and I will show you how to have full income replacement." But the 80% rule may not be as restrictive as it appears. If we reframe the discussion and approach it from a *consumption-based* perspective (also known as "spending-based") rather than income-based, you may find no change at all. A simple example will explain.

Let's assume that when you are working, your after-tax income is $100,000. Your spending needs are $80,000 per year, which allows you to live the life you want, and you are able to save the remaining $20,000. If, in retirement, your after-tax income is $80,000 (80% of your working income), do you feel like you experienced a cut in pay? From a consumption-based perspective, you will notice no change at all. You spent $80,000 before, and you spend $80,000 now. If you take an income-based approach, you may feel like you are $20,000 short, but the only difference is that you will no longer be saving.

I'm certainly not saying that you shouldn't aim for 100% income replacement in retirement. I hope everyone can achieve that amount or more. I'm merely saying that the 80% guideline is not as restrictive as it might first appear and may not represent a decrease in *consumption* at all.

Interestingly, the 80% rule may be too high of an estimate for some people. A 2013 study from David Blanchett of Morningstar looked at this issue closely and found the replacement rate ranges from 54-87%.[1]

Couples face the additional challenge of determining how their spending will change when one of them passes away. Again, having their spending disaggregated will allow them to think through each line item rather than guessing how spending as a whole will change.

There are two approaches couples can take when projecting how their spending will change. The first is more conceptual and is the same process the new retiree can use; imagine how the surviving spouse will fill their time. Depending on the age and stage of life when one spouse passes, the surviving spouse may travel or make other efforts to entertain themselves. These activities may cost more than when they were both alive. The opposite may be true if they shared an active lifestyle, and the surviving spouse decides to settle down.

There is also a more technical approach that involves determining what expenses are *fixed* and what expenses are *variable*. Fixed expenses are the same, regardless of how many people are in the household. Examples of fixed expenses include mortgage, property taxes, and homeowner's insurance. (Obviously, if you move houses, then these fixed expenses will change.) Variable expenses are based on consumption and will change if one spouse is no longer alive. The list of variable expenses includes food, health insurance, car insurance, car payments; basically, any expense that will change when a person is gone.

Ultimately, it is too personalized of a decision to speak in broad terms and provide a set percentage decrease in spending you can expect to experience. From a "needs" perspective, you likely will not "need" 100% income replacement when one spouse passes. How much your needs change will depend on you. Having accurate expense information will again make the planning process much easier.

I must make a note of caution in regards to the discussion in this chapter. Remember that the RASA is more of a conceptual exercise than a literal one. The RASA concept may imply a level of certainty that we cannot actually have. One particular challenge we face is that *we do not know what we do not know*. Determining your RASA is a helpful exercise, but it is just as subject to errors and omissions as any other forecasting process. Despite our best efforts, we can't predict how much we will spend on things that don't even exist today. I am fairly certain that when my 92-year-old grandmother planned her retirement, she didn't budget for her iPhone and Netflix subscription. While technology has improved our standard of living, and in many cases, lowered the cost of living, we will all spend money in the future on products and services that we can't foresee today.

It's clear that the quantity of what we purchase will change throughout our retirement. Let's now discuss the other piece of the spending puzzle, changes in price.

7

INFLATION

We can plan for changes in price much the way we plan for changes in quantity. Recall when we were determining our Retirement Adjusted Spending Amount (RASA), some line items increased in quantity, and others decreased, but not all increased or decreased by the same amount. The same is true of prices. Some line items are more subject to inflation than others, and projecting the same inflation rate across all lines is not the most accurate way to plan.

While we'll go into much further detail, I must make the message of this chapter clear: When it comes to spending, *you are only affected by changes in the price of the things you purchase.*[1]

With that in mind, we can start by understanding what inflation is and how it is measured. Inflation is an increase in prices that causes a decrease in purchasing power over time. As prices rise, a dollar tomorrow buys less than a dollar today.

You may think inflation is a bad thing, but a moderate level of inflation is natural and healthy for a growing economy. Higher prices tomorrow gives people an incentive to buy today. If the opposite, deflation, occurred and prices were lower tomorrow, no one would buy anything as they could get it cheaper the next day and the day after that. Sustained deflation can accelerate the collapse of an economy.

In theory, the effects of inflation are blunted while you're working, as your wages should increase as well. However, if you're retired, and your income is fixed, inflation can become a serious issue.

Consider the following example. In retirement, you live on a fixed income of $100,000, and your non-discretionary expenses total $80,000, leaving you with $20,000 of "fun money." If the prices of what you need inflate by 2% each year, after 10 years, the price of those same goods is $97,520. This leaves you with only $2,480 of "fun money." If the trend continues, the costs will grow to be larger than your income, which will require you to cut back your non-discretionary spending. Clearly, this can be a problem.

How is inflation measured? Once a month, the U.S. Bureau of Labor Statistics (BLS) publishes a figure called the Consumer Price Index (CPI). The CPI tracks the change in the price of a basket of goods and services. The percentage change in the index each year is considered inflation. For example, if the index was $1 last year, and $1.02 this year, inflation was 2%. Roughly 80,000 items are tracked that fall into the eight categories listed below. The BLS attempts to calculate the spending of a "typical" American by assigning weights to items in the basket to represent what a typical American buys.

1. Housing
2. Food and Beverages
3. Medical Care
4. Recreation
5. Apparel
6. Transportation
7. Education and Communication
8. Other Goods and Services

The BLS publishes several versions of the CPI, most notably the CPI-W, which measures the CPI for Urban Wage Earners and Clerical Workers (covers 28% of the population), and the CPI-U, the CPI for Urban Consumers (covers 88% of the population).[2] They also break CPI down by region: Northeast, Midwest, South, and West. Recently, the BLS began publishing the CPI-E, the Elderly index that attempts to track seniors' cost of living.

The CPI is a useful measurement, but once again, problems arise when we apply a group average (the economy-wide CPI) to our individual spending. If your "weights" differ from what is used to calculate the index, then *your* inflation rate (we should call it CPI-YOU) will differ from the economy-wide CPI. Often the differences are small, and CPI is "close enough," but it's worth looking at your spending a little closer to see how your inflation rate might differ from CPI.

How much do you weigh?

It's critical to understand the impacts of "weights" when calculating your inflation rate. See the following example.

Assume the CPI only tracks the prices of two goods, eggs and milk. The price of eggs increases by 10%, and the price of milk increases by 2%. Let's also assume that the typical American splits their purchases evenly, spending 50% of their money on eggs and 50% on milk. Under these assumptions, inflation for the year is 6% (50% x 10% + 50% x 2%).

Your purchases may differ. If you spend 25% of your money on eggs and 75% on milk, your inflation rate is 4% since you purchase more milk than eggs (25% x 10% + 75% x 2%).

In this example, if you design your plan to keep up with the CPI, you will overstate your inflation rate, which can drastically affect the rest of your plan, as seen in Chapter 2.

The opposite can be true, as well. If you purchase 75% eggs and 25% milk, your inflation rate is 8% (75% x 10% + 25% x 2%), and using the CPI will understate your inflation rate.

While oversimplified, the point this example makes remains, if your weights differ from those used in the CPI, your inflation rate will be different.

Before we can talk about what inflation will be in the future, we need to understand what causes it.

Inflation is primarily triggered in the following three ways. First, increases in the costs of inputs get passed on through the economy. For example, if the price of corn increases, then companies who use corn to make products will have to increase the price of their own products to remain profitable. This higher price is then passed on to the rest of the economy. Second, an increase in demand can increase prices. If more people want something, and there is no increase in supply to meet the increased demand, prices will rise. Finally, expansionary monetary policy may cause inflation. This occurs when Central Banks expand the monetary base (often incorrectly referred to as "printing" money). If there is more money in the economy going towards the same supply of goods and services, prices will rise, much like the effects of higher demand.

Aside from these factors, simply anticipating increased inflation can be a self-fulfilling prophecy. If market participants expect prices to increase, they may proactively increase the prices of the goods they sell, which in turn creates the very inflation they were anticipating.

It's important to note that while these factors *can* lead to inflation, they don't always do. Throughout the 2010s, interest rates were low, and the money supply increased with little inflation to show for it.

Inflate the debt away

Some think the U.S. government has an incentive to increase inflation. As of this writing, the national debt is over $28 Trillion.[3] In theory, the government can "print" money to pay the debt. Doing so should increase inflation and lower the debt cost, as they will be paying it down with inflated dollars. Whether or not this will happen remains to be seen.

One way to estimate inflation is to look at how much it's been in the past. Like most things, it has varied, as evidenced by Figure 7-1.

Since 1928, inflation has averaged 3.04% per year, but more recently, the number has been closer to 2%. At times, inflation has run well above the long-term average. Driven by wars, global crises, and flawed monetary policy, fortunately, these periods have been rare. Many lessons were learned from these periods, and central banks make considerable efforts to control inflation. In the United States, the Federal Reserve targets a 2% inflation rate. While they have proven to be fairly competent at meeting this target and staving off high inflation, it is always possible inflation could increase in the future.

FIGURE 7-1: Inflation By Year Since 1928

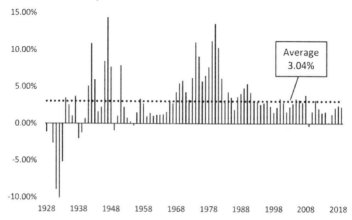

Remember the danger of relying on historical information to project the future. Relying on the past implies that the past is as good or bad as things will get. Just because we haven't seen sustained periods of deflation or high inflation does not mean it can't or won't happen.

While it is one thing to know what inflation has been and what causes it, it is an entirely different thing to be able to predict what it will be. The question that matters to you is: how should you estimate and plan for *your* inflation rate? Remember, you are affected by changes in the price of the things you consume. If I told you the price of fur coats doubled last year, would you care? If you don't buy fur coats, then no, you would not. Go back to your RASA and look at where you spend money. In *your* basket of goods and services, what is subject to inflation, and what is not? Also, remember that what your basket consists of will change over time. For example, if you travel a lot now, you may not travel as much later, meaning your exposure to the inflation of travel costs will decrease.

Looking at your basket, you may find that some of your expenses stay the same. If you have a fixed mortgage, then principal and interest do not increase each year, which means those expenses are not exposed to inflation. (Conversely, maintenance and insurance costs are exposed to inflation.) You may even find that some prices decrease. We see this with technology, as prices of computers and TVs fall even as they continue to improve in functionality. Of course, other expenses, like those related to health care, may be subject to significant price increases.

It's all part of the plan

Planned obsolescence is the process of intentionally making a product obsolete, which increases the frequency consumers must replace it. This is a tremendous source of increased expenses for consumers and can happen in several ways.

First, products can be built *not* to last. For example, refrigerators, washing machines, and printers last a fraction of the time they used to. (A 35-year printer executive once told me, "We'd have gone broke if we kept making them as good as we did.") Rather than building products that will last 20 years, companies will intentionally build them to break down much sooner, forcing consumers to buy again.

Second, companies can continuously update or "improve" their product. Rather than releasing all of their updates and features in one product, they can stagger them over time, requiring customers to keep purchasing the newest version if they want the "latest and greatest."

Finally, modifications can be made to products that require you to purchase something new if you want to continue using them. Apple used this tactic when they eliminated the headphone jack on the iPhone. If you intend to listen to music on their newer devices, you'll need to purchase an adapter or one of their handsomely priced AirPods.

There can be value in paying for quality. Paying more today for something you won't have to replace as often may save you money in the long run, but there are no guarantees. If it seems like your products aren't lasting as long as they used to, it's not an accident.

We can be fairly certain that some level of inflation will exist in the future. However, a trap to look out for is extrapolating recent inflation trends, especially when they are outliers. Let me explain why that is using long-term care costs as an example.

Assume that the cost of long-term care averages $60,000 per year and has been increasing at 10% per year for the last five years. If we were to project this 10% inflation rate into the future, in 20 years, this same $60,000 of care would cost $403,650 per year. This is only my opinion, but I do not think this is an appropriate way to budget. Projecting costs to increase indefinitely into the future disregards the laws of gravity that apply to prices as well. Prices will eventually run into some natural resistance that keeps them from rising forever. This assumption also fails to consider the capitalist system that we have in the United States. For example, if long-term care costs were to increase 10% per year in perpetuity, eventually, care would become so expensive that very few people would be able to afford it. Seeing how many people need care and the opportunity to make money if care can be provided at a reasonable price, I am confident someone will find a way to provide affordable care to capture that unmet demand.

Remember the effect inflation has on your plan. Higher inflation increases the chance you run out of money and requires lower spending or an increased return to avoid running out of money. The concept of asymmetric outcomes taught us that being underprepared for inflation is worse than being overprepared. To prepare, test your plan against a range of inflation assumptions. If you see you have a problem, it may require you to alter where you put your money, as some tools are better suited to fight inflation than others.

Tools to fight inflation

A dollar in the future will be devalued by inflation. If I promise to pay you $1,000,000 in 10 years, the higher inflation is, the less the $1,000,000 will be worth.

This can work both for and against you. If you *owe* someone a fixed dollar amount in the future, inflation will help you. Your mortgage is a great example of this. The "real" value of your mortgage decreases over time due to inflation.

This works against you if you expect to receive a fixed amount in the future. For example, fixed bond payments are devalued as inflation rises. Fixed payments made by annuities or pensions fall into this category as well.

Tools that are good for fighting inflation will rise in value as price levels increase. Real estate and stocks are amongst the most popular tools for this reason.

Gold is often thought of as an inflation hedge but has been surprisingly poor at this in recent years. Gold serves better as a "crisis hedge," performing better in times of chaos.

The U.S. Treasury offers a tool specifically designed to fight inflation, known as Treasury Inflation-Protected Securities (TIPS). TIPS are discussed in Chapter 17.

Again, you are only affected by price changes of the things you buy, and inflation is just one piece of the total spending puzzle. Your inflation rate may not represent the change in your total spending, as we must also consider changes in quantity. We'll never know for sure what inflation will be. There are ways to estimate it, but even those will likely be wrong.

One of the biggest sources of inflation in recent years has been health care costs. The most popular way to protect against these costs is through insurance. Before discussing health care, we will discuss why insurance was created and how to think about and use it.

8

INSURANCE

Insurance is like an umbrella (in more ways than one). You probably wish you didn't need it, are very grateful to have it when you do, and it can be very hard to procure once you know for sure you need it. While insurance is certainly valuable, it is one of the most misunderstood and misused tools. There are certain principles of insurance which, when understood correctly, can make the decision of whether or not to insure much easier.

To understand insurance, there's no better place to start than by asking, "Why does insurance exist?" The short answer is because the world is uncertain. Insurance protects you from a future loss that *you don't know for sure if or when* you will experience. If you did know for sure, you would either plan for or avoid the loss altogether.

It's easy to see how and why insurance was created. Imagine you and a group of people are sitting around talking one day. You turn to the group and say, "You know, it would really suck if *insert insurable event* happened. I don't think I could afford it." Someone else in the group replies, "Yeah, me too!" You all soon realize that you have the same problem. Then someone says, "Hey, what if we all pitch in some money, and if the *insurable event* happens, the pool of money will help make that person whole."

With that, the concept of risk-pooling—insurance—is born. The "insurable event" can be any number of things: my house burns down, I wreck my car, I get disabled, I die early, I need long-term care, I live too long, etc. (There are countless risks you can insure against. The unsettling joke that drug companies have invented more diseases than they've cured can also apply to insurance companies and the risks you can insure against.)

Determining how much each person should pitch in (pay in premiums) is mostly a function of 1) how big the risk is and 2) how likely they are to access the pool of money (make a claim).[1]

The first factor, the size of the risk, is straightforward. Insuring a $1,000,000 home will cost more than a $500,000 home. This is true of all insurance.

The second factor, the probability of making a claim, is made up of several parts.

There are "policyholder" factors, such as age and current health for life insurance or driving history for car insurance.

There are also "policy design" factors. A larger deductible decreases the chances of making a claim; therefore, it lowers the premiums. The length of coverage is another example. Life insurance covering one year will be cheaper than life insurance covering 10 years.

Then there are "policy performance" factors, for example, how many people make claims. If more people make claims than expected, everyone will have to pay higher premiums to help replenish the pool.

Additional policy performance factors include interest rates and investment portfolio returns. Since claims do not have to be paid right away, the pool of money must be put somewhere. The money may be invested somewhere safe that still earns a return. If the returns are higher than expected, future premiums can be lowered, or excess premiums can be returned. Conversely, if returns are lower than expected, premiums may need to increase.

While the summary above is basic and littered with oversimplifications, it is fundamentally how insurance works; a group of people pools their money to protect against a risk or insurable event. How big your risk is, how likely you are to need it, how many people actually use it, and investment returns all affect how much premiums are. Of course, an insurance company is formed to facilitate all of this.

The following are several key concepts and principles of insurance:

1. Insurance represents a transfer of risk.

When you purchase insurance, you pay premiums to an insurance company, and in exchange, they assume the risk of loss. Usually, the loss is a defined amount, but as we'll see, it can be undefined as well.

2. The more likely a claim is to be made, the higher the premiums.

While it may seem like this point is obvious and has already been discussed, it has important ramifications. There are two areas of consequence. First, certain types of insurance *in general* can be more expensive. Second, certain types of insurance *for you* can be more expensive. Long-term care insurance allows us to make both points.

Long-term care insurance is fairly expensive. Why is that? First, the cost of long-term care itself is high, so the size of the risk is large. Second, as we'll see next chapter, the chance of a retiree needing some level of long-term care in their life is also high. So long-term care insurance is expensive *in general* because the insurance company sees a big risk that people are likely to need.

Long-term care insurance (and life insurance) also requires you to be underwritten before purchasing a policy. One of the purposes of the underwriting process is to assess your current health to gauge how much of a risk you are; the higher your risk, the more likely you are to make a claim and the higher your premiums. So life insurance can be more expensive *for you*, depending on your health.

As an aside, there are two ways to respond when you see higher premiums. You can dismiss them and decline coverage, or you can listen to and evaluate what they are saying. If the insurance company is charging you more for premiums, they see something that says you're more likely to need it than others are. To be clear, I'm not saying you should buy insurance no matter what they charge; just let it clue you in on areas you need to address, even if that doesn't involve insurance.

3. Insurance isn't designed to make you rich; it's designed to keep you from becoming poor.[2]

Insurance is a form of "hedging." Hedging is a strategy to lock in a position regardless of what happens. If you have insurance and your home burns down, you are in relatively the same financial position as if it didn't because insurance replaces the value that you lost. This is how car insurance, life insurance, disability insurance, etc., all work. No one "*wins.*" You either pay premiums and don't need it or experience a loss and are made whole. You do not "gain" anything from this.

While you typically do not "gain" directly from insurance, insurance can help you grow your wealth in two ways. First, it allows you to buy assets, like houses, that you may not have been able to without the ability to insure since an uninsured loss would be devastating. Second, it can "unlock" your remaining assets. For example, rather than setting aside all of the money to cover an insurable event, insurance allows you to set aside a smaller pool of money to protect against a bigger risk. In a sense, this "frees up" those other dollars, which you can then use or invest in a way that provides a higher return than if you had to hold them somewhere safe.

While insurance *combined* with other tools can add to your wealth, insurance *alone* does not add to your wealth—it protects it.

4. You can't buy it once you know you'll need it.

This little fact is what makes the insurance decision so difficult. If your house is on fire, you can't call up State Farm and insure your home. You have to insure before you know for sure you will need it. If this weren't true, your premiums would be prohibitively high (essentially equal to your total risk).

While that is how insurance works, the question we really care about it is, "Do we need it?" Insurance makes us whole after a loss and provides peace of mind, so why is this even a question? Because preparing for tomorrow is decidedly "unpleasurable," and we could use those dollars on other more "pleasurable" things, so we seek to minimize how much we spend on insurance.

The way to decide if we need it is to ask, "Can I afford the outcome if the insurable event happens?" What does afford mean? It means you can come up with the funds to pay for the loss without having to significantly alter your lifestyle or fire sale assets. If you can afford it, then you don't *need* insurance. However, there are times where insurance can serve a purpose, even if you don't *need* it.

Asking the question, "Can I afford the outcome?" requires you to quantify the outcome. Some risks are easier to quantify than others. There are *defined risks* and *undefined risks*. With defined risks, you know how large the risk or potential liability is, for example, if your home or car is destroyed. With undefined risks, you do not know how much your future loss could be. Future health or long-term care costs are usually undefined. It's hard to answer the question, "Can I afford this outcome?" when you don't know what the outcome is.

If you cannot afford the outcome, you should at the very least explore insuring against it. In actuality, you have three choices in how you respond to a particular risk:

1. Do nothing

This is nothing more than a gamble. Doing nothing means that you do not insure, and you do not alter your saving and investing strategy to protect against this risk. If you never experience the insurable event, then you got away with it. If you do experience it, then you have no one to blame but yourself for the outcome.

2. Insure against it

Insuring requires you to pay premiums in exchange for protection that will cover you if the insurable event occurs. Insuring narrows your range of possible outcomes. It raises your floor (worst-case scenario) but also lowers your ceiling (best-case scenario).

3. Self-fund

Rather than putting money towards insurance premiums, you can attempt to "self-fund," creating your own pool of money by saving and investing money you would have spent on premiums. We can't call it "self-insure" as insurance represents a transfer of risk, and when you self-fund, you retain all of the risk.

There are two ways to execute a self-funding strategy, 1) set aside a lump sum, or 2) save and invest money over time. Both strategies have behavioral challenges, as you must actually put money aside and also not touch it. As discussed in Chapter 1, there is something innately difficult about putting money away today for a threat you may or may not experience tomorrow.

Self-funding also comes with investment risk, the chance that you don't receive the returns you expect, and sequence of returns risk, the risk that returns don't occur in the order you need them. These challenges combine to create what I call *spreadsheet risk*. Many self-fund strategies work on a spreadsheet but fail because the money expected to go in doesn't make it, or returns fall short of expectations.

Some risks, such as those relating to auto, homeowners, and health, we are required to insure against. For other risks, like death, disability, and long-term care, we have a choice. Most people decide to at least address the serious risks they face, which leaves them the choice between insuring and self-funding. This decision is a manifestation of the balancing act between fear and greed. Insurance protects us against a bad outcome. Why wouldn't we want that? Because we want more money to spend. So, on the one hand, you're exposed to a risk that you don't want to experience. On the other hand, you'd like to protect against it, but you don't want to pay insurance premiums that will detract from your spending and enjoyment today.

Obviously, if we never experience the insurable event, then self-funding will be better. It will provide us with a pool of money to either spend or pass on. But, we don't know if we will experience it or not, which is the whole reason we go through this analysis, so the self-fund approach usually tries to replicate insurance by creating the same benefit pool by investing the money we would have spent on premiums.

Inevitably when comparing insurance to self-funding, the spreadsheet comes out. We type in the premiums that we would have paid and either calculate what return we need to match the insurance pool or assume a rate of return and compare it to the insurance pool. Anyone who has done this quickly realizes there are too many scenarios and variables to look at all of them, so let's simplify the decision.

For the quantitative analysis, we need to answer four questions. 1) How much are the premiums? 2) How big is the benefit? 3) When do we need it? 4) What can we do with our money instead (rate of return)? Table 8.1 shows what outcomes favor insurance or self-funding.

TABLE 8.1: Insuring vs. Self-Funding

Criteria	Favors Insurance	Favors Self-Fund
Premiums vs. benefit spread	Bigger	Narrower
When will you need it	Sooner	Later
What rate of return you could earn	Lower	Higher

Most of these are pretty obvious. The bigger the pool is per dollar of premium, the more it will favor insurance. The sooner you need it, or the lower your investment return, the more this favors insurance as well. The self-fund approach is favored if insurance does not give you much "bang for your buck," if you don't need access to the pool of money for a while, or if you earn a high rate of return.

We can also look at the decision by comparing just two factors, investment returns and the timing of when you need insurance. Notice the symmetry in Table 8.2. If you need insurance early or the market doesn't cooperate, insurance is best. If you need it later or the market exceeds your expectations, self-funding is better. If you need it later, and the market returns are poor, it will depend on how much later and how poor the returns are. If you need it sooner and market returns are favorable, it depends just how favorable the returns are.

TABLE 8.2: Insuring vs. Self-Funding – Timing and Returns

Insurable Event Occurs	Poor Market Returns	Average Market Returns	Favorable Market Returns
Sooner	Insurance	Insurance	Depends
When Expected	Insurance	Either	Self-Fund
Later	Depends	Self-Fund	Self-Fund

There's a critical takeaway from Table 8.2 that is not a coincidence and is part of how insurance is priced. If you experience the "average" outcome, then recreating insurance is doable. This means, if you have a "better" than average experience (need it later or for less time), then self-funding will be better. If you have a "worse" than average experience, then insurance will be better.

There are important qualitative and behavioral factors we must consider. Behaviorally, we must actually save and invest the money we say we will. Qualitatively, we must consider the value of peace of mind. While the spreadsheet might show one thing, there is tremendous value in the peace of mind knowing that you're covered and don't have to worry about saving, tax rates, return sequences, etc.

We must also consider how long the risk lasts. We often save and invest rather than insure so that we can have more money left over if we don't need it. But if the risk does not go away, like with long-term care, then *we* will not spend that money; our heirs will. Any pool of money you create is reserved in case you need it, which means you can't spend it because "you never know" if you'll need it or not.

While the preceding discussion attempted to identify which strategy is best under certain outcomes, we must remember two things. 1) It relied on hindsight; you won't know if or when you'll need it or what return you will earn until after the fact. 2) It doesn't tell us which *decision* is best. We can't let the outcome determine the quality of our decisions. Having and not using insurance does not mean you made a bad decision, in the same way that not crashing your bike doesn't mean wearing a helmet was a mistake. There is value in the peace of mind knowing you were protected against a risk, even if you never use the protection. Each of us will value this peace of mind differently.

Figure 8-1 compares the range of outcomes between the three strategies we've discussed. You can see that doing nothing leaves you with only downside. Alternatively, self-funding offers the potential upside of having more money if the insurable event never happens. This figure clearly shows how insurance narrows your range of outcomes. (It does not factor in lost opportunity costs of insurance premiums.) The range is barely visible as the difference between the best-case scenario (you lose your premiums) and the worst-case scenario (you lose your premiums and deductible) is minuscule.

When deciding whether or not to insure, you must understand that there are two competing powers in the financial services industry: insurance and investment companies. Each creates products (tools) that do different things. Insurance protects against your *fear* of loss, and investments stroke your *greed* for more. Awareness of this difference will help decipher much of the messaging in financial planning.

FIGURE 8-1: Range of Outcomes for the Three Protection Strategies

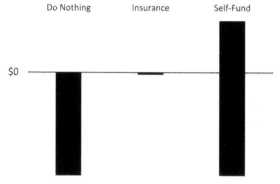

The tools these companies create take on very different risks. With insurance, the risk is that you will miss out on the upside, meaning you could have done more with the dollars you put towards premiums. With investments, the risk is that you participate in the downside, meaning you either take losses from investing or have to pay substantial costs out of pocket if the insurable event happens.

Remember, just like any other company that produces a product, each wants to sell as much as they can. They will do this by a) making their product sound as good as possible, b) making their competition sound as bad as possible, and c) training their salespeople accordingly.

The next time you come across a positive or negative opinion of insurance or investments, consider the source. Insurance companies will try to scare you about the threat they are protecting or the alternative of investing in the markets. Investment companies will tout the value of staying invested over the long run and how you'll have more money by investing. Neither is necessarily wrong.

With insurance, the story and balancing acts are always the same. An unknown exists that you don't want to experience. You want to protect your future self, but you also want to enjoy yourself now.

Let's be honest. The whole idea of insurance is painful.

Throughout our lives, we are almost certain to spend more on premiums than we'll receive in benefits. (This is also a necessary fact, as insurers need to make more money than they spend to stay in business.) But insurance can be a wonderful antidote to uncertainty. It offers asymmetric protection—more protection to the downside than upside given up. It also allows us to trade small losses to avoid huge ones—it's better to pay and lose 1% of our home's value in premiums every year than lose 100% of its value in a fire.[3] (We should also remember that preventing a big loss can have the same net effect as making a big gain.)

You could sit around all day and conjure up every conceivable risk that might hurt you, but you will not be able to protect against every one of them. You may also not be able to fully protect against the risks you do choose to insure against. This is okay, as some protection is often better than no protection and can soften the blow just enough.

When comparing your options, you should be wary of spreadsheet risk, the false comfort that comes from seeing numbers look good on a screen. Sequence of returns risk and the behavioral challenge of sticking to a savings strategy creates the gap between model and reality. When the risks are undefined, it can also be hard to know what or how much you are saving for.

In the end, you must make your decision with what you know at that moment. If you buy insurance and never use it, that doesn't mean you made a bad decision. Buying the wrong kind or amount or paying more than you need to may be bad, but protecting yourself from an event you cannot afford is not in itself a bad decision. The true value of insurance comes from limiting the range of outcomes and the certainty it provides. The cost of this certainty is reduced upside. There is value in the peace of mind of knowing you are covered. Insurance combined with other tools may add to your wealth, but insurance alone will not. Always remember the tug of war that exists between insurance and investment companies.

Next, we discuss the costs we most commonly insure—those related to health care.

9

HEALTH CARE

While we all know that costs related to health care are one of the most significant sources of expenses for retirees, "health care" is a broad term. We can separate these costs into two categories, 1) major medical, which includes doctors and hospitals and the type of care you're used to receiving, and 2) long-term care, which I'll further define in a few pages. (When we use the term "medical" in this chapter, we are referring to any *non*-long-term care treatment.)

Both forms of health care share the same challenge when planning:

1. We don't know if or how long we will need care.
2. We don't know how much the care will cost.

That is a double whammy of uncertainty and is the epitome of an *undefined risk.* You may need a little care or a lot of care, and the care could cost a few hundred dollars or a few hundred thousand dollars.

While the topic of health care deserves a longer discussion, this chapter aims to provide a background on the source of these expenses and an overview of ways that we can protect ourselves from them. When it comes to medical expenses, we don't have much choice but to insure. For the majority of retirees in America, their health insurance is provided through Medicare. Let's start with a brief overview of the basics of Medicare and discuss how it can be used to limit your range of exposure to medical costs.

MEDICARE

The following is not Medicare enrollment advice. The program has many specifics and frequently changes. There are exceptions to most of the points made in this chapter. Please consult a Medicare expert before making any enrollment decisions.

Medicare is the health insurance program offered by the government that is available to most Americans beginning at age 65. There are two forms of Medicare—Original Medicare and Medicare Advantage. Each consists of different "Parts," as shown in Table 9.1.

TABLE 9.1: Original Medicare vs. Medicare Advantage

Original Medicare	Medicare Advantage
Part A	Part A
Part B	Part B
Part D	Part C
Supplement	

Notice that both forms of Medicare include Parts A and B. Part A covers hospitals and inpatient care. If you are "Medicare eligible," meaning you have worked and paid into the system for 40 quarters, then Part A will be premium-free.* This is the case for the majority of Americans. Part B covers doctors and outpatient care. Part B charges a premium, and the exact cost depends on your income level. These premiums increase each year, typically to adjust for inflation. To give you an idea of the size of premiums, in 2021, Part B premiums range from $148.50 to $504.90 per month per person, depending on the individual or couple's income.

It is imperative that you sign up for Medicare on time. If you're eligible for Part A, then enrollment is "automatic" at age 65. Part B, however, is not automatic. For every year you're late to enroll, Medicare can assess a permanent 10% penalty. This means that if you are two years late to enroll, you will be paying 120% of your regular

---

* The "system" is defined as paying FICA taxes, which are further discussed in Chapter 10. FICA tax consists of 6.2% to Social Security and 1.45% to Medicare.

premiums for as long as you live. The rules on when you must enroll will vary depending on whether you are already receiving Social Security and whether you are working and have health insurance through your employer. Work with someone who understands Medicare to determine which programs to enroll in and when you need to do it.

Medicare Part A and Part B are designed to cover 80% of your medical costs, meaning you are liable for the remaining 20%. This leaves you a choice between two options to cover the difference: Original Medicare, or Medicare Advantage.

If you choose Original Medicare, you are eligible to purchase a Medicare Supplement or "Medigap" policy. There are several types of Medicare Supplements to choose from, and each varies based on the level of coverage provided. Policies that reach 100% coverage are obviously more expensive than policies that don't.

Medigap policies are offered by private health insurance companies such as Aetna and UnitedHealthcare. Medigap plans are categorized alphabetically and standardized across carriers, meaning Plan M with one company provides the same coverage as Plan M offered by a different company. They are only differentiated by price. It is important to note that Medigap premiums will increase as you age.

To receive prescription drug coverage on Original Medicare, you will need to sign up for Part D, which also charges a premium based on your income level and will increase with inflation over time.

Medicare Advantage works differently. If you choose Medicare Advantage, you will sign up for Part C instead of a Medigap and Part D plan. Part C plans are also called "Advantage Plans," hence the name Medicare Advantage. These plans often provide more extensive coverage than Medigap policies, and many include prescription drug coverage. Some Advantage Plans may not even charge a premium.

At this point, you may wonder why anyone would choose Original Medicare. One of the biggest reasons is access to doctors. Original Medicare is accepted by any doctor that takes Medicare, while Advantage Plans are only accepted by doctors in your network.

Deciding between Original Medicare and Medicare Advantage is a personalized decision beyond this book's scope. The discussion so far has been a high-level overview, but there is much more to consider, and again, you should consult a Medicare planning professional before making any decisions.

Let's reset. There are two forms of Medicare, Original and Advantage. Part A and Part B apply to everyone and cover 80% of your medical costs. The decision you have to make is how to cover the remaining 20%. Purchasing the right Medigap or Advantage plan could provide you nearly 100% coverage of medical (non-long-term care) costs.

The difference in premiums between a lower and higher coverage Medigap plan can be significant. You may be tempted to sign up for a lower coverage plan, with the thinking that as you age and become more likely to need care, you can switch to a higher coverage plan. Unfortunately, it's not that easy. In order to switch from a lower coverage (and lower premium) policy to a higher coverage (and higher premium) policy, you must pass medical underwriting at that time. To put it bluntly, you probably won't pass. The process includes completing a questionnaire with a list of health conditions. If you have *ever* had any of the conditions listed, you are ineligible to switch coverage. The list is so extensive that even the healthiest among us are unlikely to answer "No" to all questions.

This means if you want to have higher coverage later, you need to pay for it now. This puts us back in the uncomfortable position of deciding whether to pay high premiums for insurance we will not use now and may not use ever or save money today and risk being exposed to high health care costs in the future.

The following tables and chart help us visualize the difference between 80% and 100% coverage, whether obtained through a Medigap or Advantage plan. If you are 80% covered, your total cost exposure is equal to your premiums plus 20% of any health care costs. With 100% coverage, your only exposure is the cost of your premiums (plus applicable deductibles).

TABLE 9.2: Difference in Exposure - 80% vs. 100% Coverage

Health Care Costs	Total Exposure	
	80% Covered	**100% Covered**
$	Premiums + 20% of costs	Premiums

Let's use a hypothetical example. Assume that premiums for 80% coverage are $8,000 per year, and premiums for 100% coverage are $12,000. Table 9.3 quantifies the difference in total exposure.

TABLE 9.3: Difference in Exposure - 80% vs. 100% Coverage

Health Care Costs	Total Exposure		
	80% Covered (Premiums + Costs)	**100% Covered (Premiums)**	**100% vs 80% Coverage**
$0	$8,000	$12,000	$4,000
$100,000	$28,000	$12,000	($16,000)
$200,000	$48,000	$12,000	($36,000)
$500,000	$108,000	$12,000	($96,000)

FIGURE 9-1: Partial vs. Full Coverage Out of Pocket Cost Comparison

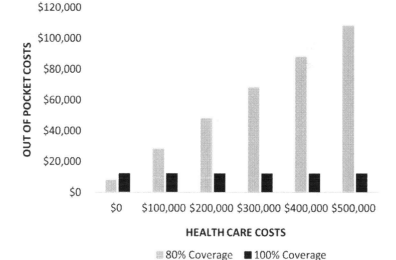

If no care is needed, you will save $4,000 per year if you have 80% coverage. However, if a higher amount of medical care is needed, 100% coverage can save you substantial amounts of money.

From a planning perspective, it's much easier to plan for premium increases over time than for future unknown health care costs. We know our premiums will increase as we age, and if we are off in our projections, it likely will not have a material impact on our plan. For example, if you expect premiums to be $5,000, but they end up being $6,000, the difference is only $1,000. (Even if we're off by 100%, the difference is only $5,000.) However, predicting your future health care costs is much more perilous. Say we plan for $50,000 of future health care costs, but the actual total could be $100,000 or $250,000. Coming up with an additional $200,000 could prove troublesome.

Obviously, 100% coverage is beneficial if you need it, but you won't know if you will or not. You must balance what is more important to you, limiting your range of exposure to medical costs or having more money to spend today by choosing lower-cost coverage.

Medicare is not a perfect system, but overall, it provides quality health care coverage. Medicare covers doctors and hospitals and some forms of rehabilitative care. What Medicare does not cover, however, is most types of long-term care.

LONG-TERM CARE

Imagine you are retired and out on your yacht with your friends. It's a beautiful blue-sky day with a light breeze and passing clouds. You're all taking turns looking through binoculars at whales breaching in the distance. When it is your turn, you see something rippling in the water on the horizon. You soon realize it is a torpedo, and it appears to be headed straight for your boat! You think to yourself, "Well, it's still pretty far away. Maybe I can maneuver around it," or "Maybe it won't hit me if I stay where I am." For the rest of the day, the torpedo is on your mind. When you are ordering lunch, you say, "Yes, I'll have the…" and you pause to look over your shoulder to check where the torpedo is. This torpedo represents long-term care and what it can do to your retirement. You can have a seemingly rock-solid plan, but if you don't have a plan for long-term care, you will constantly be looking over your shoulder, waiting for the torpedo to hit.

While financial planning professionals and academics recognize long-term care as a serious threat, many individuals either don't understand long-term care or don't take it seriously. The truth is, for some, long-term care will be no big deal, and for others, it will completely ruin their retirement. Because of this disparity, it will be time well spent to discuss the topic further.

What is long-term care?

Long-term care is a range of health care services that assist you in performing certain activities that you've always done but may now struggle with or be unable to do. These certain activities are called the "activities of daily living" (ADL). Known as the "six ADLs," they will become familiar to you. They are:

1. Walking
2. Eating
3. Dressing
4. Bathing
5. Toileting
6. Continence

The threshold to begin receiving care (also the threshold for most long-term care insurance policies to commence paying benefits) is an inability to perform two of the six ADLs.

Another way to qualify for care is cognitive impairment. Cognitive impairment overrides the "two of the six ADLs" requirement. You may be able to perform all six ADLs, but severe enough cognitive impairment will allow you to qualify for care.

Many people hear cognitive impairment, dementia, and Alzheimer's and either don't know the difference or consider them all the same. Figure 9-2 illustrates the distinctions. Alzheimer's is a type of dementia, which is a form of cognitive impairment. All people who have Alzheimer's have dementia and cognitive impairment, but not all people who have cognitive impairment have dementia, and not all people that have dementia have Alzheimer's. Cognitive impairment is becoming increasingly common and is now one of the biggest threats to retirees. The average long-term care claim for an Alzheimer's patient is currently around eight years. Not only is this disease emotionally taxing, but it can also be financially devastating.

FIGURE 9-2: Different Categorizations of Cognitive Impairment

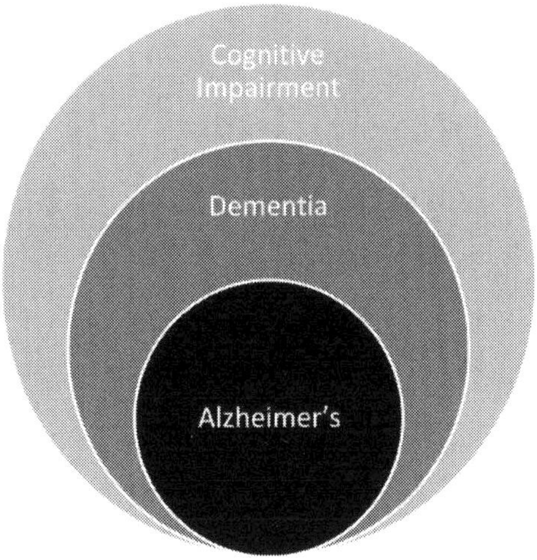

What are the types of long-term care?

The most common forms of care are listed below in ascending order of severity:

1. Adult Day Care
2. In-Home Care
3. Assisted Living
4. Nursing Home
5. Memory Care
6. Hospice

For many, the first thought that comes to mind when they hear long-term care is a nursing home. While a nursing home is one form of long-term care, many people do not reach the level of nursing home care. More commonly, people start with in-home health care, and if their condition worsens or a spouse passes away, they will move into assisted living. A few from this group will advance to a nursing home.

How much does long-term care cost?

In short, it can cost a lot—exactly how much varies by location and level of care.

Table 9.4 shows the national averages in 2020, as calculated by the insurance company Genworth.[1] There are significant differences in cost depending on where you live, the quality of the facility, and the level of care you receive. Unfortunately, there are facilities you would never wish to send a loved one to that are included in the "average."

TABLE 9.4: National Avg. of Current (2020) and Projected (2040) LTC Costs

	Costs in 2020		Projected Costs in 2040 2% inflation[2]	
Type of Care	Monthly	Annual	Monthly	Annual
Adult Day Care	$1,603	$19,236	$2,382	$28,584
In-Home Care	$4,546	$54,912	$6,800	$81,596
Assisted Living	$4,300	$51,600	$6,390	$76,675
Nursing Home, Semi-Private	$7,756	$93,072	$11,525	$138,300
Nursing Home, Private	$8,821	$105,852	$13,108	$157,291

In 2016, PricewaterhouseCoopers (PwC) performed an extensive study of long-term care costs. They evaluated the lifetime long-term care costs for those who need care and assigned a probability of reaching certain cost thresholds, as shown in Table 9.5. According to this study, half of these people will experience care costing $100,000, and nearly 20% will need care costing $300,000. They found the average lifetime cost of long-term care to be $172,000.[3] All of these figures are burdensome for one person. Married couples run the risk of experiencing this chart twice.

TABLE 9.5: Probability of Reaching LTC Cost Thresholds

Threshold	Probability	Threshold	Probability
$50,000	65%	$350,000	15%
$100,000	52%	$400,000	12%
$150,000	39%	$450,000	9%
$200,000	30%	$500,000	7%
$250,000	24%	$750,000	2%
$300,000	19%	$1,000,000	<1%

Who cares about the caregiver?

Many families choose to provide care themselves for a family member who needs assistance. The caregiver could be a spouse or an adult child. While admirable, there are very real but often hidden costs the *caregiver* must consider. These costs are financial as well as emotional and physical.

If the caregiver has a job of their own, caregiving can lead to lost time at work and decreased job performance. If the caregiver is older, there may be physical limitations as well. For example, if a spouse needs assistance getting in and out of bed or the bathtub, can the caregiver lift that person?

Allow me to speak from experience. Caregiving can be very stressful and can even lead to resentment. It can be a lot for one person to handle. If you plan on providing care for a loved one, be sure to have a plan to care for yourself as well.

How likely are you to need long-term care?

There are two ways to look at it. There's the statistical way, which is the summary of everyone, and there's the anecdotal way, which is based on our experiences and opinions.

We know statistics don't tell us everything, but they can give us a baseline. The consensus, reached by blending studies performed by the U.S. Department of Health and Human Services, AARP, PwC, and Morningstar, is about a 2 in 3 chance of needing *some level* of long-term care.[4] That might seem high, but if you reframe it by instead asking, "What percentage of people over the age of 65 will need help with either eating, bathing, dressing, toileting, continence, or walking at some point in their life?" then two out of three seems reasonable.

Anecdotally, I find people take two approaches. The first is looking at family history. If they have firsthand experience with long-term care, they are acutely aware of the problem long-term care poses. If they don't have a history of it, some think this makes them exempt.

The other approach is basically the "strong-man" (or woman) approach. I've heard countless times, "It won't happen to me," "I'll never go in a home," or "I'll take matters into my own hands before that happens to me." While I believe they all mean it when they say it, I also understand that, as humans, we are terrible at imagining ourselves in the future. This is in part due to the effects of the *end of history illusion*, which essentially means we can't picture ourselves changing (whether growing or shrinking) much from our current state.[5] The truth is, we may not be able to imagine it now, but even the strongest of us are likely to eventually need some help.

How long do people typically need care?

According to the American Association for Long-Term Care Insurance, half of all claims last less than one year. For the other half, the average is 3.9 years, and of all claims, 15% last longer than five years.[6] What is this telling us? We typically need care either for a short amount of time or for a relatively long amount of time, or to put it more bluntly, we either die pretty quick or hang around for a while. We are most concerned with the possibility of needing care for an extended amount of time. Most retirees can afford three to six months or maybe even a year or two of long-term care expenses. However, it is when people need care for more extended periods that retirements are torpedoed.

Let's pause and summarize what we know so far. Long-term care is a threat you are likely to experience on some level. It may or may not be problematic. If you need care for a short amount of time, it won't be bad, but if you need care for a long time, it could significantly change your lifestyle.

The challenge of planning for long-term care can be captured in three points.

1. *Care is very expensive.* If you need care, it could devastate you financially. Not only that, but since we don't know how much care will cost or how long we will need it, long-term care represents an undefined risk. We can use averages, but as we've discussed, averages don't capture the full range of possible outcomes and misrepresent what your experience could be if you do need care.

2. *Insurance can be expensive.* If long-term care insurance were cheap, you would protect yourself. Since it is a bigger financial commitment, it becomes a harder decision.

3. *You don't know if you will need care or not.* You would rather not spend money on insurance or protection you may never need.

So what are our options to protect against long-term care? The government does offer some assistance, but it is not as beneficial as you might hope. As we saw, Medicare does not cover most forms of long-term care. Medicare will cover up to 100 days of rehabilitative care in a skilled nursing facility, but this is not the same type of care we have been discussing thus far.

While Medicare does not cover most long-term care costs, Medicaid will. The idea of the government paying your long-term care bills may be appealing, but it comes with substantial tradeoffs. The following is an oversimplified summary of how Medicaid can assist.

To qualify for Medicaid, you must have very few assets and a low income. For example, in Texas, as of this writing, the asset limit for a single person is $2,000, and the income limit is $2,349 per month. For married couples, the figures change to $3,000 in assets and $4,698 per month of income.[7] If you attempt to "give your money away" to children or others to meet these requirements, the Medicaid "look-back" provision will apply. For example, assume you give $200,000 to your children so you will qualify for Medicaid. Medicaid can look back over the previous five years to see what money you have gifted and can "clawback" those gifts to recover the funds from your children before Medicaid pays anything towards your care. When it comes to the quality of care, you must make tradeoffs as well. You have little say over what facility you receive care from. There are *many* more rules and criteria, all of which vary by state. Consider Medicaid to be a "last resort." Be grateful it is there but plan to avoid it if at all possible.

If the government is not paying for your care, your options for protection are the same as we discussed in Chapter 8: do nothing, insure against it, or self-fund.

The "do nothing" approach is nothing more than a gamble. If you lose this gamble and need care, your outcome ranges from a significant decrease in savings to straight-up running out of money. Medicaid is always a possibility for those who choose to do nothing. If you never need care, your payoff is that you'll have more money to spend since you didn't save for long-term care or spend money on premiums.

As you know, the second option, self-funding, can be executed one of two ways. Either you a) set aside a pool of funds from the beginning or b) craft a savings plan to build a reserve. Both methods can work but have some inherent challenges. First, if you plan to save and invest, you must actually save and invest. Second, if you're relying on market returns, you take on investment risk—you must earn the returns you expect to earn—and take on sequence of returns risk—that the returns occur in a favorable order. Third, since the risk of long-term doesn't end, you must resist the temptation to spend the money you save. Imagine that you're 90 years old and you've accumulated $500,000 in your self-funded pool. Do you spend it? How can you be sure you won't need it for care? You will simply never know.

Then there is insurance. Long-term care insurance usually comes in the form of a monthly benefit that will pay for a certain length of time. (For example, you may have a $5,000/month benefit that pays for 48 months (4 years), for a total benefit pool of $240,000.) These benefits are typically paid tax-free, and some policies will offer inflation protection, meaning the benefit amount increases over time.

There are two types of long-term care insurance, 1) traditional and 2) "hybrid" (sometimes called "Asset-Based Care").

Traditional is what most people think of when they think of long-term care insurance, and it works much like car insurance, meaning you either "use it or lose it." The policyholder pays premiums in exchange for a long-term care benefit that you can use if you need care. If you never need it, the benefit expires, and the insurance company keeps your money.

The advantage of traditional long-term care insurance over hybrid insurance is that the starting premiums are usually much lower. Notice that I said "starting" premiums. Premiums for most traditional policies are not guaranteed, meaning they can be increased. In the past, policyholders have received multiple massive premium increases that border on criminal and has earned traditional long-term care insurance a deservedly bad reputation. These premium hikes can be as high as 50% or more, and it's not uncommon for premiums to grow to be three or four times the initial amount. These increases lead many policyholders to surrender their coverage, often around the time they are most likely to need care.

Hybrid policies are a little more complex, but the complexity comes with favorable features. It, too, offers a monthly benefit of up to a certain amount in total. But the unique structure of hybrid policies makes it a "How will you use it?" rather than a "use it or lose it" policy.

Hybrid policies create a death benefit and cash value, much like certain kinds of life insurance. There are three benefits to this structure. First, if you don't use all of your benefit and die, your heirs will receive a death benefit. Second, if you change your mind and decide to surrender the policy, you will receive the cash value (minus any surrender charges). Third, this structure allows the premiums to be guaranteed, avoiding the main issue with traditional.

The tradeoff, as you might imagine, is higher starting premiums.

So which option should you choose? Based on features alone, hybrid long-term care insurance appears to be the perfect solution. 1) Protection if you need it. 2) Money back if you change your mind. 3) Death benefit if you die. As a way of embracing uncertainty, hybrid policies are fantastic. It diversifies you away from relying on the market. It provides optionality if you change your mind. And it adds redundancy if you do need care.

Of course, features alone are not reason enough to make a purchase, and nothing is perfect. Just because you get some or all of your money back with a hybrid policy doesn't mean it's automatically better. If premiums are 20 times higher than traditional, traditional is likely better. Accurately comparing traditional and hybrid is difficult because we never really know for sure what traditional premiums will be in the future since they are not guaranteed.

Long-term care insurance can be a big financial commitment, which inevitably leads people to compare it to self-funding. It's the same conversation every time. "I don't want (or can't afford) to pay for long-term care, but I also don't want to 'waste' money on insurance I'm not going to use. What if I save and invest the money instead?"

Once again, just tell me when and how long you'll need care, and I'll tell you which strategy is best. Of course, the whole reason we need insurance in the first place is that we can't answer those two questions, but let's see when what answers lead to which conclusions.

The quantitative decision comes down to the same factors discussed in Chapter 8. 1) The premium and benefit amounts, 2) when you need care, 3) how long you need care, and 4) what rate of return you could earn if you did not pay premiums.

Table 9.6 details which outcomes favor which strategy. Remember that sequence of returns risk will likely apply as well. (When accumulating, losses in the later years, when your account balance is at its highest, will have a greater effect than losses in the early years.)

TABLE 9.6: Comparing What Outcomes Favor Which Protection Strategy

Criteria	Favors Insurance	Favors Self-Fund
Premiums vs. benefit spread	Bigger	Narrower
When you need care	Sooner	Later
How long you need care	Longer	Shorter
What rate of return you could earn	Lower	Higher

The greater the benefit amount per dollar of premium, the more that favors insurance. Because insurance creates an immediate benefit pool, insurance is typically the superior strategy if you need care soon. This makes sense as your money would not have much time to grow using the self-fund strategy. If you need care for a significant length of time, then the size of the insurance pool is also hard to match.

If you need care later on, then you will have more time for your investments to grow, and unless you need care for a long time, saving and investing is likely to be equally as good as insurance, assuming you earn your rate of return, and returns occur in the right order.

If you never need care, you didn't need insurance, but obviously, that is not knowable when these decisions have to be made. Hybrid policies do allow for considerable cost recovery but should not leave you with more money than saving and investing the premiums would if you never need care.

Of course, this entire exercise is misguided. The purpose of insurance is to keep you from becoming poor, not to outpace an investment account. Hybrid long-term care policies provide this protection, but the desire for efficiency leads us to try to maximize outcomes. The decision is really simple. Do you want to make sure you're okay if you need care or pass on more money if you don't? (I say pass on rather than spend because the purpose of self-funding is to create a pool of money in case you need care. Since you don't know for sure if or when you'll need it, *you* usually cannot "spend" this money.)

From a qualitative perspective, we must not forget the behavioral challenge of saving and investing. The spreadsheet may tell you to self-fund, but you still must actually save, invest, *and* earn the necessary rate of return. People are much more likely to quit on a savings strategy than they are to quit paying premiums.

What is the best way to protect against long-term care? Do you need insurance? I don't know. Here is what I do know:

Long-term care is a threat to your retirement that you are more likely to experience than you probably realize. It can be uncomfortable to think about, but the *time to think about it is before you think it's time to think about it.* If you wait until you start needing care to plan for it, it's likely too late.

To protect yourself from long-term care costs, you have three options: do nothing, self-fund, or insure against it. If you never need long-term care, you don't need insurance. If you need care 20 years from now and only need it for a year or two, you can probably self-fund and be just fine. If you need care sooner than that or for longer than two to three years, insurance will probably be best. If you can tell me when you'll need care and for how long, I can tell you which option is best. Unfortunately, there's no way to know. There is an option that protects against all three outcomes, but you have to give up a little upside to have it.

As much fun as it is to think about long-term care, it can be even less fun to think about taxes. Let's do so next.

10

TAXES

T he simplest definition of a tax is a payment that must be made to the government. Taxes can be assessed on how much you own (property tax), how much you make (income tax), how much you pass on (estate tax), how much you buy (sales tax), and so on.

We care about taxes because, while necessary, they reduce how much we can spend. Because taxes are a law of man rather than nature, taxes are ever-changing. What is written today will soon be out of date. Thus, the focus of this chapter is not to memorize the rules but to understand the mechanics and identify the variables that matter so that you can assess how you'll be affected when they change.

The tax code is quite complex. This discussion will not cover every exception and caveat. Given this, your specific situation should be discussed with a tax professional before any decisions are made.

Because the tax code is complex, understanding it can be a challenge. Many of the concepts are interrelated and circular, meaning an understanding of A requires an understanding of B while an understanding of B requires an understanding of A. Nevertheless, we must start somewhere, which we will with income taxes.

What are income taxes? When we *receive* money, a *portion* of it must be paid in taxes. There are many ways to receive money. We can *earn* it by working and receiving a salary. We can be given it (gifts). We can also win it (lotteries, gambling). The money we already have can also earn money from interest, dividends, and growth.

Regardless of how we receive the money, from a tax perspective, what we want to know is:

1) *How much* of the money I receive is subject to tax?
2) *What rate* (percentage) is the money I receive taxed at?
3) *When* is the money I receive subject to tax?

Of course, many nuances affect the answers to those questions. To understand the nuances, we must first understand the basics. We'll start with a simple example of how earned income (salary) is taxed and slowly add complexity.

When you go to work, you *earn income*. Your earned income is subject to two kinds of tax.

1. *Federal Insurance Contributions Act (FICA) tax*

FICA taxes fund Social Security and Medicare. The Social Security portion is 6.2% and assessed on the first $142,800 of earned income. The Medicare portion amounts to 1.45% and is assessed on all earned income. As we'll see in Chapter 13, how much FICA tax you pay determines how much your Social Security benefit is.

2. *Income taxes*

Income taxes can be assessed at the federal level (which is what we'll focus on) as well as at the state and local levels.

Let's assume you earn a salary of $150,000. The calculation below shows how much FICA tax you will pay.

TABLE 10.1: FICA Tax Calculation

	Income subject to tax	Rate	Taxes Due
Social Security tax	$142,800	6.2%	$8,854
Medicare tax	$150,000	1.45%	$2,175
Total FICA Tax Paid			$11,029

As for federal income taxes, we must first determine how much of our income is subject to tax, called our *taxable income*. The total of all our income is called our *gross income*. Fortunately, not all our gross income is subject to tax, and some of the expenses that we incur throughout the year can be *deducted* (which reduces how much is subject to tax and thus how much tax we have to pay). There are many expenses that can be deducted, for example, mortgage interest, charitable contributions, medical expenses over a certain threshold, etc.

There are two ways to determine how much you can deduct. The first is to keep track of all these expenses and list (*itemize*) them out. Or, instead of going through all of that, you can deduct a fixed amount called the *standard* deduction. In 2021, the standard deduction is $12,550 per person ($25,100 for married couples). You will choose whichever of the two (itemized or standard deduction) is higher.

To determine our taxable income, we subtract our deductions from our gross income. In this example, let's assume we are married and take the standard deduction.

TABLE 10.2: Calculate Taxable Income

Step 1:	Total of all income:	$150,000
Step 2:	Subtract deductions:	($25,100)
Step 3:	Taxable Income:	$124,900

Now that we know how much of our income is subject to tax, we must next determine what rate we will pay. Each year, the IRS publishes *ordinary income* rates, shown below. There are two important things to note about these rates.

TABLE 10.3: 2021 Ordinary Income Tax Brackets

Rate	Income Threshold	
	Single	**Married Filing Joint**
10%	$0-$9,950	$0-$19,900
12%	$9,951-$40,525	$19,901-$81,050
22%	$40,526-$86,375	$81,051-$172,750
24%	$86,376-$164,925	$172,751-$329,850
32%	$164,926-$209,425	$329,851-$418,850
35%	$209,426-$523,600	$418,851-$628,300
37%	$523,601+	$628,301+

First, the rates are not fixed; they are *marginal*. Marginal means that as you make more money, the tax rate you pay on the *additional* income increases. Think of these marginal rates as a ladder. The first "rung" of income is taxed at one rate, the next rung at a higher rate, and so on. It's important to understand that moving up a rung (colloquially referred to as a "higher tax bracket") only affects additional dollars received, not all of the money received.

Second, there are different income thresholds depending on your *filing status*, such as single or married filing jointly. (There are other filing statuses, such as head of household, but these two capture most people.)

To calculate how much tax we must pay, we simply "climb the ladder," as shown below.

TABLE 10.4: Step 5: Calculate Tax Due Based on Marginal Rates

Rate	Married, Joint	Calculation	Tax Due
10%	$0-$19,900	$19,900 x 10%	$1,990
12%	$19,901-$81,050	$61,150 x 12%	$7,338
22%	$81,051-$172,750	$43,850 x 22%	$9,647
24%	$172,751-$329,850	-	-
32%	$329,851-$418,850	-	-
35%	$418,851-$628,300	-	-
37%	$628,301+	-	-
	Total Tax Due		**$18,975**

It may seem like a simple question, but if I asked you, "What is your tax rate?" there are actually three answers you could give me.

1. *Marginal.* 22%. This is the tax rate that will be paid on the next dollar received. Once you reach the income threshold for that rate (i.e., the maximum number shown for each bracket), you are bumped into the next highest rate.
2. *Effective.* 15.2%. Taxes Paid ÷ Taxable Income. This tells you what percentage of your *taxable income* you paid in tax.
3. *Average.* 12.7%. Taxes Paid ÷ Gross Income. This will tell you what percentage of your *gross income* you paid in tax.

Understanding the difference between these three tax rates is important when planning. If you are receiving additional income *this* year, you want to know your marginal tax rate, as that will apply to the next dollar you receive. If you know your taxable income for *next* year and would like to estimate your tax liability, your effective tax rate will help you calculate this. If you know your gross income, which includes non-taxable income, before any deductions are taken, then your average tax rate will be helpful.

When it comes to income, it's not just about how much you make; it's more important to know how much you keep. To see how much of our $150,000 we keep after FICA and income taxes, see below.

TABLE 10.5: Total After-Tax Income (FICA and Federal Income Tax)

Total Income	$150,000
FICA Tax	($11,029)
Income Tax	($18,975)
After-Tax Income	$119,996

So, money comes in, you can deduct some of it, and you pay tax on the rest. From there, you either can spend the money, or you can save it. What happens to the money you save?

Here's a general rule: you do not pay tax on the money you have already paid tax on. If you save $100 and put it in a checking account, you do not pay tax again when you pull that $100 out. But what if our money earns money? We could earn interest at the bank, or we could buy an asset, and the price could appreciate, or we receive dividends. Since income taxes apply to the money we receive, we must pay tax on this "new money."

Let's start with price appreciation (gains). First, we must understand how we determine what the gain is. Gain is the difference between the current value (price) and our *basis*. Basis is a tax term that essentially means the amount of "after-tax" money (money you've already paid tax on) you used to purchase it. For now, our basis will equal the price that we paid.

Next, we must understand the difference between unrealized and realized gains. Assume you purchase a stock for $100, and the price soon rises to $150. At this point, you have an *unrealized gain* of $50.

It is unrealized because you have not sold it. You do not pay tax on unrealized gains. Consider why this is. In this example, if you had to pay tax on the $50 gain, with what money would you pay tax?

A key concept in taxation is the *wherewithal to pay*, meaning having the funds available to pay tax. In our example, if you do not have other money available, you would have to sell the stock just to pay the gains on it. Recognizing this is unfair, the IRS does not require us to pay tax on unrealized gains. This means that we pay tax on *realized gains*, which are recognized when we sell. After we sell, we have the wherewithal to pay the tax due. (Consider also that values change, and paying tax on unrealized gains would require yearly corrections.)

Next, we must determine what tax rate we pay on our realized gains. This depends on how long we held the investment. If we held the investment for less than one year, it is considered a *short-term capital gain*, and these gains are included in our taxable income, and we pay tax at the ordinary income rates previously shown.

If we held the investment for longer than one year, it is considered a *long-term capital gain (LTCG)*, and there is a different set of tax rates that apply, shown below. These rates are noticeably lower than ordinary income rates. How much ordinary income you have determines which LTCG rate you pay.

TABLE 10.6: 2021 Long-Term Capital Gain Tax Brackets

	Income Threshold	
Rate	Single	Married Filing Joint
0%	$0-$40,400	$0-$80,800
15%	$40,401-$445,850	$80,801-$501,600
20%	$445,851+	$501,601+

Let's recap. When we earn a salary, we pay FICA tax. To determine our income tax due, we must determine our taxable income. To determine our taxable income, we first calculate our gross income, which includes salary and short-term gains. We can deduct some of this income, either by itemizing or taking the standard deduction. To calculate how much tax we pay, we run our taxable income through the appropriate ordinary income rate table, and any long-term capital gains are subject to LTCG rates.

We can use the discussion so far as our "base" example of taxes. As mentioned, there are many exceptions. The two most common exceptions come from how contributions, gains, and distributions related to *tax-deferred* and *tax-free* accounts are treated.

A 401(k) or Traditional IRA is an example of a tax-deferred account. How they work is in their name, you *defer* taxes. How do you defer taxes? Let's go back to our earlier example. What if we contribute $5,000 of our earned income to an IRA? This $5,000 contribution is not included in taxable income that year; it is deferred. This deferral has a similar effect to deductions in that it reduces your taxable income and the tax you pay in the year you contribute. The difference, however, is that you still eventually pay tax on the money you defer versus deductions you do not.

What happens if our $5,000 grows? Any gains in a tax-deferred account, even if they are realized, are also deferred.

When do we pay taxes? We only pay tax when the money is *distributed* from a tax-deferred account. An example of distributing money is withdrawing it and putting it into a checking account so that you can spend it. It's crucial to understand that transfers *between* tax-deferred accounts are not taxable. For example, if you transfer money from your 401(k) to a Traditional IRA or between two Traditional IRAs, there is no taxable event. Likewise, buying and selling investments inside a tax-deferred account is not a taxable event either.

This tax deferral can be beneficial, as we'll detail later, but it comes with two restrictions. First, there is a limit to how much you can contribute to tax-deferred accounts. The exact limit changes each year and depends on the type of account (e.g., 401(k), IRA, SEP-IRA, etc.) Second, money in tax-deferred accounts is subject to a 10% penalty if withdrawn before age 59 ½.

The other exception to our basic example is related to tax-free accounts, such as a Roth IRA. Here, the tax treatment is the opposite of a tax-deferred account. With tax-free accounts, contributions are made with after-tax dollars, meaning you do not deduct the income you contribute to a tax-free account, but after that, you never pay taxes again. There is no tax due on growth and no tax due when you distribute or spend it. Roth IRAs also have contribution limits, and any growth is subject to the 10% penalty if withdrawn before age 59 ½.

From a tax perspective, there are three kinds of accounts. 1) Tax-deferred, such as 401(k)s and IRAs. 2) Tax-free, such as Roth IRAs. 3) Taxable, such as checking, savings, or anything else that's not tax-free or tax-deferred. Table 10.7 summarizes the differences in how contributions, gains, and distributions are treated in these accounts.

TABLE 10.7: Difference in Taxation at Contribution and Distribution By Tax Status of Account

	Tax-Deferred	Taxable	Tax-Free
Contributions	Tax-deductible	Non-deductible	Non-deductible
Growth	Deferred	As realized	Not taxable
Distributions	Fully-taxable	Growth is taxable	Not taxable

With this understanding, we can begin discussing some concepts specific to retirement.

One of the biggest differences in retirement is where our income comes from. Using our definition of retirement—that we stop going to work and our money goes to work for us—we make an important assumption: that we no longer *earn income*.

FICA tax only applies to earned income, so if we stop earning income, we no longer pay FICA tax. For example, distributions from a tax-deferred account are subject to income tax but not FICA tax. This can result in us keeping more of the same amount of gross income when retired than when we're working.

While most retirees no longer earn income, they do start receiving Social Security. A portion of your Social Security benefit is likely to be included in taxable income. The portion that is included depends on how much *provisional income* you have. The formula for determining your provisional income is shown in Table 10.8.

TABLE 10.8: Calculating Provisional Income

½ of your Social Security Benefit

+   Adjusted Gross Income (Wages, Tax-Deferred Withdrawals, etc.)

+   Tax-Exempt Interest Income

=   Provisional Income

After you've determined your provisional income, Table 10.9 will help you determine the maximum portion of your benefits that could be taxable. This amount will then be included in taxable income to be taxed at your marginal ordinary income rate.

TABLE 10.9: Social Security Tax Brackets

Portion of Benefits Taxable	Single	Married Filing Jointly
0%	$25,000	$32,000
50%	$34,000	$44,000
85%	$34,000+	$44,000+

For example, if you are married and have provisional income of $100,000, and your Social Security benefit is $50,000, at a maximum, $42,500 ($50,000 x 85%) could be included in taxable income. Note that this calculation is marginal, and each individual or couple's calculation will vary.

In addition to Social Security, most retirees rely on their savings to generate income. Very often, their savings are held in tax-deferred accounts. As I've mentioned, any money pulled from a tax-deferred account is included in your taxable income. Aside from withdrawing money to live on, there is another reason that a retiree might distribute some of their tax-deferred accounts—because they are forced to.

You might be forced to pull money out because of Required Minimum Distributions (RMDs). RMDs require you to begin withdrawing money from your tax-deferred accounts in the year that you turn 72 and continue to make distributions as long as you're alive. There is a set percentage that you must withdraw each year, and the amount increases as you age, as shown in Table 10.10.

TABLE 10.10: Required Minimum Distribution % by Age

Age	RMD %	Age	RMD %	Age	RMD %
72	3.91%	87	7.46%	102	18.18%
73	4.05%	88	7.87%	103	19.23%
74	4.20%	89	8.33%	104	20.41%
75	4.37%	90	8.77%	105	22.22%
76	4.55%	91	9.26%	106	23.81%
77	4.72%	92	9.80%	107	25.64%
78	4.93%	93	10.42%	108	27.03%
79	5.13%	94	10.99%	109	29.41%
80	5.35%	95	11.63%	110	32.26%
81	5.59%	96	12.35%	111	34.48%
82	5.85%	97	12.16%	112	38.46%
83	6.13%	98	14.08%	113	41.67%
84	6.45%	99	14.93%	114	47.62%
85	6.76%	100	15.87%	115	52.63%
86	7.09%	101	16.95%		

Why do RMDs exist? Simply put, because you've never paid tax on money in your tax-deferred accounts, and the government would like to generate some revenue.

Some retirees satisfy their RMD requirement every year when they make withdrawals to spend money in order to live. For others, complying with the requirements can be a headache. There are two things to look out for. First, money taken as an RMD is included in taxable income. This can bump you into a higher marginal tax bracket, as mentioned, which can affect your qualification for other tax breaks, increase the LTCG rates you pay, and affect how much of your Social Security is taxable. Second, you don't want to forget to take an RMD. If you fail to take an RMD, the IRS can assess a 50% penalty on the funds that you should have withdrawn.

What happens to your money when you die? (Or what happens to the money you receive if someone passes money on to you.) *There are a slew of exceptions in the area of estate planning. The following is very general.* As you should expect by now, it depends. The total value of everything you own is called your *estate*. When you die, your estate is subject to the *estate tax*. But, similar to income, not all of it may be subject to tax. An *estate tax exemption* makes a portion of your estate "exempt" from the estate tax. In 2021, the exemption is $11.7 million per person ($23.4 million for married couples). This means if the value of your taxable estate is less than this amount, then there are no estate taxes due.

While estate taxes may not be an issue, income taxes still apply to inherited accounts. Yet again, how income taxes are assessed depends on what type of account it is.

We can start with the simplest, tax-free accounts. Tax-free accounts, for the most part, remain tax-free to those who receive them.

Those who receive tax-deferred accounts must still pay income taxes. Beneficiaries have several options for paying the tax. For example, they can pay it all upfront or stretch it out over a number of years. Tax laws surrounding this area are constantly changing.

Taxable accounts are again treated differently and are easiest understood with an example. The idea that we don't pay tax on money we already paid tax on remains. It is how gains inside of taxable accounts are treated that things differ.

Let's return to the earlier example, where we purchased a stock for $100 that is currently worth $150, showing an unrealized gain of $50. If we die and pass this on, what do our beneficiaries do with the gain?

Currently, there is a favorable concept called *step up in basis*. Remember that when you buy a stock in a taxable account, your basis is essentially equal to what you pay for it. Your beneficiaries, however, are allowed to "step up their basis" to the current market value. In our example, this means that their basis could become $150. If they went to sell the stock for $150, there would be no gain, and thus, no taxes due. As of this writing, the step-up in basis feature is under scrutiny and may soon be changed.

Choose wisely

If you want to pass money on when you die, which accounts you pull money from while you're alive is important. Suppose that your child is working and in a higher tax bracket than you. Remember that when they inherit your tax-deferred accounts, they will have to pay tax at their rates. Conversely, they will not pay as much tax on your taxable accounts because of step-up in basis.

In this case, pulling money from your tax-deferred accounts while you're alive is a nice way of doing a bit of tax arbitrage. You will pay tax at your lower rates and pass on more money in the accounts they will pay less tax on.

If the situation is reversed, and you are in a higher tax bracket than they are, the opposite may be best.

Estate planning often involves drafting wills and setting up trusts. The two most common types of trusts are *revocable* and *irrevocable*. The differences are crucial to understand. At the very least, I highly recommend you explore them. Revocable trusts are relatively painless to set up and allow you to be sure that your money will go where you want it to when you die.

There is something else crucial to keep in mind—the rules that will apply to you are the rules that are in place when you die. While the estate tax exemption is relatively high today, it could be significantly lower in the future. Remember this when making permanent estate planning decisions.

Taxes are obviously an important topic. They reduce how much of your income you keep and can increase how much you must pull from savings to create the same after-tax income if rates increase. As we saw in Chapter 2, slight increases in taxes alter the outcome of your plan and can increase your chances of running out of money.

It is understandable then that people give considerable attention and energy trying to minimize the amount of tax they pay. I feel compelled to share a few thoughts on this.

Taxes are a part of life. While we should aim to minimize them, we cannot eliminate them. Some people can get so obsessed over taxes that they miss the big picture. It's better to make $100 and pay $20 of tax than it is to make $75 and pay $0 of tax. As the saying goes, "Don't let the tax tail wag the dog."

So how do we minimize taxes? Remember, in any given year, two variables determine how much tax you pay: 1) how much is taxable and 2) what tax rate you pay. Thus, to minimize taxes, we try to minimize these variables.

Let's discuss how to minimize our taxable income first. Your taxable income is equal to your gross income minus deductions. This means there are two ways to lower your taxable income, 1) lower your gross income or 2) increase your deductions.

One way to minimize our gross income in a given year is to defer it, which we'll discuss shortly. Many times, however, there is very little we can do about our gross income. For example, if we have a pension, annuity, or Social Security, we have little control over when we receive those (other than when we start).

We have slightly more control over our deductions. Planning your deductions is where a good tax professional can be worth their weight in gold.* Be careful, though. It can be easy to get in trouble by being overzealous with deductions.

Now, let's discuss how to lower our rate. There are again two ways for this to occur. 1) Statutory tax rates themselves are lower. 2) Our taxable income is lower (moving us into a lower tax bracket). We have little control over what tax rates will be, so our focus is again on #2.

Of course, increasing deductions will do this, but here our focus is on timing. The concept behind timing is simple. For the income that

---

* This ultimately depends on the weight of the tax-planner. As of this writing, an ounce of gold is worth $1,940. If your tax-planner weighs 200 pounds, at 16 ounces per pound, that is 3,200 ounces. This equates to $6,208,000 worth of gold. Your tax-planner may or may not be worth their weight in gold.

you can control, you want to time it when you will pay as low of a rate as possible. This means two things. If you expect your tax rate to be lower in the future (either because rates themselves are lower or you'll have lower income), you want to defer as much as possible. If you expect your tax rate to be higher in the future, you want to pay as much now as possible. Think about it with numbers. If you have $100 and must pay 20% tax, it would be beneficial to defer it to next year if your rate will be 10%, and beneficial to pay it today if the rate will be 30% next year.

Let's talk about deferral first. The idea of deferring taxes due today to when rates will be lower in the future is the logic behind why people contribute to tax-deferred accounts. There is an overarching assumption that retirees will be in a lower tax bracket than when they're working, but there are two reasons this may not be true.

First, tax rates themselves may rise. As of this writing, historically speaking, tax rates in the U.S. are pretty low. Some argue that the size of the national debt will inevitably force rates to rise, although this argument has been made for several decades and has yet to materialize.

FIGURE 10-1: Highest Marginal Tax Rates Over Time

Another reason your tax rate may not be lower is that while you may have lower gross income, your taxable income may not be much lower because you may have fewer deductions. When working and raising a family, many taxpayers enjoy deductions related to dependents and mortgage interest on their home. If the kids move out and the house is paid off, these deductions can go away.

So what if we expect rates to rise? How do we "pull-forward" future income and pay tax today? Again, we can't pull forward our pension, annuity, or Social Security income, so what we're talking about here is money in tax-deferred accounts. There are two ways to do this. 1) Withdraw the money, pay the tax, and put it in a checking account. 2) Withdraw the money, pay the tax, and put it in a Roth account. There are several ways to execute the second strategy, such as a "Roth Conversion" or "Backdoor Roth."

Of course, there are things to look out for. First, you want to be sure you don't send yourself into too high of a tax bracket, negating the benefits of paying the tax early. Second, if you convert funds before you are 59 ½, you must pay any tax due with money outside of the converted funds; otherwise, you may be subject to the 10% early withdrawal penalty.

Whether these strategies, deferring or pulling forward income, are beneficial or not ultimately depends on whether tax rates are higher or lower in the future. If tax rates are the same when you contribute and distribute, there is no net difference between tax-deferred and tax-free accounts. Table 10.11 shows an example when tax rates are at 20%.

TABLE 10.11: Comparing Tax-Deferred and Tax-Free Accounts

	Tax-Deferred	Tax-Free
Contribution	$5,000	$4,000*
Growth (50%)	$2,500	$2,000
Ending Balance	$7,500	$6,000
Tax on Withdrawal	($1,500)	($0)
After-Tax amount	$6,000	$6,000

*Both contributions involve $5,000 of earned income. However, you had to pay 20% tax on the money contributed to the tax-free account, leaving $4,000 to be contributed. Contributions to the tax-deferred account are deductible, so the entire $5,000 is contributed.

This raises one last point. If you have tax-deferred accounts, the value of your personal balance sheet is likely inflated as a portion of your IRA belongs to the government, not you. If you have $1,000,000 in a 401(k), you will have to pay tax eventually. If you have $1,000,000 in a Roth, that money is all yours.

The conversation related to taxes could go on for days. This chapter provided just a brief overview. As I've said, consult a tax planning professional before making any decisions.

From a planning perspective, remember what taxes do—they reduce how much we keep. This means we either have less money to spend or have to withdraw more money to create the same after-tax income. All else being equal, higher taxes increase our chances of running out of money.

Outside of pulling forward or deferring income in certain accounts, there is little you can do to control taxes. The best you can do is be aware of how you will be affected when they inevitably change. Taxes will inevitably change because they are the government's most potent tool to incentivize behavior, and the behavior the government chooses to incentivize will change.

Remember, taxes are a part of life. Paying taxes isn't always a bad thing; it (usually) means you had money coming in. Our goal should not be to eliminate taxes; rather, it should be to not pay more than we need to.

A word of warning

Taxes are a sensitive and emotional topic, and consumers jump at the opportunity to lower their tax bills. The industry knows this and has come up with myriad "strategies" to do so. Some of these strategies are beneficial; others are predatory. Minimizing taxes is a good goal but should not be your only goal. Some of the greatest scams and frauds in finance are built on the premise of minimizing taxes.

11

SUMMARY OF OUTFLOWS

A tremendous amount of thought goes into planning your outflows in retirement. You must consider changing life stages, changing interests, changing quantities of consumption, changing prices of things you consume, unknown expenses such as long-term care, and changing tax rates. Even after putting in all of that thought, you are still likely to be wrong. Ultimately, there is no way to accurately predict these variables years into the future. This emphasizes the fact that retirement planning is not a "set it and forget it" process. You must build in flexibility so that you can reassess and adjust.

When you create a model based on assumptions and forecasts, the more actual (real) numbers you can include, the more accurate your model and plan will be. If your spending is higher or lower than originally anticipated, the sooner you can update your plan, the sooner you can adjust the other parts of your plan to allow for these changes.

My recommendation to you, if you do not do so already, is to start keeping track of your expenses. With the number of computer programs and smartphone apps available today, this process is easier than ever. I use a program that, after some initial setup, takes five minutes per week to categorize my spending. The information you will glean is invaluable. You will begin to see a complete and accurate picture of where your money is actually going, and many times will identify waste that can be eliminated that you weren't aware of. Having this information makes the RASA process both easier and more reliable.

Many people create a "budget," but few people keep "actuals." A budget without tracking actual expenses is essentially worthless; it's nothing more than a dream. You can create the most detailed and rosy budget, but if you don't keep track of what actually happens, then what good is that? I will never forget early in my career meeting with an engineer who had a marvelous budget typed out in about size 8-point font on a sheet of paper that appeared to be two feet wide and three feet long. He was pouring over it, trying to understand why he didn't have an extra $20,000 to save each year. He kept repeating, "It's in the budget, it's in the budget." Finally, I asked him, "Do you keep track of your actual expenses?" Sheepishly he replied, "Well…no." We both just laughed. A budget is great, but it's only worth anything if you follow it and keep track of your progress.

Consider again the different factors you must consider when planning your spending: inflation, changes in quantity, taxes, changing health, unexpected expenses. For some of these, there are tools available that we can use to protect ourselves. Others are beyond our control. Embrace this and test your plan against a range of different outcomes, ensuring you protect against the asymmetrically worse outcome of running out of money.

Now that we understand what our outflows are made of, we need to discuss how to generate the inflows to cover them.

12

INTRODUCTION TO INFLOWS

I have mentioned several times that either your plan for inflows can be a function of your outflows, or your plan for outflows can be a function of your inflows. In other words, you can base your income on how much you spend or base your spending on how much your income is. Which option you choose may depend on where your income is coming from.

Inflows consist of sources from both inside and outside of your plan. Outside sources include Social Security and pensions. Inside sources are produced from your savings and include interest, dividends, growth on investments, and real estate income. Some sources are guaranteed; others are not.

To understand why I refer to them as inside and outside sources, a simple example can explain. If I were to create a personal balance sheet of all your assets and liabilities on one page, where does Social Security come from? It comes from "outside" your balance sheet. On the other hand, if you were taking withdrawals from an IRA, they would come from "inside" your balance sheet.

We often do not have much control over outside sources. Inside sources, however, offer considerable flexibility, and there are many tools we can use. Which tool or tools you choose will ultimately depend on how much income you need, how long you need it, and how much risk you are willing to take.

As we discuss the different tools and strategies, keep in mind that the decision is not "one or the other." They can (and many times, should) be mixed and used together. For example, we've discussed the value of distinguishing your must-haves and nice to haves. Many people prefer to have their must-haves covered by guaranteed sources, and their nice to haves covered by strategies with more upside. Whatever mix you choose, the point is this: You do not have to plan for all of your income the same way.

We will begin our discussion by looking at outside sources before examining the many different inside sources.

13

SOCIAL SECURITY

How would you like a guaranteed income that increases with inflation every year and lasts as long as you're alive? Well, if you've paid FICA taxes for 40 quarters (10 years), then you've got one.

Much about Social Security, we cannot control. What we can control, however, is when we begin receiving benefits. To understand how to make that decision, let's learn more about how the program works.

Social Security, like most government programs, is littered with caveats and exceptions. Once again, we will not be covering all of them. Consult a Social Security "expert" before making any decisions.

To determine how much your benefit will be, Social Security uses your 35 highest-earning years to calculate your Primary Insurance Amount (PIA). Earnings are indexed for inflation, meaning $100,000 earned 30 years ago is worth more in the calculation than $100,000 earned today. There is a maximum amount of earnings subject to the Social Security portion of the FICA tax ($142,800 in 2021). Accordingly, there is a maximum Social Security benefit amount ($3,148 per month at full retirement age in 2021). Both of these figures increase each year. Someone who earned the maximum and someone who earned $1,000,000 every year will have the same Social Security benefit since they both paid the maximum FICA tax.

What age you begin receiving benefits affects how much your benefit will be. First, you must determine your full retirement age (FRA). You can find yours using Table 13.1.

TABLE 13.1: Full Retirement Age by Year of Birth

Year of Birth	Full Retirement Age
1941	65 and 8 months
1942	65 and 10 months
1943-1954	66
1955	66 and 2 months
1956	66 and 4 months
1957	66 and 6 months
1958	66 and 8 months
1959	66 and 10 months
1960 and later	67

You are eligible to receive 100% of your PIA at full retirement age. You can begin receiving benefits as early as age 62 or as late as age 70. Your benefit is reduced between 5-6.67% every year you take it *before* FRA and increased 8% for every year you take it *after* FRA. The adjustments are pro-rated monthly, so your benefit is determined based on the month you begin. Table 13.2 shows what percent of your PIA you will receive if you begin receiving benefits at different ages.

TABLE 13.2: Percent of Benefit Received by Age Benefits Started

Begin Benefits at Age:	% of PIA Received if:	
	FRA 66	FRA 67
62	75%	70%
63	80%	75%
64	86.7%	80%
65	93.3%	86.7%
66	100%	93.3%
67	108%	100%
68	116%	108%
69	124%	116%
70	132%	124%

One caveat to be aware of is if you start receiving benefits before FRA and are still working, a portion of your benefit will be reduced. This reduction does not occur if you receive benefits at FRA or later.

There are several features unique to married couples. First is the spousal benefit. It is common for one spouse to have worked or earned significantly more than the other. The spouse with the lower benefit is allowed to receive the *higher of* 1) their own benefit or 2) half of the higher-earning spouse's PIA.

Table 13.3 shows what each spouse will receive as a percentage of the higher-earning spouse's PIA if they begin receiving benefits between ages 62 and 70. This example assumes both spouses have an FRA of 67. Notice that spousal benefits are reduced if they are taken before FRA, just like normal, but they *are not* increased above 50% if taken after FRA.

TABLE 13.3: Percent of Higher Earning Spouse's Benefit Received By Age Benefits Started

Begin Benefits at Age:	% of Higher Earning Spouse's PIA Received	
	Higher-Earning Spouse Own Benefit	Lower-Earning Spouse Spousal Benefit
62	70%	32.5%
63	75%	35%
64	80%	37.5%
65	86.7%	41.7%
66	93.3%	45.8%
67 (FRA)	100%	50%
68	108%	50%
69	116%	50%
70	124%	50%

The second feature unique to married couples is survivor benefits. Normally when you die, Social Security benefits stop, and there is no "unused" benefit that is passed on. For married couples, survivor benefits allow the higher of the two benefits to be passed on to the surviving spouse when one spouse dies. For example, if one spouse is receiving $2,500 per month and the other $1,500 per month, the $2,500 per month benefit will continue to be paid when either spouse passes. Different rules will apply for both spousal and survivor benefits if one spouse is considerably younger (not yet 60 for survivor benefits and not yet 62 for spousal benefits). Since their benefit is passed on, the higher-earning spouse has an extra incentive to have as high of a benefit as possible, especially when we consider how much higher joint life expectancy is.

As mentioned, benefits are inflation-adjusted. Social Security calls this a cost-of-living adjustment (COLA). Benefit payments are increased for inflation each year based on the prior year's CPI-W index. At first glance, the increases shown in Table 13.4 may not seem like much, but over time they add up. For example, a $2,000 per month benefit beginning in the year 2000 would have grown to over $3,000 per month by 2021.

TABLE 13.4: Cost-of-Living Adjustment (COLA) Since 2000

Year	COLA (%)	Year	COLA (%)
2000	2.5%	2011	0.0%
2001	3.5%	2012	3.6%
2002	2.6%	2013	1.7%
2003	1.4%	2014	1.5%
2004	2.1%	2015	1.7%
2005	2.7%	2016	0.0%
2006	4.1%	2017	0.3%
2007	3.3%	2018	2.0%
2008	2.3%	2019	2.8%
2009	5.8%	2020	1.6%
2010	0.0%	2021	1.3%
2022	5.9%		

So that's the overview of how Social Security works. How much you pay in FICA taxes determines how much your benefit will be. Your benefit increases every year that you wait. Once you begin receiving benefits, a cost-of-living adjustment is applied each year. When you die, your benefit stops unless you're married, and there is no "unused" benefit that is passed on.

We have no control over everything we've discussed so far; they're just the rules of the game. However, we do have control over when we begin receiving benefits, which we'll talk about next.

The decision of when to begin receiving benefits is usually a battle between the cumulative approach and the needs or income approach.

The cumulative approach tries to determine what claiming age allows you to receive the most money in total. This analysis is very straight-forward.

Recall the difference in benefit amounts if you start them at age 62 versus 70. The question becomes, "Do I take the lower benefit for a longer period or wait to take the higher benefit?" The answer is log-ical; the longer you live, the more beneficial waiting to begin receiving benefits will be. How long do you have to live for the amounts to "break-even," meaning it will be more beneficial to have waited? It may surprise you that by design, if you live to your life expectancy, the total benefits received will be about equal regardless of what age you began receiving them. That means that if you live below your life ex-pectancy, starting benefits earlier will be better, and if you live past your life expectancy, starting benefits later will be better.

The following is a basic example of how cumulative benefits re-ceived will change over time based on what age you started receiving them. Assume a retiree has a full retirement age of 66 and a primary insurance amount of $2,000 per month. Table 13.6 shows the cumu-lative benefits received as of a certain age (the columns) if they had begun receiving benefits at different ages (the rows). For simplicity, we will assume no cost-of-living adjustments.

TABLE 13.5: Hypothetical Social Security Benefit

Assumption	Amount
Full Retirement Age	66
Primary Insurance Amount	$2,000 per month
Cost-of-Living Adjustment	0%

TABLE 13.6: Total Benefits Received Depending on Age Benefits Began

		Accumulated Benefits Received by Age:				
		70	75	80	85	90
Start Receiving Benefits at Age:	62	$144,000	$234,000	$324,000	$414,000	$504,000
	64	$124,776	$228,756	$332,736	$436,716	$540,696
	66	$96,000	$216,000	$336,000	$456,000	$576,000
	68	$55,680	$194,880	$334,080	$473,280	$612,480
	70	$0	$158,400	$316,800	$475,200	$633,600

You can see that the benefit "break-even" point (when the accumulated benefits received are nearly equal) is around age 80. This will not always be the case. When you include cost-of-living adjustments, the break-even age is usually between ages 78 and 82.

This analysis only considers total dollars received and does not factor in any reinvestment of benefits if you started receiving them earlier. So what if we do invest the benefits we receive early? JP Morgan has provided a helpful chart to analyze this decision.

The two meaningful variables should be obvious, how long you live and what rate of return you earn. Figure 13-1 shows the results. Start by determining your expected longevity on the x-axis and your expected return on the y-axis. The chart will tell you which age is best to begin receiving benefits where the two intersect.

FIGURE 13-1: Best Time to Claim Social Security Based on Expected Longevity and Rate of Return

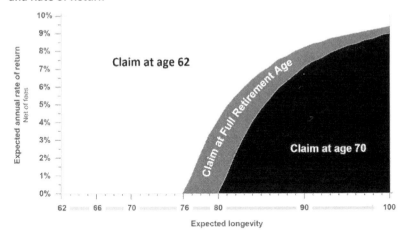

But this assumes you don't ever spend your benefit. What if you're like most retirees and rely on Social Security as part of your income to meet your spending needs?

Remember the two biggest sources of retirement income, Social Security and personal savings. For some, they cannot generate enough income from their savings and must begin receiving Social Security out of necessity. For those, the decision is very simple, start receiving benefits when you retire.

What about the people who do have enough savings to generate the income they need? For them, the decision is, "Do I spend my savings and let Social Security grow, or begin receiving Social Security and let my savings grow?"

Since Social Security does not pass on any unused benefit at death, most people understandably want to preserve their savings as much as possible. Whether claiming early or late is better thus depends on how long you live. In the early years, claiming Social Security and not spending your savings will be beneficial. But in later years, the lower Social Security benefit will require you to spend more of your savings. The reverse logic is true too. Delaying Social Security and spending some of your savings early will draw down your savings, but the higher Social Security benefit later allows you to spend less of your savings.

In the end, it all depends on how long you live and what your money is doing instead. Similar to the analysis in Figure 13-1, if your money is earning a high rate of return, taking Social Security early may be beneficial. But if you think you might live a while, and your money won't earn outsized returns, delaying Social Security as long as possible will likely be the best choice.

It's not all the same

Human behavior and the cumulative approach can lead to a shortfall despite receiving the same amount of money.

The situation you want to avoid is beginning benefits early, spending it when you don't really need it, and being short later in life when you do. The person who waits doesn't get to spend it early but won't be short later in life when they need it. You both may receive the same "cumulative" amount, but from a needs perspective, it's far different.

The decision of when to begin receiving benefits should not be made in a vacuum, meaning, you must consider the other parts of your plan—where your income is coming from, what your spending needs are, the mix of non-discretionary and discretionary spending needs, how much you have in savings, what your savings are invested in, etc. Ultimately, the quantitative analysis will depend on longevity, COLA, and the rate of return you could earn. I'll simplify the decision with this: If you'll die early, take it early. If you'll die later, take it later. If you don't know when you'll die, protect against the worst outcome (living longer). It's better to die early and miss out on unused benefits than to live a long time and run out of money.

One factor to at least consider is what happens if your benefit is reduced due to cuts in the Social Security program as a whole. The possibility of this happening is real, but let's look at the factors affecting why a little closer.

Social Security and Medicare are funded by the FICA tax, and these dollars are put into the Social Security Trust Fund. The trust accumulates assets over time and pays existing beneficiaries from incoming FICA taxes as well as earnings on the trust's assets. The Social Security Trust Fund is currently paying out more in benefits than it receives in taxes and interest, meaning the trust's assets are drawing down. Based on projections made in November 2020, the trust is projected to be depleted in 2034. This does not mean Social Security will no longer be around; it simply means the system will only be able to pay out what it takes in. As of this writing, payouts are projected to be 75-80% of benefits in 2035.[*][1]

Understanding what has led to this issue can help us devise ways to solve it. No single factor is responsible.

When the program began in 1935, life expectancy at birth was 58 years for men and 62 for women, and for those 65 years old, life expectancy was 78 years for men and 80 for women.[2] Full retirement age

---

[*] These projections do not incorporate the full impact of government stimulus measures taken in response to the COVID-19 pandemic.

at the time was 65. Since then, life expectancy at birth has increased to 79 years, and life expectancy for those age 65 has grown to around 84.³ Full retirement age, on the other hand, has risen to between 66 and 67, an increase of only one to two years. The rise in longevity without a corresponding increase in eligibility age has led to the program paying benefits much longer than initially designed.

Another issue is that the number of payers versus receivers has changed drastically. In 1945, 42 people paid into the system for every one person receiving benefits. As of 2013, only 2.8 people are paying in for every one person receiving.⁴ Part of this change is due to the increase in people eligible for program benefits. In 1935, only older Americans were eligible. As of 2021, older Americans, spouses, minor children of retired workers, disabled workers, and more can receive benefits from the trust.

A final factor that has contributed to the funding problem is the inclusion of annual cost-of-living adjustments. At inception, benefits were increased for inflation every few years. Beginning in 1972, the program began making yearly cost-of-living adjustments. While this is an improvement for those receiving benefits, it makes the program that much more expensive.

There is no single factor that has caused Social Security's funding issues. The preceding is not an exhaustive list but rather an overview of the main culprits. Options to "fix" the problem include reversing what has caused it, increasing FRA, limiting the type of people who can receive benefits, and getting rid of COLAs. There is also the option of raising the FICA tax rate or minimum base as well.

I'm not foolish enough to speculate on what is actually going to happen to fix this problem. Whatever action is taken, some groups of people will feel shortchanged.

However, what you should think about is what will happen to you if your benefit is cut. I recommend looking at what a 20% or 25% decrease in your benefits beginning in the year 2035 will do to your plan. If a 20% decrease results in an "Aw shucks, but I'll be okay" moment, you probably don't need to do anything. If a 20% decrease results in an "Oh boy, I'll be in trouble!" reaction (likely because you'll have to spend down your savings), then you need to plan around it by saving more, spending less, or being prepared to produce more income from "inside sources."

The decision of when to begin receiving Social Security benefits is ultimately a personal one. The math says the lower your expected investment return and the longer your life expectancy, the better it is to wait to take your benefit. However, some choose to take benefits early, if for no other reason than the argument "take it while you can get it." While it certainly would be a shame to delay receiving benefits until 70, only to pass away a year or two later, it would be a greater shame to run out of money later in life because we started receiving benefits earlier than we needed them.

When making the decision, consider what other funds you have available to live on if you do defer your benefits. If you start receiving benefits rather than spending savings, what are your savings invested in? If they are just sitting in cash, using that money and letting Social Security grow may be the better plan. However, if drawing down your savings while you defer Social Security leaves you in a tight position, then it may be best to begin taking benefits earlier.

Everybody's circumstances are unique to them. There are many intricate rules to Social Security, which is why I always recommend finding a professional competent on the subject to help you. The Social Security office cannot offer advice, but they can answer questions about how the program works and what your options are.

Social Security is not a perfect program, but it remains a great source of retirement income for older Americans. In a way, it is "America's pension." Pensions were once much more common than they are today, but many still remain. For those who have a pension, let's briefly discuss how they fit into your plan.

14

PENSIONS

Years ago, if employers wanted to provide their employees with a retirement benefit, they offered them a pension. Pension benefits traditionally come in the form of an income stream that lasts as long as the employee (or former employee) is alive. When the employee dies, benefit payments stop unless the pension offers "survivor" benefits. Survivor benefits allow the income to continue until the surviving spouse passes away. Much like Social Security, there is no unused benefit passed on when the employee or surviving spouse passes.

Pensions are a form of defined-*benefit* retirement plan. This means the benefit to the employee is "defined," and the burden of making the benefit a reality rests with the employer. Compare this to a 401(k), which is a type of defined-*contribution* plan. In this case, the contribution of the employer is defined, and the burden of making the benefit a reality lies with the employee.

While pensions are a fantastic tool for the employee, running a pension and keeping it solvent is a difficult task for the employer. A brief explanation of how pensions work will elucidate this challenge. (We will face the same type of challenge when creating long-term income from our investment accounts, as we'll discuss in Chapter 21.)

When a company runs a pension, they must first determine how much they will need to pay in the future. They do this by deciding a) how much they will pay each employee in benefits and b) how long they expect to pay them. Typically, benefit amounts are a function of the employee's salary and length of service to the employer. Most pensions will pay as long as the employee is alive, which means the company must estimate how long they expect their pensioners to live.

Multiplying the amount they expect to pay each year by how long they expect to pay will determine the pension plan's obligation. This number is understandably quite large. Companies do not set aside enough money to meet this obligation all at once. Instead, they set aside a smaller amount (known as the plan assets) and aim to grow it over time to meet their future obligation. This requires another estimate to be made, what rate of return they will earn.*

So the pension makes two major assumptions: 1) how long they will have to pay (i.e., how long people will live) and 2) what rate of return they will earn.

Here is why pensions get in trouble. First, they underestimate how long people are living. When people live longer than expected, the pension obligation (what they owe) increases. Second, pensions often earn a lower rate of return than anticipated, meaning the plan assets (what they own) grow less than expected. You don't have to be an accountant to understand it's not a good thing if what you owe increases and what you own decreases.

When this happens, the company is left with only a few choices. They can either a) increase funding to the pension, which takes away money from the existing business and shareholders, or b) decrease benefits to current and future recipients. As we have seen all too often, many pensions elect to reduce benefits, even for the employees already receiving benefits.

Obviously, a lifetime income stream is a great tool to have, but it is not without risk to the employee (you). The first risk is what we just discussed, that the pension will reduce benefit payments. A pension is nothing more than a promise made by the company. Unfortunately,

---

* If you're familiar with how present value calculations work, this concept will make sense. They are simply discounting their future obligations to a present value.

companies break their promises all the time, leaving retirees with benefits that are drastically lower or eliminated altogether.

The second risk is that you will die early and not receive many or any benefits at all (much like the risk with deferring Social Security). Some pensions will offer lump-sum payments instead of a lifetime income stream. The lump-sum option gives you a pool of money you now control, rather than an income stream you do not control—think of it as if your pension turned into a 401(k). You can now manage this money as they would a 401(k) or IRA.

Deciding between the lump sum and income options may be the most significant financial decision you ever make and should not be taken lightly. When considering the pension lump sum, it's easy to be wide-eyed when faced with all of those zeroes—it can be a big number! Imagine being offered the chance to have a check for $500,000 or $1 Million be deposited in your IRA. You'll have to give up your $20,000 or $40,000 income stream, but that big number can be tempting.

You must weigh the options carefully. If faced with the choice between an income stream or a lump sum, take yourself through the following process:

Step 1: *How long am I likely to live?*

Under most circumstances, this is an unknown. If you have reason to believe you may not live to your life expectancy, the lump sum option can make sense. With most pensions, when you die, the income stops, and there is no unused benefit to pass on. The lump-sum option allows you (or, more precisely, your beneficiaries) to receive some of the future income you will miss out on if you pass away early.

Step 2: *How much will it cost to recreate my pension?*

Pensions provide a lifetime income stream that ceases at death. This is also how many annuities work (we will discuss annuities in depth in Chapter 23). To determine the value of your pension, you can compare your pension payout to how much income you could create using annuities. The following two examples explain.

Example #1:

Pension Income	$50,000	Annuity Income	$50,000
Pension Lump Sum	$1,000,000	Annuity Premium Required to Create Income	$900,000

In this scenario, you could choose the pension lump sum option of $1,000,000, put $900,000 into an annuity to create the same income stream the pension would have created, and still have $100,000 leftover do with as you please. In this situation, it makes sense to take the lump sum and recreate it using annuities.

Example #2:

Pension Income	$50,000	Annuity Income	$50,000
Pension Lump Sum	$800,000	Annuity Premium Required to Create Income	$900,000

In this scenario, the pension provides a higher income than you could recreate by putting the lump sum in an annuity. This outcome leads us to ask a third question.

Step 3: *How likely am I to receive my benefits?*

As mentioned, pensions can and do cut benefits. Annuity payments, however, are guaranteed by large insurance companies. (Guarantees are backed by the claims-paying ability of the insurance company.) In this case, it is worth asking if the reduced payout from the guaranteed annuity is worth more than a higher payout from the pension that is not guaranteed and could be reduced in the future.

One argument for choosing the annuity, even when the pension pays more, is to frame the reduced income as an insurance premium. Think about it with an example. Assume your pension offers $50,000 per year, and the annuity offers $45,000. Your pension is not guaranteed; the annuity is guaranteed. You could have $50,000 of non-guaranteed income, or for the price of $5,000 per year (the difference between the pension and annuity), you can have $45,000 of guaranteed income.

You can gauge how at risk your pension payout is by reviewing your plan's annual report. This report provides details on plan assets and obligations and will calculate a "funded ratio." While not a perfect measure, the funded ratio tells you what percentage of the plan's obligations are met by the plan's assets. While you would love for your pension to be 100% funded, very few are. A funded ratio below 100% is not an immediate cause for alarm, but a funded ratio of say 60% should cause concern.

Some pensions receive government support if they run into trouble. The Pension Benefit Guaranty Corporation (PBGC) assists certain private-sector pensions. While these protections are helpful, it's not the same as a full guarantee and is not a process you want your pension to go through.

Some people will forgo the income options offered by both the pension and annuity, and instead, will choose the lump sum option to manage and create income on their own. This introduces a much higher level of risk and is a different strategy altogether. In Chapter 21, we'll have a complete discussion on how to create income from your investments.

These three steps are a good starting point for deciding between an income stream or a lump sum, but further analysis must be done if faced with this choice. The decision is especially delicate as it typically represents a significant portion of a person's savings. Finding a competent and unbiased professional to help you think through the decision is crucial. Be careful, though. Looking to move a pension can be a bit like swimming in the ocean with a bleeding leg; you are sure to attract some sharks. In the chapter on advisors, we will discuss what to look for when choosing an advisor and how we define competent and unbiased.

Pensions and the lifetime income they offer are excellent tools that become more valuable the longer you live. If you have concerns about your pension's ability to meet its obligations, explore your lump-sum options. If you do not have a lump sum option, unfortunately, you are limited in your choices and must take the income and hope it lasts.

15

INTRODUCTION TO
INSIDE SOURCES

We have so far reviewed how to determine our spending needs and looked at the most common outside sources of income. The gap between these two must be filled by our inside sources, which is our personal savings.

We've also touched on the fact that for most of our lives, we are accumulating wealth, and when we accumulate, we focus on our balances (how much we have saved). Understandably, people carry this "balance focus" into retirement. Countless commercials reinforce this by asking, "What's your retirement number?" which is really asking how you need to have saved to retire. The problem is, retirement involves *distributing* wealth, and in my opinion, asking "What's your retirement number?" stops one step short of the more relevant question.

While knowing the balance of your savings is necessary and provides a starting point, it doesn't tell us what we really need to know. Consider the following exercise.

Of the following two questions, which of these is *easier* to answer? I'm not asking which you would rather have, but for which question does a "Yes" or a "No" come to your mind quicker.

1. I have $2,000,000 saved. Is that enough money to retire?
2. I have $100,000 of income guaranteed for the rest of my life. Is that enough money to retire?

Most of us can answer #2 quickest. We are used to thinking in terms of monthly and annual amounts, whether it be salary, mortgages, car payments, etc. We know right away whether that number is high, low, or just right. The $2,000,000 may sound nice, but the answer depends. It depends on how old you are, how long you will live, how much you need to spend, what current interest rates are, what rate of return you will earn, and so on.

This is why I say the question about your retirement number falls one step short. While having savings is important and necessary, it's not always about how much you've saved. It's far more important to know what your savings can do, meaning 1) how much you can spend and 2) how long it will last. This shift from a balance focus to an income focus goes against the muscle memory we have built our entire lives, but it makes the retirement planning process more effective.

You see, $1,000,000 in cash, in bonds, in stocks, in annuities, even in life insurance cash value, will provide far different amounts of income. Some tools may have higher growth potential but lower income potential. Some tools allow us to answer the questions of how much I can spend and how long it will last with certainty, while with others, we must rely on projections.

That being said, rate of return is still important. Your savings must be held somewhere, and unless you are stashing them under a mattress, your money will earn some rate of return. It could be positive, or it could be negative. As we showed in Chapter 2, what return you earn has an enormous impact on all of the other parts of your plan. The following chapters will discuss the different tools we have to choose from, how they work, what they are good for (and not so good for), and where appropriate, what rate of return we can expect to earn.

Let's start by first gaining a better understanding of the tradeoff between risk and return.

16

RISK AND RETURN

Higher risk, higher return. It's been mentioned several times in this book and is a commonly understood principle of finance. On the surface, it appears simple, but there's more we need to understand about this seemingly straightforward relationship.

Let's recall the definition of return we gave in Chapter 3. Return is simply the difference between what you put in (buy) and what you get out (sell). If you get out more than you put in, your return is positive, and if you get out less than you put in, your return is negative. We discussed several ways to measure return, and while there are multiple ways to calculate it, there's less debate about how we define it.

When we try to define risk, however, we start to see a disconnect between academia and the real world. If I asked you what makes an investment "risky," you'd probably tell me, "The chance that I lose money." I agree with you. But finance likes to measure things and needed a way to measure the chance of losing money. How do they measure the chance that you will lose money, which happens in the future? They can't. Since they can't measure the future, they look backward. When they looked back, they found they could measure how much the price of an investment changed and settled on this as their measure of risk. They call this volatility.

Most people agree that how much the price of something changed does not truly capture risk. Volatility as a measure of risk was agreed upon out of convenience rather than accuracy. While there are issues with volatility, it is not completely worthless, as we'll see shortly.

So, return is the difference between what you put in and get out, and risk is the chance that the difference is negative. Now, let's understand why the risk and return relationship exists. Because investors dislike risk (the possibility of losing money), they must be bribed with the prospect of higher returns. (Notice the squishiness of the word "prospect." Returns are expected, potential, possible…uncertain.)

Since return is the difference between what you put in and get out, there are two ways to earn a higher return, 1) put in less and 2) get out more. We usually have little control over how much we can get out, so we respond to higher risk by paying less, which boosts our expected return. We can again rephrase the risk and return relationship. The less certainty there is about how much we'll get out, the higher the return we'll require to take this risk, and the less we'll pay. The more certain we are, the less return we require, and the more we will pay.

Reviewing the historical performance of stocks, bonds, and cash shows evidence of the positive relationship between higher risk and return. In the past, stocks have returned more than bonds, and bonds have returned more than cash. This isn't by accident, and I can almost guarantee you that this will continue to be the case in the future (over the long run). Why can I do that? Because the risk and return relationship is, in a sense, self-regulating. The following example will explain why that is and how the risk and return relationship is established.

In the U.S., where is the safest place you can put your money? In the bank. How much do you expect to get out when you put money in the bank? All of it. How certain are you? Since U.S. banks are insured by the FDIC, you are very certain. Since you have a lot of certainty, your return for putting money in the bank is very low.

What if, instead, you consider purchasing a bond. How much do you expect to get out when you purchase a bond? Bonds are like loans in that their terms are strictly defined. When you buy a bond, you know exactly how much you can possibly get out—your principal plus some interest. The question then becomes, how certain are you to receive that money? The answer is a reflection of who you are loaning to. You're more certain the U.S. Treasury will repay you than Blockbuster Video. The more certain you are, the more you will pay, which will lower your expected return (called *yield* when referring to bonds). (The higher the price you pay, the lower the yield. The higher the yield, the lower the price.) Regardless of who you loan to, you will not pay so much that you will earn less purchasing the bond than you would by storing cash in the bank. Otherwise, you wouldn't take the risk of buying the bond in the first place. Because you won't pay that much for a bond, the relationship is self-regulating. As soon as bond yields drop to the point that you would earn less buying a bond than you would by putting cash in the bank, people will stop buying and start selling bonds (lowering demand and increasing supply) which will cause the bond price to drop and the yield to rise.

The same thing happens with stocks. When you own a stock, as an owner of the company, you are paid last. When the company thrives, you keep the leftovers and reap the rewards in the form of dividends and price increases, but when the company struggles, if there's nothing left over, you don't receive dividends, and you suffer the pains of price decreases. So as an owner, you aren't sure how much you can get out, meaning you don't know for sure how much or if the company will pay dividends and certainly don't know how much you can sell your shares for in the future. To take this kind of risk, you need to make sure you expect to earn more than you would buying bonds; otherwise, you wouldn't take the risk of being an owner.

Let's say you can earn 5% owning a bond. If the price of a stock rises to a point where you think you can earn only 4% by owning it, you won't take that risk because you could buy a bond and earn more with far less risk. Once again, investors will stop buying and start selling the stock until the price of the stock drops to a point where investors are offered a higher expected return by owning the stock than owning a bond.

The self-regulating nature of returns also introduces what I call the *relativity* of returns. There is no way to know what the future *absolute* returns will be—will stocks return 5%, 10%, 15%, we don't know—but we can be confident in the *relative* returns to each other—stocks will continue to earn more than bonds and bonds more than cash (over the long-run).

As mentioned, history has corroborated the idea that higher risk relates to higher returns. Table 16.1 shows the different average returns of cash, bonds, and stocks over the last 90+ years. This data is used to create the risk and return chart seen in Figure 16-1.

TABLE 16.1: Historical Returns 1928-2020

	Compound Return	Simple Average
Large Cap Stocks	9.79%	11.64%
Corporate Bonds	6.99%	7.25%
Government Bonds	4.95%	5.21%
Cash (Treasury-Bills)	3.32%	3.36%
Inflation	2.95%	3.02%

FIGURE 16-1: Risk and Return Chart

In my opinion, this visual is harmful, as it oversimplifies the risk-return relationship. In fact, it doesn't show any risk at all; it just shows the relationship of average returns. It perpetuates the attitude of "Need more return? Take more risk. Voila!" Understand this: if riskier investments reliably produced higher returns, they wouldn't be riskier![1]

We know that finance measures risk in terms of volatility and that volatility is a measure of how much prices change. So, how do we measure volatility? In earlier chapters, we established that investments do not return their average every year. Instead, they vary, meaning they return somewhere "around" their average. The amount around the average is measured by standard deviation and is what we use as our measure of volatility.

On their own as a predictive tool, averages and standard deviation are limited in what they tell us. However, when we combine them with the theory of normal probability distribution, they can be useful.

The theory of normal distribution, as it relates to investment returns, is simple. If you were to plot the yearly returns of an investment over time (creating a histogram), they should form the shape of a "bell," with the average being in the middle, and returns "distributing" around the average in a neat and tidy fashion, shown in Figure 16-2.[2] (Note that many distributions form the shape of a bell, and a "normal distribution" is just a type of bell curve. The term "bell curve" is often generalized to refer to a normal distribution unless specified otherwise.) The theory of normal distribution tells us that returns will be within one standard deviation 68% of the time, within two standard deviations 95% of the time, and within three standard deviations 99.7% of the time. The higher the standard deviation, the wider the range of outcomes.

FIGURE 16-2: The 68-95-99.7 Rule for the Normal Distribution

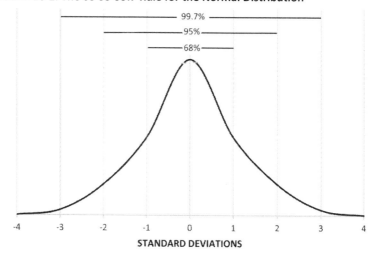

STANDARD DEVIATIONS

We can combine all of this information to make projections of future returns. For example, suppose your investment averages a return of 10% and has a standard deviation of 5%. Rather than expecting it to earn 10% every year, we can expect that 68% of the time, returns will be between 5% and 15% (±5% from the average of 10%), 95% of the time, returns will be between 0% and 20%, and 99.7% of the time between -5% and 25%.

Table 16.2 compares the (simple) average historical returns and standard deviations of cash, measured by the 3-month U.S. Treasury Bill, bonds, measured by the 10-year U.S. Treasury Bond, and stocks, measured by the S&P 500.[3] You can see from the table that there is a positive relationship between volatility and returns.

TABLE 16.2: Average Returns and Standard Deviation

	Average Return	Standard Deviation
Cash	3.3%	3.4%
Bonds	5.2%	7.6%
Stocks	11.6%	19.5%

While this is interesting historical data, finance is forward-looking, and problems arise when we use historical averages and standard deviations to project future returns. There are two main issues.

First, using historical returns is often a flawed method of projecting future returns. We discussed at length in Chapter 3 the problems of using history to project the future. The investing mantra "past performance is not a guarantee of future results" tries to capture this, but we can do more to understand why that is true.

Let's assume that you know exactly how much you could sell a stock for in the future, $100. The stock price was $50 but is now $90, providing a return of 80%. If you still expect to sell the investment for $100, your current expected return is barely 11%, but if you base your expectation on historical returns, you expect to earn 80%, which would require you to sell it for $162.

There can also be an upper limit to how much a company can grow. Take Apple, for example. At the time of this writing, Apple is worth over $2 Trillion, roughly 1,100 times the amount it was 40 years ago when it first went public. Will Apple continue and repeat its past performance, growing another 1,100 times in the next 40 years?

This discussion introduces a curious relationship between historical returns, risk, and future returns. Remember, the more you pay, the lower your expected return. Given this, when stocks get more expensive, we would expect people to want them less. But the stock market makes us do funny things. With stocks, when recent returns have been high, people think future returns will be high and will pay more. So they pay more, which lowers their expected return (which also increases their risk), yet think their future returns will be high because they were in the past. Rather than being cautious as prices rise, we gain more confidence. As Howard Marks explains, "Normally people buy when things are on sale. On Wall Street, people buy when it's more expensive." We will revisit this phenomenon in Chapter 19.

A complicated relationship

We are all taught and typically understand the traditional relationship between supply, demand, and price. All else being equal, higher demand or lower supply increases prices, and lower demand or higher supply decreases prices. But George Cooper, in his book *The Origin of Financial Crises*, shows that this relationship differs depending on what we are buying.[4]

With traditional goods, the traditional relationship holds. If demand for bread increases, prices will rise until the number of people willing to buy bread lowers to meet the supply. Likewise, when prices rise, other bread makers will increase their supply which will help lower the price to some "equilibrium" level.

With asset markets, for example, stocks and real estate, this relationship isn't always so straightforward.

When investors buy an asset for investment purposes, they do so for the asset's ability to generate income (dividends) or deliver capital gains (increase in price). If they buy for the purpose of capital gains, inherent in that reason is the belief that the price must be undervalued if it will rise in the future.

If the price of an asset begins to increase, this gives the investor confidence in their belief that the price will rise. This higher price does not necessarily cause the investor to sell, which would have increased the supply and lowered the price. Since there is no increase in supply, the price may continue to rise.

In goods markets, items are purchased for consumption. In asset markets, items are purchased for their potential to change in price. This makes the nature of how market participants respond to price changes fundamentally different.

Some of this behavior is grounded in logic and can be explained by what is called an *information cascade* (similar to a feedback loop). Richard Meadows uses the following example in his book, *Optionality*.

> Let's say you and I are at an auction house, and the contents of a mysterious black box go under the hammer. I bid $50, purely for the hell of it. You have no idea what's in that box either, but you think I must know something, so you bid $100. Now I think you know something, and raise my own bid to $200. A third person enters the gallery, sees the two of us engaged in a heated bidding war over a mysterious box, deduces that we must have information about its contents, and enthusiastically enters a bid at $400. None of us are aware that we're promising increasingly ridiculous sums for a box of old straw and mouse droppings.[5]

Information cascades cause the following cycle: People buy because the price goes up, and the price goes up because people buy. At some point, this cycle must end.

I say these cascades are grounded in logic because it's understandable why we take cues from other people's actions. If someone yells "Fire!" it's probably best to exit the room. But this *herd mentality* (further discussed in Chapter 29) can work against us when investing.

The second issue with using historical averages and standard deviation to project returns is that markets are not normally distributed, meaning they do not obey the tidy bell curve distribution. The corollary of this is enormous, as many planning systems and models rely on the assumption that markets are normally distributed. Since markets are *not* normally distributed, "outliers" happen far more frequently than the friendly bell curve suggests. That means a model built on the theory of normal distribution understates the probability of extreme outliers, which leaves us less prepared when they do occur.[6]

We have seen the failure of this assumption several times in history. If you look at the bell curve in Figure 16-2, returns greater than three standard deviations should happen only .03% of the time. But in reality, events that were "ten sigma" (sigma being the term for standard deviation, so something ten deviations from the average, or supposedly next to impossible) happen, and financial strategies built on the expectation of their impossibility explode. Events like Black Monday in 1987 should happen once in the history of the universe. The creation, rise, and subsequent blowup of the investment firm Long Term Capital Management in the 1990s is a textbook example of the flaws of assuming markets are normally distributed. Renowned economist Eugene Fama wrote his thesis on this issue, and he found that price movements of more than five deviations happened 2,000 times more often than expected.[7]

There is an overarching conceptual issue with using volatility (standard deviation) as a measure of risk. Volatility defines price movement as risk, regardless of which direction prices move. In theory, a stock that repeatedly increases 50%, then decreases 25% (which would lead to a decent gain), is "riskier" (because it is more volatile) than an investment that loses 10% every year.[8]

We also must be careful not to think that higher standard deviation *causes* higher returns. This way of thinking suggests that an investment should return a lot in the future simply because its price changed a lot in the past.

A positive of using standard deviations is that it helps us shift from a mindset of average returns to a range of returns. Like in our earlier example when we showed how we expect that 68% of the time returns will be between 5% and 15%, 95% of the time between 0% and 20%, and 99.7% of the time between -5% and 25%.

We can carry this way of thinking in ranges into creating a revised risk and return chart. The previously cited Howard Marks created a risk and return chart that integrates the bell curve, shown in Figure 16-3. Rather than a dot indicating what return to expect, Marks' graphic puts little bell curves turned sideways to remind us that really, we'll earn a distribution around that average return. I find this visual much more realistic, as it attempts to illustrate the range of possible outcomes. (Of course, the actual ranges are even wider than shown here, but it communicates the point of thinking in ranges.)

I believe this graphic should be seared into every investor's mind. We must remember that higher upside comes with the risk of lower downside.

FIGURE 16-3: Risk and Return Chart With Range of Possible Outcomes[9]

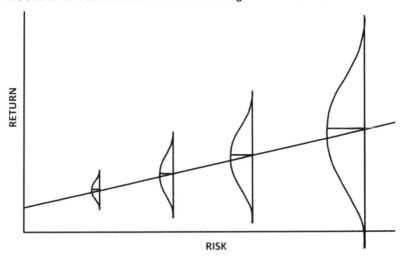

We now understand what risk is, how finance tries to measure it, and what returns are. But we must ask a curious question, why do we care about risk? Answering that question can help us understand *when* we should care about it. Here, volatility is actually helpful.

We care about risk when we do not want to lose money. To lose money, we have to get out less than we put in. To get money out, we have to sell. When we sell, we sell at the current market price. So, to lose money, we have to sell when the price is below what we paid for it. Duh, right? Here's the point. Market prices, especially of stocks, move around all over the place (because they're volatile, remember?). They *temporarily* decrease quite often. But if we are not selling, do we care about temporary drops? (Do we and should we care often have different answers.) If we don't plan to sell, then why care if the price drops temporarily?

We shouldn't. But if we do care, and panic and sell during a temporary drop, then we turn it into a permanent drop. If we use volatility as our definition of risk, then this explains why it's recommended to "reduce risk" (reduce volatility) as we near the time we need our money (sell). Doing so decreases the chance of turning a temporary loss into a permanent one.

This concept will become a core tenet of the coming chapters. If you are investing for the long-term, then you'll care a lot less about temporary "losses." If you are investing your money for income, requiring you to frequently sell, then you care a lot more. If selling more often, then it is advisable to take less risk to decrease the likelihood of turning temporary price decreases into permanent ones.

There are many factors that affect how you should manage your money. There are quantitative factors, such as how long until you need your money, what portion of your overall portfolio it represents, and what the rest of your portfolio is invested in. There are also qualitative factors, such as what the money is for and how you feel about risk. I believe we can boil it down to two questions. 1) Can you afford to lose it? 2) When do you need it?

To determine if you can afford to lose it, you should first ask, what is it for? Use our discussion of non-discretionary and discretionary expenses as a guide. If the money is for your mortgage, you will treat it differently than if it is for a fifth car. Next, imagine what position you will be in if you do lose money. If you lose 25% of your investments and can no longer pay your mortgage, you probably can't afford to lose it. If losing 25% of your investments means that you take one less vacation or pass on a little less to your kids, the question then becomes, do you care? Some people will; some won't. As a rule, if you can't afford to lose it, you shouldn't put it at risk. (This is one of those "I can't believe I need to even say this" things. Think about the alternative. "I can't afford to lose it, but I want the upside, so I'm going to risk it anyway.")

We also need to ask, when do we need it? Let's say that the money is for *next month's* mortgage. If we can't afford to lose it, we should keep it somewhere safe. If we need it for the mortgage in five years and can't afford to lose it, then we shouldn't put it somewhere we can lose it in the next five years. However, if we need it in 30 years, then we care less if it is worth less in five years.

The takeaway is this: Limit volatility when you cannot afford to lose money and you near the time you need it. As we'll discuss in later chapters, most people's trouble investing comes from mismanaging these two factors.

What's the return (on my) policy?

This chapter so far has discussed the most common places we put our money: cash, bonds, and stocks. We should also briefly discuss insurance and how it fits in.

Remember, insurance is used to protect your downside, not pursue the upside. We don't usually buy insurance to earn a rate of return, and I get uneasy when I start hearing rate of return and insurance used together. There are two types of insurance, however, that can blur that line, life insurance and annuities. Each behaves slightly differently and is difficult to plot on a traditional risk and return chart.

First, they each protect against different risks, life insurance against a short life and annuities against a long life. Life insurance pays a death benefit that is typically (but not always) a fixed amount, which means the longer you live, the lower the rate of return. Annuities, in the traditional sense, pay an income for as long as you are alive, and thus the longer you live, the higher the rate of return.

Measuring either of them by the traditional definition of risk (volatility) is difficult. For traditional annuities and fixed death benefit life insurance policies, there is no volatility. Your risk is that the company cannot pay it. Given the regulations surrounding the insurance industry, a guaranteed benefit from a highly rated insurance carrier can be one of the safest things in finance, although anything is possible. For variable or indexed life insurance and annuity policies, there is volatility that can be measured by more traditional standards, which we'll discuss briefly in Chapters 23 and 24.

SUMMARY

Risk and return. Typically, you can't have one without the other, and nearly every financial fraud tries to break this relationship. Risk and return are a proxy for the eternal battle between greed and fear. We all want the upside, but we have to be sure we can afford the downside, or more accurately, the downside during the time that we might need to sell it. At the end of the day, there is no way to know what future returns will be. If you can't afford to lose money, it doesn't matter if an investment can go up 50% if it can also go down 50%.

Risking money you can't afford to lose to earn a higher return is known as "reaching for yield." Warren Buffett gave some sobering comments on this topic in a February 2020 interview on CNBC:

"If you need to get 3% and you can only get 1%, the answer is... you should always adapt your consumption to your income. Reaching for yield is really stupid. But it is very human. People say, "Well, I saved all my life and I can only get 1%, what do I do?" You learn to live on 1%, unfortunately. You don't go and listen to some salesman come and tell you, I've got you some magic way to get you 5%." [10]

As you near the time you need the money, if you can't afford to lose it, begin to cut back on your risk. Remember, prices of volatile investments move around a lot, and the more often you need to sell a highly volatile investment, the more you increase the chance of turning a temporary loss into a permanent one.

The flip side of this is, if you don't need the money for a while, or can afford some variation in values, then don't overreact to temporary price movements.

While it is admirable that finance has tried to boil down risk into one concise number, it's ultimately an impossible endeavor. We each have different definitions of what is risk is, for both qualitative (e.g., experience, temperament) and quantitative (e.g., age, wealth, income, time horizon) reasons. What might be a horribly inappropriate investment for one person can be a completely prudent investment for another. A 40-year-old with a steady high salary saving for retirement will evaluate a volatile investment far differently than an 80-year-old spending down their savings in retirement.

With this deeper understanding of risk and return, we can now explore the most common tools available to us—cash, bonds, stocks, annuities, life insurance, and real estate. The discussion will center on how each tool works and how it can be used. Where appropriate, we will discuss how to estimate what rate of return we can expect to earn.

17

CASH

As we just saw, in the U.S., cash held in the bank is considered the safest place to put your money. The FDIC insures deposits of up to $250,000 per institution, which means there is little risk of losing your principal. While cash is the safest, it also offers the lowest return of the tools we will discuss. The "return" your cash earns comes in the form of interest paid by the bank in exchange for depositing your money. How much interest the bank pays is the result of many complicated market interactions that can all be tied back to the actions of the Central Bank (in the U.S. called the Federal Reserve). Below is a brief discussion of these interactions.

How and why interest rates change

An economy is made up of those who have capital (money) and those who need capital. For an economy to grow, capital must be put to work, such as hiring workers, building plants and factories, investing in R&D, etc.

Interest rates are the price of money. If you're buying (need capital), you want the price to be low, and if you're selling (have capital), you want the price to be high. When interest rates are high, those who need capital may find it too expensive to borrow, and those who have capital may earn enough at the bank that they have no reason to put their capital at risk, which means no economic activity.

If an economy is sluggish, the Central Bank can encourage spending and investment by lowering the price of money (interest rates). (This is often called "stimulating the economy.") When interest rates are lower, it becomes less expensive for those who need capital to borrow and less lucrative for those who have capital to hold it in the bank. This causes capital to be deployed, projects to be started, and hopefully, results in economic growth.

The reverse is true when the Central Bank needs to slow an economy down. While intentionally slowing growth may sound counterintuitive, economies can "overheat," leading to higher inflation that may soon rage out of control. To slow an economy, the Central Bank raises interest rates, making it more expensive to borrow and more enticing to save.

So, how do Central Banks lower or raise interest rates? They do so by controlling the economy's money supply. When they increase the money supply, there is more competition to deploy capital. More competition and supply leads to lower prices (interest rates), more capital being deployed, and higher growth. When they decrease the money supply, the opposite occurs, less money, higher prices (interest rates), and less economic activity.

To increase the money supply, the Central Bank (usually) purchases U.S. Treasuries with money that was not previously in the economy (some call this "printing money," although this is an entirely electronic process now.) To decrease the money supply, they sell securities. When the Central Bank does not redeploy the dollars they received from selling, money is removed from the economy.

The biggest benefit to holding cash is the optionality that it provides. This optionality comes from its liquidity. Liquidity refers to how quickly something can be turned into spendable cash. When people are in a crunch, a lack of liquidity may cause them to sell assets and investments at temporarily lower prices. Having cash available can help them ride through the tough times and avoid having to fire sale assets. This optionality also makes cash opportunistic—it provides dry powder to capitalize on opportunities when they present themselves.

How much interest different cash instruments pay often depends on how liquid they are. All else being equal, the less liquid something is, the higher the interest rate. Cash in the bank is about as liquid as it gets (other than cash in your pocket) and pays a very low interest rate. Certificates of Deposit are cash instruments but with a longer maturity, meaning you may not be able to access your principal held in a CD for a year or two without a penalty. Because your money is less liquid, the bank will offer a higher interest rate on a CD than it will on a checking account that you can withdraw from on-demand.

The greatest threat to cash is inflation. While interest rates typically move with inflation, inflation can run higher than interest rates, which will erode the purchasing power of your cash.

Will the real interest rate please stand up?

It's important to understand the difference between nominal and real interest rates. The nominal interest rate is the "stated" rate. For example, a checking account that pays 5% interest has a nominal interest rate of 5%. The "real interest rate" is the inflation-adjusted rate, which is calculated by subtracting inflation from the nominal rate. If your nominal interest rate is 5% and inflation is 3%, then your real interest rate is 2%. Why does this matter?

Not understanding this difference can lead to what is called the *money illusion*. This occurs when we mistake inflation for an increase in wealth or purchasing power. If our checking account pays 10% interest, but inflation is 9%, our real wealth does not increase 10%; it increases 1%.

A safe solution to the inflation problem is Treasury Inflation-Protected Securities, called TIPS. TIPS are short-term instruments that provide either inflation-adjusted interest payments or inflation-adjusted principal payments. Depending on your reasons for owning TIPS, one will be more appropriate than the other.

TIPS yields will generally be lower than regular Treasuries of the same maturity by the amount of *expected* inflation. For example, if a regular 30-year Treasury is yielding 3% and future expected inflation is 2%, 30-year TIPS will yield 1%. Comparing Treasury yields to TIPS is a good way of determining expected inflation.

How much cash you should have is not always a straightforward answer. There are rules of thumb, for example, six months to a years' worth of expenses. But ultimately, it's yet another balancing act, between the qualitative and quantitative, safety and efficiency.

From a quantitative perspective, the biggest reason to own cash is to avoid having to fire sale assets in case of emergency, turning a temporary loss into a permanent one. Emergencies include a loss of income, covering insurance deductibles, and paying for any spending shocks. From this perspective, the answer to how much cash you should have is a function of the rest of your plan—what your other assets are invested in (how liquid, how volatile), what your spending needs are, and where your income comes from. For example, if all of your spending needs are met by guaranteed sources of income, then you don't need to set aside as much to meet your living expenses.

From a qualitative perspective, the answer is a matter of personal preference. Many will have a "sleep well at night" number, i.e., how much they need to have saved to feel comfortable. I've heard some say their number is "anything above $0," while others have said "not a dollar below $100,000."

Once again, there isn't always a right answer. Having a lot of cash on hand may appear inefficient at one moment and the source of incredible opportunity at the next.

While we can think of cash held in the bank as a "loan" to the bank, if we want to earn a higher return, we can also loan money to governments and corporations by purchasing a financial instrument called a bond, which is what we will discuss next.

18

BONDS

Renowned bond investor Bill Gross says, "Bond markets have power because they're the fundamental base of all markets." Sounds important, yet, bonds rarely get much attention.

To understand the role of bonds in your portfolio requires an understanding of how they work. Any confusion surrounding bonds is mostly a result of the unique math and terminology used, such as face value, maturity date, coupon rate, and yield to maturity.

Bonds are often compared to making a loan, which is accurate, but there are slight differences. At its simplest, buying a bond is like purchasing an I.O.U. In exchange for your money today, you are promised to receive predetermined cash flows in the future.

A bond is a type of *security* that a government or company, called the *issuer*, sells to the public to raise money for their operations. Before they sell the bond, the issuer must determine what they are selling.

Let's say that the issuer creates a bond that promises to pay $100 (*face value*) in 10 years (*maturity date*) and 5% interest per year (*coupon rate*) along the way. This creates a 10-year bond with a $100 face value and a 5% coupon rate. The issuer then takes this security to the market and asks, "How much will you pay us today for our promise to make these payments in the future?" How much someone is willing to pay for this promise determines the bond's price.

As a purchaser of bonds, you expect to receive two things in the future: 1) the face value and 2) coupon payments. Since both are fixed and determined when you purchase the bond, you can calculate precisely what rate of return, or yield, you expect to earn from owning the bond. Rather than a dollar amount, this return, known as the *yield to maturity* (YTM), is often how bond prices are quoted.

Simply put, YTM is the annualized return you will earn if you hold the bond to maturity (meaning you do not sell it). Since you know exactly how much you will receive and cannot receive any more than that amount, the more you pay for the bond, the lower your YTM (return) is. This is a key principle of bonds that we will revisit.

The YTM will often differ from the coupon rate of the bond. This can lead to a lot of confusion, as it can seem like there are two interest rates. Here is the difference. Coupon rates are fixed and predetermined. YTM depends on the price you pay. The following examples show how YTM is determined.

Let's say you purchase a bond with a face value of $100, a 10-year maturity, and a 5% coupon rate. This means that in 10 years, the issuer will give you $100 and pay you $5 of interest every year until then. If you purchase this bond at the same price as its face value, $100, the *yield to maturity (YTM)* is 5%. We can understand why by thinking through each piece of the bond. If you pay $100 today to receive $100 in 10 years (the face value), your return would be 0%. Since you will also receive $5 per year (in coupon payments), which is 5% of your purchase price of $100, then your return is 5% each year.

If you pay more than $100 for this bond, your YTM will be lower. Since you paid more than $100 to receive $100 in the future, your return on the face value is negative. Your return on the coupon payments is less than 5% since you are receiving $5 of coupon payments on a principal amount greater than $100.

The same logic explains why paying less than face value means your yield to maturity will be higher. You're paying less than $100 to receive $100 in the future and receiving $5 of coupon payments on a principal amount less than $100.

Understand that while the YTM will fluctuate, just as the price of any investment does, the yield that *you* earn after you purchase a bond does not change. As long as you receive the payments promised when you purchased the bond, your YTM will stay the same.

Next, we must understand what affects the price of a bond. Recall from our discussion in Chapter 16: the lower the risk, the higher the price, which means the lower the return (YTM). Three main factors affect bond prices.

1. Maturity
2. Credit risk
3. Interest rate risk

1. *Maturity*

Typically, the sooner you are paid back, the less risky the bond. This means that bonds with shorter maturities, for example, 10 years, will have a lower YTM than ones with a longer maturity, such as 30 years.

If you plot the yield of bonds by the length of maturity, you will usually produce something like Figure 18-1, called an upward sloping *yield curve*. Occasionally, the yield curve can become "inverted" or downward sloping. This implies you are less likely to be paid back in the short term and more likely to be paid back in the long term. There is an old joke that inverted yield curves have correctly predicted 30 of the last three recessions. While they often get attention in the media as a sign of impending economic doom, this is not always the case and shouldn't necessarily cause panic.

FIGURE 18-1: Yield Curve

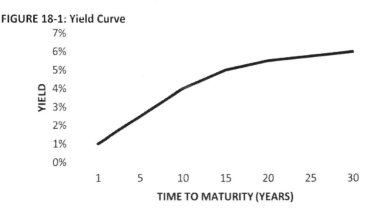

2. *Credit Risk*

Credit risk asks the question, "How likely am I to be paid back?" The more likely you are to be paid back, the less risky the bond is, and the higher the price of the bond will be relative to other riskier bonds. The higher the price you pay, the lower your YTM. Therefore, the safer the bond, the lower the yield.

The safest (lowest credit risk) issuer of bonds is the U.S. Treasury. Bonds issued by the Treasury are known as "Treasuries."* Since the Treasury can "print" money to pay their debts, Treasuries are considered "risk-free" in the world of finance. This means that Treasuries should have the lowest YTM for bonds of the same maturity. To understand why, consider two bonds with identical face values, coupon rates, and maturity. The U.S. Treasury issues one, and AT&T issues the other. Who is more likely to pay you back? The U.S. Treasury. Because a bond issued by the Treasury is less risky than one issued by AT&T, you'll pay more for the Treasury (or pay less for the AT&T bond), meaning it will have a lower YTM than the AT&T bond.

There are companies that rate the credit risk of bonds, most notably S&P, Moody's, and Fitch. Each has its own scale but typically follows an A, B, C grading system, with the safest bonds receiving the highest grades (A). They can be categorized into investment-grade and junk bonds. Lower risk bonds receive higher grades, e.g., "investment grade," and have lower yields.

Throughout this book, when I say that "bonds are yielding 1%," I am referring to Treasuries. Treasury bonds set the floor for bond yields, and yields increase as you take on more credit risk. The difference in yields between Treasuries and corporate bonds is called the credit spread. This spread can widen and shrink. Generally speaking, a tighter spread is considered healthy. As economic conditions deteriorate, investors may have concerns about corporations' abilities to

---

* Treasuries have different names based on the length of maturity. Maturities less than 52 weeks are called Bills (known as T-Bills). Maturities between two and ten years are called Notes. And maturities greater than ten years are called Bonds. In this chapter we will refer to all of them as Treasuries.

meet their obligations. Investors will sell corporate bonds, which lowers their price and increases their yields, and buy Treasuries, raising their price and lowering their yields. As people gain confidence in corporate bonds, the process reverses, and the spread tightens.

Sometimes spreads can tighten out of desperation. When Treasuries yield next to zero, people purchase corporate bonds simply to earn a higher return. When this happens, you are taking more risk and receiving less compensation per unit of risk.

Figure 18-2 shows how yields have differed for bonds of different risks. The lowest yielding has been short-term Treasuries, followed by longer-term Treasuries. Highly rated corporate bonds are followed by the riskiest debt, known as "junk bonds," which are not pictured.

FIGURE 18-2: Comparing Bond Yields of Different Risk

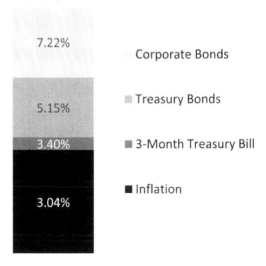

3. *Interest Rate Risk*

Interest rates in the market also play an essential role. The yield of your bond will move as the interest rates in the market move—if interest rates in the market decrease, so will the YTM of your bond. For example, if your bond currently has a YTM of 5% and interest rates in the market for a comparable bond fall to 3%, people will be willing to pay more for your bond that yields 5%. The price of your bond will increase until the YTM equals 3%.

If any of these three factors change, the price of your bond will as well. If it appears more or less likely you will be paid back, the price of your bond will rise or decrease accordingly. Remember that the YTM you will receive is fixed when you purchase the bond. If you hold the bond to maturity, price changes will not affect you. For example, if rates move up or down, the value of your bond could decrease or increase by 20%, but if you hold until maturity and still receive the face value and coupon payments, you will not recognize any gain or loss.

One final question needs to be asked, "How much will the price of a bond change?" A term called *duration* answers this question.

While more complicated than this, duration is a measure of how long the bond's payments will last. It is quoted in years but is not the same as the length of maturity. That being said, longer-term bonds typically have a higher duration than shorter-term bonds. The main point is this: The higher the duration, the more the price of the bond will be affected by changes in interest rates. For example, a bond with a duration of 2 years may only lose 2% of its value if interest rates increase by 1%, while a bond with a duration of 15 years may lose 15% of its value.

Let's recap what we've covered. Bonds make pre-determined payments over a set period of time. The price of your bond depends on when you'll be paid back (maturity), how likely you are to be paid back (credit risk), and what interest rates in the market are (interest rate risk). The longer the duration, the more sensitive the price of the bond is to changes in interest rates.

How do bonds fit into our portfolio? Usually, we own bonds for two reasons, 1) a steady source of income and 2) lower volatility. Each of these is still a viable reason but is challenged when yields are low.

The first problem is that the yield itself is not high enough to provide the income necessary for most retirees. This is the same problem with holding cash at the bank; there's simply not enough interest to "live off the interest." If the income from the bond yield alone is not enough, you may need to sell some of your bonds to generate the required income. This introduces us to the next problem.

When you sell a bond, you do so at the current market price. As we just discussed, bond prices decrease as interest rates increase. When yields are near 1%, how much lower can yields go? There is not much room for yields to drop, which means there is little opportunity for bond prices to increase. There is, however, a lot of room for bond prices to decrease if interest rates were to rise. This means when yields are too low, they have more downside potential than upside, which is not ideal.

To get an idea of how much bond prices can fluctuate, we can use a simple example. Assume you purchase a 10-year bond with a 5% coupon rate at a YTM of 1%. If we assume that the lowest yields can drop is to zero percent (this is not true, they can go negative), then the most the price can appreciate is 8.7%. Table 18.1 shows how the value of this bond will change if rates were to increase. You can see that a 3% increase in interest rates results in a 21.6% decrease in price. Remember, many people buy bonds for their safety, not realizing that the potential to lose money is real if they need to sell them.

TABLE 18.1: Example of Price Changes of a Bond

Change in Interest Rates	Change in Price
1% decrease	8.7%
1% increase	(7.9%)
2% increase	(15.1%)
3% increase	(21.6%)

Not all bad

Owning bonds when rates are rising is not always a bad thing. If we own bonds and hold them to maturity, then any decrease in price does not affect us, and if we *reinvest* our interest payments, we get to reinvest at the current higher rates. So, if you hold bonds to maturity and are reinvesting your interest payments, rising rates are beneficial.

The third problem with owning low-yielding bonds is the unlikelihood of them returning their historical average. As we showed earlier, bonds have historically averaged around 6% per year and have been an especially great investment for the last 30+ years as interest rates have continued to fall and bond prices have continued to rise. The best proxy for future bond returns, while not perfect, has been the YTM at the time of purchase. This means, with interest rates near zero and yields on most Treasuries around 1%, there is almost no conceivable way for bonds to return their 6% historical average going forward. (This is just as true when yields are 2% or 3%.) Many plans use historical returns to validate their strategies, and we should be wary of using historical bond returns when planning.

The final challenge of owning bonds is inflation. As we discussed in Chapter 7, any tool that provides fixed payments in the future is vulnerable to inflation. Since bonds provide fixed coupon and face value payments, they are especially susceptible. Recall that TIPS (Treasury Inflation-Protected Securities) exist to combat this risk and eliminate the risk of your returns being completely eroded by inflation.

It's easy to fall into a trap when it comes to bonds. Cash doesn't provide enough return, so we turn to bonds. If bond yields are low, we either purchase a bond with a longer maturity or higher credit risk to earn a higher yield. The longer the maturity, the more it will be affected by changes in interest rates. The higher the credit risk, the higher the chance we won't be paid back. As a result, many people take on more risk in search of higher yield, which, as Warren Buffett told us in Chapter 16, is "really stupid."

To potentially earn an even higher return, the next place to turn is to stocks, which is what we'll discuss next.

19

STOCKS

While the bond market runs the show behind the scenes, front and center in the media and our minds are stocks. Everyone is familiar with stocks, but fewer truly know how they work. When people think of stocks, charts and graphs are just as likely to come to mind as ownership in an underlying business is. Let's return to the basics.

When you buy a share of stock, you are buying an equity (ownership) stake in a business. How much you are willing to pay for your stake depends on how much money you expect to get out of it in the future. As an owner, there are two ways to get money out of the business. The first is through dividends, which are paid when the business generates more cash than it needs. The second is through capital gains, which occur when you sell your shares to someone else for more than you paid for them. In theory, the value of your shares should reflect the health and prospects of the business, so if the health and prospects of the business are better when you sell it than when you bought it, then your shares should be worth more. If not, they could be worth less, and if things get too bad, they could become worthless.

Potentially losing your entire investment is a big risk. To minimize the chance of this happening, you may choose to spread out your risk by diversifying your investments and becoming the owner of multiple companies. When diversified, if one of your companies fails, you may lose the value of that portion of your investment, but the other companies should make up for this loss. It is very unlikely that every company you own will go out of business, especially if you diversify across companies in different industries or sectors.

What are we actually diversifying?

Every stock carries two risks: 1) company-specific risk and 2) market risk. We can remove company-specific risk by diversifying, but we cannot avoid market risk.

Assume that you own shares of Coca-Cola. There are a lot of risks unique to Coke (company-specific). If consumers switch to Pepsi, Coke's business will suffer. To mitigate this risk, you can diversify and buy Pepsi as well. But what if people stop liking soft drinks and switch to beer? You can invest in a beer company. You can further diversify by owning a bunch of beverage makers, but then, you have a lot of sector-specific risk. You can then buy technology stocks to diversify the sector risk. If you then realize you own mostly large companies, you can buy small and medium-sized companies. If you realize you own all U.S. companies, you can buy global companies, and on it goes.

You can continue this process of diversifying away company-specific risk until you own enough companies that it no longer affects your portfolio. What you cannot diversify away by buying other stocks are market risks, such as interest rates, recessions, and wars. There will always be some risk in investing—otherwise, there's no return. If we diversify to the point that we offset every risk, we are left with a "perfect hedge," giving us a return of 0%.

Recall from Chapter 3 that while diversification limits the chance of total loss, it also limits the chance of the home run. When you diversify, you own both the winners and losers. Clearly, if you owned only the winners, you'd be better off, but the whole reason we diversify is that we don't know who the winners and losers will be. When diversifying, you'll always do worse than the biggest winner (and conversely, better than the biggest loser). If you own the S&P 500, and Apple is the best-performing stock, you'd have done better if you owned only Apple. If you diversify globally, and U.S. stocks do best, you'll do worse than if you owned all U.S. stocks. This doesn't mean you made a bad decision; it's just how diversification works.

Diworsification?

If diversification guarantees that your portfolio will do worse than the best-case scenario, then why do we do it? Once again, it's because markets are unpredictable. The following example demonstrates the value of diversification.

Assume you are offered a choice between two coin flips.

Option A: Heads, you win $100. Tails, you lose $80.
Option B: Tails, you win $100. Heads, you lose $80

Which option should you choose? If you choose Option A and it lands on heads, you will be the big winner, but if it lands on tails, you will be the big loser. If you choose Option B, the opposite is true.

What if you could accept both? Now, if the coin lands on heads, Option A will pay you $100, and Option B will cost you $80, for a net gain of $20. If it lands on tails, Option B will pay you $100, and Option A will cost you $80, for once again a net gain of $20. By diversifying, you eliminated the chance of the big $100 gain, but you also eliminated the chance of the big $80 loss, and in the process, assured yourself a gain of $20.

There are countless ways to diversify, for example, by sector (e.g., energy, health care, technology), size (e.g., small-cap, mid-cap, large-cap), or geography (e.g., U.S., international, global). Years ago, if you wanted to diversify, you would have to buy individual holdings of different companies. This process was time-consuming and expensive. With the invention of mutual funds and, more recently, exchange-traded funds (ETF), you can now own multiple companies inside a single holding. Taking this even further, index funds allow you to purchase a single investment that mimics an entire index, such as the S&P 500. This means you can effectively become an owner of 500 (or more) different companies in one transaction. (The differences between mutual funds and ETFs are important but not for this conversation.) From here on, when we refer to "stocks," except where noted, we will be referring to the asset class as a whole, not individual companies.

How diversified is your diversified index fund?

Index funds are the most common way investors choose to diversify, and the most popular index to track is the S&P 500. The S&P 500 Index tracks the 500 (or so) largest U.S.-based publicly traded companies. (The value of the companies in the index represents approximately 80% of the total US equity market and around 50% of the global equity market.)

The S&P 500 is a *market-cap weighted* index. Market capitalization is a measure of a company's total value and is calculated by multiplying a company's number of shares by the share price. Market-cap weighted means the portion of the index that each company represents is equal to their portion of the market's overall value. For example, if the market's total value is $100, and Apple is worth $5, then Apple represents 5% of the index.

This can lead to the index being much more top-heavy than many investors realize. As of December 31, 2020, five companies, Microsoft, Apple, Amazon, Alphabet (Google), and Facebook, represent over 20% of the index.[1] When those large companies are performing well, the index will soar. However, if these giants struggle, they will bring down the rest of the index even if the rest of the overall market is fine.

An alternative to a market-cap weighting is *equal weight*, meaning all stocks have the same weight. This means the price change of the smallest company carries the same weight as the biggest.

There is also the antiquated and nearly worthless way of indexing, known as *price-weighted* (the Dow Jones is the most notable user of this relic). A price-weighted index uses each stock's share price to determine its weight in the index. This means a company worth $100 million dollars with a share price of $100 will move the index more than a company worth $100 billion and a share price of $10.

From an information perspective, market-cap, equal-weight, and price-weighted are just different ways of slicing the same pie. From an investment strategy perspective, history offers mixed results as to which is better. When smaller companies perform better, equal-weight indexes outperform market-cap-weighted and vice versa. In the 2010s, larger companies had a tremendous run, and the S&P 500 was one of the highest performing indexes. As we'll see, investors love to chase past performance, so the S&P 500 is incredibly popular in discussion these days.

Of the asset classes we have discussed so far—cash, bonds, and now stocks—stocks have clearly provided the highest returns. We saw in Chapter 16 that stocks have returned 9.79% compounded annually since 1928, while government bonds have returned just 4.95%. This begs the question, since stocks offer the highest return, why does conventional wisdom tell retirees they shouldn't have all of their money invested in stocks? The traditional answer is volatility, but as we showed in Chapter 15, it really depends on whether you can afford to lose money and when you need it.

Let's take a minute to understand what causes volatility in stocks. Since volatility is a measure of the change in price, the question really becomes, what causes a stock's price to *change*? To understand what causes the price to change, we should first discuss how we determine the price of a stock to begin with. We'll discuss three common ways.

1. How much cash you expect to get out of the business (Future *expected* cash flows)

At the end of the day, a business exists to make money, and if it doesn't, it will eventually fail. When you invest in a company, you do so with the hope of getting more money out of it than you put in it. One way to value a company is to determine how much money you expect to receive from it in the future. To get money out of the business, it must generate more cash than it needs to operate. When a company distributes excess cash, it pays a dividend. We can then value the business by projecting how much in dividends we expect to receive.

Say, for example, that you expect to receive $10 in dividends for the next 10 years for a total of $100. You could value the company at $100. Doing so, however, would give you a return of 0%, as you are paying $100 today to receive $100 over the next 10 years. Since you are taking risk, you would like to earn some sort of return. Suppose that you would like to earn a 10% return. You can calculate what price you would have to pay today to earn a 10% return when you receive those dividends. (This is called discounting future cash flows to a present value.) Doing this will give you a price of $61.45. If you purchase the stock at $61.45 and you receive the dividends you expect, you will earn a 10% annualized return over the next 10 years.

It's helpful to understand how the math works—the higher your expected return, the lower the price today. If instead, we said we wanted to earn a 20% return, the price would change to $41.92. This also means the lower the price, the higher our expected return.

The 10% figure used in this example is known as the discount rate since that is what we used to discount future cash flows to today's value. The discount rate is also equal to our expected return. (It makes sense then that the higher the discount rate, the lower the price.) The two terms are used interchangeably. In this discussion, I will use the term expected return.

How do you determine what your expected return should be? Your expected return should compensate you for the risk you are taking. Since stocks are riskier than bonds, your expected return should be higher than the return you can earn on bonds. If it's not, you won't take the risk of owning stocks if you can earn the same amount owning bonds.

How much higher your expected return is than bonds is called the *risk premium*. The exact risk premium varies based on the specifics of the company. The riskier the company, the higher the risk premium.

(We can take this one step further to bring together all the topics we have discussed so far. Stocks should return more than bonds, and bonds should return more than cash. How much interest cash in the bank pays depends largely on the interest rates set by the Federal Reserve. If interest rates rise, bond yields rise, and risk premiums rise, meaning stock prices fall. If interest rates fall, the reverse happens.)

In this type of analysis, two factors affect the stock price: 1) future cash flows and 2) your expected return. For prices to increase, there must be an increase in future cash flows (e.g., dividends) or a decrease in your expected return (discount rate). Dividends increase if revenues rise or expenses fall, and your expected return decreases if interest rates drop or you are willing to accept a lower risk premium.

Remember, if your expected return increases, the price you pay today will fall. If your expected return is lower, the price you pay today will rise. This means, *the more you pay for a stock, the lower your expected return is.*

It's important to note that this valuation is based on *future* cash flows. What if we expect the dividend to increase by 10% each year? Now we will value the company at $95.62. If one year, the company's dividend only increased by 5%, the company's value will fall, as the actual cash flows differ from the expected cash flows. This can lead to some confusing headlines "Dividend rises 5%, stock price falls." The stock market is always future-looking, and we can't react to the headline alone. *What matters is the news compared to our expectations.*

The metric used in this type of analysis does not have to be dividends. It can be, amongst others, free cash flow or net income. The specifics are not important for our discussion.

Not all companies generate excess cash that we can use to determine a value. In that case, what else can we do?

2. Compare it to others (Relative valuation)

Another way to value a company is to compare it to the valuation of similar companies. This method involves using "multiples," which is similar to how your home is appraised. You choose a common metric, such as price per square foot, and apply it to your home. When valuing stocks, the most common multiple is the price-to-earnings ratio (P/E ratio). See the following example.

Company A has earnings of $10 and a share price of $200, giving it a price-to-earnings multiple of 20 (Price of $200 ÷ Earnings of $10). If Company B has earnings of $5 per share, how much should we pay for it? We can value it *relative* to Company A. Since Company A has a P/E ratio of 20, if we apply this multiple to Company B's earnings of $5, we can value Company B at $100.

P/E ratios are a reflection of investors' confidence in a company. For example, the riskier the company, the less we'll pay for it, and the lower the multiple will be. Conversely, if we expect the company to grow, we'll pay more for it, and the multiple will be higher.

It's again useful to understand the math and the relationship between multiples and expected return. The higher the multiple, the higher the price, and therefore the lower your expected return. The riskier the stock, the lower the multiple you will pay, the lower the price, and the higher your expected return. The higher the multiple, the lower your expected return.

Similar to discounting cash flows, there are many metrics we can apply a multiple to, such as sales, assets, even the number of customers (for example, daily users of a social network). The appropriate metric will vary based on the industry and maturity of the company.

3. Whatever the current price is (Because you think you can sell it to someone else for more)

Sometimes, we buy a stock for no other reason than we think someone else will pay us more for it in the future. This is known as the Greater Fool Theory—there will always be a fool greater than us to pay more. This way of thinking, spurred on by the information cascades discussed in Chapter 16, often leads to bubbles, as buying begins to occur for no reason other than the price is going up.

In Chapter 16, we also talked about how supply and demand for assets work differently than supply and demand for goods. When people see asset prices rise, they become emboldened (or, if they didn't buy before, they regret not buying) and often want more, even though they take on more risk by buying at higher prices. People infer past results to be an indication of future performance and become willing to buy at any price. Understand this: even a great company can become a bad *investment* if the price is too high.

The Dark Art of Investing

There is another valuation method (or at least, method of identifying trading opportunities) that has largely been debunked yet remains popular since it appeals to our desire to recognize patterns. It is known as *technical analysis*.

Technical analysis attempts to predict the direction of future prices based on a study of past market data. It typically involves analyzing charts and graphs.

An example of technical analysis is calculating the "moving average," e.g., averages based on prices for the last 50 or 200 days and comparing it to the price today. When the price breaks above the moving average, further increases might be expected. If it drops below, then the opposite.

There is a wide range of applications for these methods, some more legitimate than others. Charts help visualize data and can illuminate behavior we might otherwise miss. That being said, don't fall for an elementary version of technical analysis: seeing a pattern of up and down prices and thinking the stock will do something just because it fits the pattern. Patterns are a part of nature and don't always have a deeper meaning.

If any of these factors—cash flows, dividends, sales, customers, interest rates, etc.—change, then prices will change too. At the end of the day, the price of anything is determined by the balance between supply and demand—the greater the demand, the higher the price. Since prices are a function of supply and demand which are a function of needs and emotions, and needs and emotions change—prices will change too. That's normal. It would be worrisome if they didn't, and there isn't always a burning reason why prices change. The financial media loves (and needs) to publish a reason for market movements every day, but sometimes there isn't an explanation. I joke, but I am serious when I say that some days a stock's price moves because an investment manager wakes up in a bad mood and sells more shares than people are looking to buy. Prices won't always be tied to fundamentals either. The fundamentals (e.g., sales, net income, cash flow) may say one thing, but if enough people want to buy something, the price will rise to the highest bid.

Understanding Financial Media

It's popular to hate on the media, but they're usually just doing their job. Financial media companies are businesses, and like any business, their goal is to make money. Media companies create content and make money by either selling ads on their platforms or gaining subscribers. The more people that consume their content, the more ads they can sell. Therefore, their incentive is for you to consume (read or watch) their content. To do this, they need your attention.

Humans pay attention to things that are remarkable or unexpected. Consequently, the news is filled with these remarkable and unexpected outliers. We don't hear about how John lawfully stopped at a red light or how Jane's investment portfolio returned the same as the market last year. We hear about the "newsworthy" stuff, the terrible crashes, or the person who crushed the market by buying at the bottom and selling at the top.

In a 24/7 world, there is always pressure to have something to say. There isn't always 24 hours' worth of "news," so the media turns to opinions and explanations of the day's events. In finance, the reason something happened isn't usually immediately clear, but the media is forced to declare reasons almost instantly. Not only do they have to react fast, but they must react with something—no one pays to hear, "I don't know what happened." Consequently, it is in their interest to come up with a reason, even if it is wrong.

Two cognitive biases help explain how the media can affect our investing behavior. The *availability bias* makes us think that things we can easily recall are more likely to happen, and the *illusory truth effect* makes us think the more we hear something, the more it is true. Since the news is filled with outliers, we frequently hear of outliers. We begin to think that outliers are common and subsequently develop flawed expectations, thinking we too should crush the market, and as a result, we try to time the market or swing for the fences and take more risk than we should.

As we've seen, making decisions about the future based on a flawed understanding of the past or present will eventually catch up to us. Financial media tries to be helpful, and much of it is. But we must remember that what is shown in the news is not what is happening everywhere, and we should give it time before blindly accepting quick reactions as valid explanations for the day's events.

Consider this: the three driving factors of stock prices are 1) future cash flows, 2) interest rates, and 3) emotions. Given that all three are wildly unpredictable, it is no wonder that stock prices are wildly unpredictable. This unpredictability leads to the volatility we see.

While stock returns are unpredictable year-to-year, they are surprisingly consistent over longer periods (notice I still didn't say predictable). This consistency reemphasizes the importance of your holding period in determining how you invest your money and why conventional advice tells you to take less risk the nearer you are to needing money (having to sell).

On any given day, the U.S. stock market has gone up 50% of the time. Over one year, it has gone up 68% of the time, and over 20 years, 100% of the time.[2] While interesting, this tells us nothing about how much the market has gone up or down in these periods.

Figure 19-1, adapted from Burton Malkiel's excellent book *A Random Walk Down Wall Street*, shows the range of returns in the S&P 500 over various holding periods. In any single year, the market has gained as much as 53% (1954) and lost as much as -37% (2008). Over five years, the worst the market has returned is -3% per year, and the best it has returned is 29% per year. You can see that the longer the time horizon, the tighter the range of outcomes. Over 25 years, stocks have historically returned on average between 8% and 17% per year. The white ovals represent the average return for each holding period.

FIGURE 19-1: S&P 500 Returns Over Various Holding Periods[3]

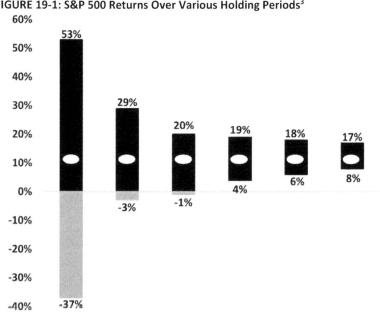

Don't get lost in the middle

Historical returns are usually calculated on a calendar year basis, meaning from January 1st to December 31st. Intra-year swings (e.g., from March to September) can be even more extreme than those shown in Figure 19-1. For example, in the spring of 2020, the market was down nearly 40%, yet ended the year up 11%. Measuring returns on a calendar year basis hides the intra-year volatility. This will be important when we discuss how to generate income from investments in Chapter 21.

An appreciation of Figure 19-1 is crucial to how you view stocks as a part of your portfolio. Much like standard deviation, this chart can help us think in ranges. For example, if I'm investing for the next five years, I don't expect to earn 10% per year (the average); I expect to earn *between* -3% and 29% per year, paying particular attention to the downside (we can all afford the upside). Remember, these numbers are based on history, so the best or worst that has happened doesn't mean that it is the best or worst of what will or can happen.

Even the best fall down sometimes

Stock returns are more consistent over the long run, but they still swing drastically year-to-year. Figure 19-2 shows how far yearly returns were from the average (14.9%) during the best 30-year period in the S&P 500's history (1975-2004).

This graph shows that even the best periods still experience significant price swings, which emphasizes three points. 1) When investing for long-term growth, don't overreact to short-term swings. 2) When relying on the market for income, this volatility magnifies sequence of returns risk. 3) Yearly stock returns rarely match their long-term average.

FIGURE 19-2: Yearly Returns from the Average (1975-2004)

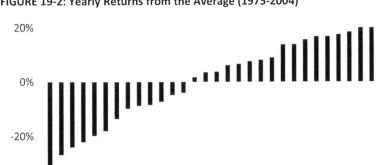

The previous two charts show us that we can reasonably rely on stocks to provide positive returns over the long run, but we have no idea what they will do in any given year. So what then can we do to project stock returns? There are three primary methods: 1) Historical Averages, 2) Current Valuations, 3) Random Variable Projections.

1. Historical Averages

We've discussed several times the flaw of using historical averages. First, you won't experience the average; you will experience somewhere around the average. Second, using historical averages assumes the best and worst of what can possibly happen has already happened. Remember, history tells us what happened, not what could have happened. This means the historical average is not the average of all possible outcomes; it is the average of what did happen. Third, it may be impossible for a stock to return its historical average. A company worth $500 billion that has grown 100 times in the last 20 years is less likely to grow 100 times in the next 20 years.

This last comment raises an important point. Returns of individual stocks, and returns of investment funds (which consist of individual stocks selected by an investment manager), are subject to different limitations. It may be reasonable for a $100M company to double every year for several years, and it may be completely unreasonable for a trillion-dollar company to double even one year. However, at least in theory, an investment fund could double every year if the manager correctly picks which stocks to buy and sell. This difference will be important when we discuss reversion toward the mean in Chapter 28.

2. Current Valuations

Recall from our previous discussion, the higher the price of a stock, the lower its expected return. Therefore, the more expensive a stock or the market is, the lower we expect future returns to be. There is empirical evidence to support this idea.

We just discussed the PE ratio and how it is a measure of how "expensive" a stock is. The PE ratio is based on the last year's earnings, which can include short-term factors that are not indicative of long-term performance (e.g., a really bad quarter). To adjust for these short-term factors, the cyclically adjusted price-to-earnings ratio (CAPE ratio) was created.[4] Rather than using current earnings, the CAPE ratio uses the last 10 years of earnings to derive a more consistent earnings level. The CAPE ratio can be calculated for the market as a whole.

Researchers have found that as the CAPE ratio increases, future returns in the following 10 to 15 years decrease. (It remains a very poor predictor of short-term performance.) When the CAPE ratio is in the top 20 percentile, returns over the next 10 years have averaged a 3.2% real return. When the CAPE ratio is in the bottom 20 percentile, returns have averaged an 11% real return over the next 10 years.[5]

While we still have no idea what returns will be from year to year, we can glean some idea of what they will be in the intermediate-term by looking at valuations today. As of August 30, 2021, the market's CAPE is 39.1 (highest since the early 2000s),[6] placing it firmly in the top 20 percentile. Does this mean stocks will underperform over the next 10 years? We'll just have to wait and see.

Buy the top?

I've said several times that buying at lower prices increases your expected return. This is simple math. But price alone does not tell the full story. It is possible to have a higher expected return even if you pay the highest price ever.

We must understand the distinction between *price* and *value*. Suppose a stock is trading for $25 and has $1 dollar of earnings (a P/E ratio of 25). A few years later, it is trading for $100. If you buy it for $100, is your expected return lower? Suppose that current earnings are $50, giving it a P/E Ratio of 2. The price of the stock may be higher at $100, but it is a much better value, and therefore has a much higher expected return.

Grasping the idea of value can explain why buying the market at all-time high *prices* does not necessarily lead to lower future returns. History does suggest, however, that buying at all-time high *valuations* can lead to lower future returns, as shown by the discussion on the CAPE ratio.

3. Random Variable Projections

We've established that investment returns are not the same every year, meaning they are variable, and we also don't know what they will be, meaning they are random. So to project returns going forward, we need to generate random variable returns to plug into our model.

To do this, we would need to know the average return, the range of possible returns, and how often returns fall within that range. Fortunately, we have this information with historical averages, standard deviation, and the theory of normal distribution (the bell curve).

By most calculations, stocks have historically averaged approximately a 10% annual return with a 20% standard deviation. If they follow a normal distribution, this means that 68% of the time, returns will fall between -10% and +30%, 95% of the time between -30% and +50%, and 99.7% of the time between -50% and +70%. How do we use this information to project random variable returns?

Imagine you had a bin full of ping pong balls with different percentages written on them. The average of all the balls is equal to the stock market's average return, 10%. If you were to pull one ping pong ball from the bin, you could draw a ball with anywhere between -50% and 70% written on it. The balls are distributed according to a normal distribution, so 68% of the time, the ball will be between -10% and 30%, 95% of the time between -30% and 50%, etc. Now, imagine you pull a ball from the bin 30 times and write down what is written on the ball each time. Each number you write down represents a return that you could use in your model.

This is one way of randomizing your return sequence, which is more realistic than simply using a linear average. While realistic, you probably realize that you would get completely different results if you repeated the exercise. But what if you could repeat the exercise, again, and again, and again, tracking the results until you've run every possible sequence? This would give you the full range of outcomes, and you could determine the probability of ending up with certain amounts. Your chart would look something like Figure 19-3.

FIGURE 19-3: Example of Monte Carlo Simulation Results

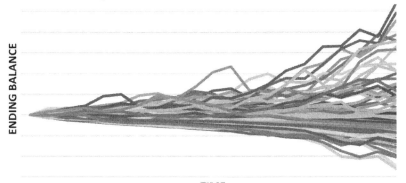

ENDING BALANCE

TIME

This is much the way it is done in practice, but statistical software is used instead of ping pong balls. The most common analysis is a Monte Carlo simulation. While it's a powerful tool, Monte Carlo simulations should come with a warning label. You must understand both its limitations and how to interpret the results.

Like any model, Monte Carlo simulations are limited by the quality of inputs. For example, suppose you input a 10% average return and a 20% standard deviation. If actual returns averaged 8% and the standard deviation was 22%, the contrast in outcomes will be enormous, despite what may seem like a tiny difference. If you recall from our rate of return discussion in Chapter 2, a 1% or 2% change in the assumed rate of return has a drastic effect on your plan's outcome. The adage, "garbage in, garbage out," summarizes this point. If the inputs into your model are not accurate, the outputs will not be either.

We must also remember our conversation about markets not being normally distributed. Monte Carlo simulations usually rely on the bell curve and will not include extreme outliers.

Monte Carlo simulations are an incredible tool that can be used in many productive ways. An early version of it was vital to the success of the Manhattan Project (which helped build the first atomic bomb), and casinos rely on these simulations to calculate their expected wins and losses. Given how profitable the gambling operations of casinos are, the simulations clearly work. These simulations work for casinos because the range of outcomes is completely defined, i.e., the casino knows all of the possible outcomes, meaning they do not run the risk of extreme outliers that investing in the market does.

That being said, Monte Carlo simulations are dangerous when retirees and advisors over-rely on its results. We will especially see this when we discuss ways to create income from a portfolio of stocks in Chapter 21. It is easy to be swayed by the complexity of the analysis, but even the most complex calculations will be wrong if the inputs are bad. As former GE CEO Ian E. Wilson said, "No amount of sophistication is going to allay the fact that all of your knowledge is about the past and all your decisions are about the future."

With so much noise surrounding stocks, understanding the core fundamentals is crucial to parsing what is helpful and what is nonsense. The big takeaway: stocks go up over the long run and up and down in the short run. Unfortunately, we'll never know which way. The less you pay, the higher your expected return, unless the price is low because it's a value trap (which we'll further define later).

Stocks are the highest returning but also the most volatile investment most people own. To reduce this volatility, we usually add bonds to the portfolio. Next, we'll discuss how a blended portfolio of stocks and bonds works together.

20

BLENDED PORTFOLIO

We know that how we manage our investments depends on when we need the money and whether or not we can afford to lose it. The standard advice is that the closer we are to needing to sell, the less risk we should take. Taking less risk usually involves decreasing our ownership of stocks and increasing our ownership of bonds. The resulting blended portfolio benefits from lower overall volatility while maintaining the potential to grow. Bonds have two favorable features that make them a valuable part of a blended portfolio: 1) lower volatility and 2) their correlation with stocks.

The benefit of lower volatility is obvious. When bonds go down, they don't go down as much. This fact alone can soften the blow to your portfolio when things get rocky.

Correlation is just as impactful but requires a little more involved conversation. Correlation is a measure of how much two things move together. If they move together exactly the same, they have a correlation of 1. If they move completely opposite of each other, they have a correlation of -1. If you own two investments with a correlation of -1, any gain will be offset by a loss in the other (this is known as a "perfect hedge"), which is helpful if you don't want your account balance to change, but counterproductive if you want it to grow. From a diversification standpoint, you want correlations near zero, which means they have no predictive relationship to each other.

How do stocks and bonds correlate? First of all, the correlation is not constant and changes over time. Figure 20-1 shows how returns and correlations of stocks and bonds have moved from 1980-2020. However, historically, there has been a general pattern.

FIGURE 20-1: Correlations of Stocks and Bonds (1980-2020)[1]

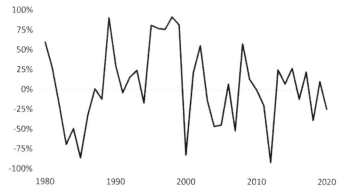

When things are calm, correlations are positive. This is a good thing as both stocks and bonds can rise.

When things are bad, correlations can be negative, which is also a good thing. This means when stocks are down, bonds might be up.

When correlations turn negative, it's usually the result of a "flight to safety," meaning people sell stocks to buy bonds (which are considered "safe.") During a flight to safety, the value of stocks decreases while the value of bonds increases. These gains on bonds can partially offset losses on stocks in your portfolio.

Stock and bond returns in 2008 provide a real-world example. When stocks were down -37%, bonds were up 8%. A portfolio of 60% stocks and 40% bonds (60/40) was consequently down roughly 22%. That's not great, but it's a lot better than being down 37%. Diversifying with stocks and bonds limits the huge upside but also limits the huge downside, which is often the main focus in retirement.

When things are *really* bad, however, the correlation can flip back to positive. As the old saying goes, "In times of crisis, all correlations go to 1." When that happens, you have nowhere to hide. When stocks are down big, so are bonds. Financial models that rely on historical correlations usually blow up when these relationships break.

So far, we have been using the term "bonds" very generally. The correlations we've been talking about are for Treasuries. Corporate bonds are riskier and more likely to have a positive correlation with stocks, especially when things are bad.

So, let's assume you do need to take less risk and begin building a blended portfolio. How much of your portfolio should be invested in bonds? The answer is fairly subjective and a point of much debate in the industry. However, there are some popular rules of thumb.

Some say bonds should equal your age, so if you're 70 years old, you should have 70% of your portfolio invested in bonds. Others say 120 minus your age is how much you should have in stocks, so a 70-year-old would have 50% in stocks and 50% in bonds. The default answer is typically a 60/40 portfolio.

A quick aside to clear up some terminology. Rather than saying "a portfolio of 60% stocks and 40% bonds," it is common to say a "60/40 portfolio." When referenced this way, the percentage of stocks is listed first, followed by the percentage of bonds. You will see this later when I reference 30/70, 50/50, and 60/40 portfolios.

Ultimately, how much of your portfolio should be invested in bonds depends on the factors we've already discussed: when you need the money and how much you can afford to lose. The answers to those questions depend on the rest of your plan—the purpose of the investments, how much income you need, and how much risk you are willing to take.

If you're relying on your investments to generate income, then owning bonds and lowering the volatility of your portfolio is likely a good thing. But, what if all of your income is provided by Social Security, a pension, and other guaranteed sources of income? Should you still be as concerned about volatility? If all of your income is provided by guaranteed sources, and your investments exist for long-term growth, then you may not need to own many bonds.

When designing your portfolio allocation, it is important to consider your entire plan. Imagine you have $1,000,000 saved, and $500,000 of it is in an annuity designed to provide lifetime income. How should you allocate the remaining $500,000 of investments? If you invest in a 60/40 portfolio ($300,000 in stocks, $200,000 in bonds) your entire portfolio is now much more like a 30/70 mix, since annuities are similar to bonds ($500,000 annuity + $200,000 bonds = $700,000 of "bond-like" money; $700,000 of "bond-like" money ÷ $1,000,000 of investments = 70%).

If instead, you were to invest your remaining $500,000 in stocks, the portfolio would be more in line with a 50/50 mix. It may feel strange to invest your remaining $500,000 entirely in stocks, but if you do not make this adjustment, you may find yourself taking less risk than you need to, which may cause your portfolio to lag over time. You can't simply say, "I'm 65 years old, so I have to be invested 60/40," without considering the other parts of your plan.

We must also remember that prices change. Soon after building a 60/40 portfolio, it will no longer be 60/40. If the growth of stocks outpaces the growth of bonds, your portfolio may creep up to 70/30 or 80/20. When this happens, we must *rebalance*. Rebalancing has tax implications, introduces sequence of returns risk, and years ago was a source of significant transaction costs. If enough investors rebalance at the same time, for example, at the end of the quarter, overall prices in the market may move as well.

The mechanics of rebalancing is simple; sell some of the asset class that is larger than its original allocation and buy more of the smaller asset class. How often you rebalance, when you rebalance, etc., is part of a longer conversation, and a professional can be of great help.

As we've seen, with bond yields currently as low as they are, many investors are increasing their allocation to stocks to earn a higher return. This can work when the market cooperates, but it leaves you even more exposed to downturns in stocks. Yet again, we are reminded of Warren Buffett's previous comments about reaching for yield. If we can't afford to take additional risk, then we shouldn't take it.

Stocks and bonds go together like apple pie and ice cream in most people's minds. We can use them for growth and to generate income. Let's look closer at how to generate income from our investments.

21

CREATING INCOME FROM INVESTMENTS

We now understand how bonds work, how stocks work, and how stocks and bonds work together. How we choose to allocate our money amongst these tools (and others) depends on how long until we need it, what we are managing it for, and whether or not we can afford to lose it. This chapter focuses on how to generate income using cash, bonds, and stocks. We'll look at how to generate income using insurance and real estate in Chapters 23-25.

Let's remember why we're having this conversation. If we need more income than our outside sources (e.g., Social Security and pensions) will provide, we need to use our savings. There are many ways to generate income from our savings. Income can come from principal, interest, a combination of principal and interest, dividends, growth, a combination of principal and dividends and growth, etc. *(Whether or not principal should count as "income" is a game of semantics. By the literal and taxable definitions, principal is not income. But as a source of funds to meet our spending needs, it is. So while principal is not truly income, for this chapter, we will discuss it as if it is.)* Which of these different ways you choose to generate income will again depend on your circumstances, most importantly, how long you need it, how much you need, where the rest of your money is held, how much risk you're willing and able to take, and how much you want to leave behind.

Of course, some of these questions we know the answer to, and some we have to assume. Recall from Chapter 2 that the way to plan our income can go in two directions. We can answer those questions to decide where to put our money or decide where to put our money to answer those questions. Since everyone is different, we'll have a more general conversation about how these tools and strategies work.

The main distinction between the different income strategies is risk. Here, we can define risk as unpredictability that leads to a higher chance of running out of money. The relationship is simple: higher income comes with higher risk. The less predictable or reliable our income, the more we can have, but the higher the chance we run out.

Let's climb the ladder of predictability to understand how much income we can expect and what the risks are. *Please note: the absolute numbers in these examples are not the point. We want to understand the relative and directional relationships between the strategies.*

We'll start with the safest place we can put our money, the bank. Let's assume that the bank is currently paying 1% interest. If we deposit $1,000,000, we'll earn $10,000 of interest every year. If this meets our needs, the risk-averse among us will stop right here. We'll receive $10,000 of interest and won't have to spend any principal. The risk to this strategy is that the interest rate decreases, but there is little risk of losing our principal or running out of money.

To earn more income, we need a higher yield, which we can achieve by taking more risk, which means purchasing a bond. The type and length of maturity of a bond we purchase depends on how long we need income. Let's assume we need income for 30 years, so we purchase a 30-year Treasury bond yielding 2%. Now we'll earn $20,000 of interest per year and receive our principal back at the end.

If we're buying a bond from the U.S. Treasury, we're not concerned about *not* receiving the interest payments and principal we're promised. But if we want to earn more income (a higher yield), we can take more risk and buy bonds from issuers with a lower credit rating. Of course, the tradeoff for the higher yield is a higher risk that we don't receive some or all of the money we are promised. In other words, the risk that the issuer defaults, and we run out of money.

If the interest paid by the bank or bond issuers isn't enough, we can generate more income by spending part of our principal. When we plan to spend our principal, properly planning for longevity becomes very important. If we are spending principal, it will eventually run out, and if we deplete our principal, we can no longer generate income. So if we deplete our principal before we die, we run out of money. This creates a tricky balance. Planning for a shorter retirement allows us to project a higher income, but it also increases the chance of depleting and outliving our money.

In the remaining examples, we assume a 30-year retirement. The exact length again doesn't matter. The relationships between the different strategies are the same whether we have a 10, 20, 30, or 40-year retirement.

Returning to our example of putting money in the bank, if we earn 1% per year while spending our principal, we can spend $38,364 per year before depleting our account after 30 years. While this is a very easy strategy to execute, the risk again is that the bank lowers how much interest they pay, jeopardizing our strategy.

Just as before, we can take more risk to generate more income, which involves buying bonds and spending principal. The challenge of doing so with individual bonds is that most bonds don't give us our principal back until the bond matures. This means we cannot access our principal until maturity, and thus we can't spend our principal along the way as we can with money in the bank. We can, however, use bond funds (i.e., a basket of bonds, similar to how a stock ETF works), which allow more frequent buying and selling of principal. (A "bond ladder," which involves buying bonds of different maturities to provide access to principal and income along the way, is another example of trying to handle this issue.) But, recall from our discussion of bonds in Chapter 18, the price of bonds swings with interest rate movements. This means there are two risks to this strategy. 1) The same risk of default (although we diversify away much of this risk when buying a bond fund). 2) The risk of selling at losses if interest rates rise, which creates sequence of returns risk.

For the sake of this example though, we will assume that everything goes smoothly and we are able to spend our principal and earn 2% every year for 30 years. This will allow for an income of $43,774, which is the highest we've seen so far.

We can generate even more income by taking even more risk, and on the next rung up the risk ladder are stocks. Stocks are trickier than savings accounts and bonds because stocks don't pay interest. Some stocks pay dividends, which we'll discuss at the end of this chapter, but if stocks don't pay dividends, then the way to generate income is to sell them. The challenge, of course, is that the price of stocks is constantly changing, so we never know for sure what price we can sell at, which makes sequence of returns risk even more of a threat. This also means we can't simply plug in a return number and amortize it as we previously did with interest on the bank account and bonds. (If we did the same exercise using historical stock returns of 11%, we could spend $103,626 per year. I wish.) We must then find a way to estimate how much we can spend.

There are three related methods to estimate how much we can spend from a portfolio of stocks and bonds. 1) Historical approach. 2) Historical approach accounting for valuations. 3) Dynamic approach.

The historical approach defines certain parameters, namely, what we're investing in (the allocation between stocks and bonds) and how long we expect to live, and then simulates the strategy against historical scenarios and return sequences. This method allows us to evaluate what has usually and always worked. An example will make this clear.

Let's assume we want to invest in a 60/40 portfolio for our 30-year retirement. Technically, we also need to assume how much we want to have left. For simplicity, we'll assume we want to deplete the money we are putting towards this strategy. (If we want to leave a remaining balance, that amount becomes our threshold for what we call "running out of money," even though the account may not truly be depleted.)

Before we look at the results, I must add one layer of complexity. None of the examples we've looked at so far have factored in inflation. For example, the $43,774 we can generate buying bonds and spending principal will have decreasing purchasing power as time goes on. The finance industry has recognized this. When using the historical approach, withdrawals are usually adjusted each year for inflation. Adding this layer of complexity is beneficial to the retiree but also makes it harder to compare to the previous strategies we've discussed.

Okay, so what is the highest inflation-adjusted amount we can withdraw for 30 years from a 60/40 portfolio?

FIGURE 21-1: Highest Safe Withdrawal Rates by Year – 60/40 Portfolio

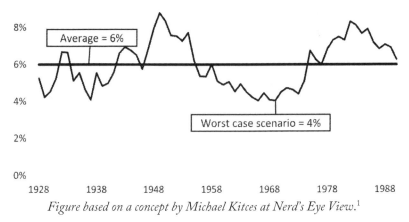

Figure based on a concept by Michael Kitces at Nerd's Eye View.[1]

Figure 21-1 shows the results going back to 1928. First, notice the results are stated in terms of percentages, called an *initial withdrawal rate*. Stating the results this way makes it scalable as we can apply it to a beginning balance of $100,000, $1,000,000, or any other amount. I must also clarify the importance of the word *initial*. If you see an initial withdrawal rate of 5%, this does not mean you withdraw 5% every year. It means, whatever 5% of your initial balance is, is the amount you withdraw. If you have $1,000,000 and a 5% initial withdrawal rate, you withdraw $50,000 from then on, regardless of the current balance. If we adjust for inflation, which we will in these examples, then in year 1, we withdraw $50,000, and in year 2, we withdraw $50,000 + inflation, and so on. The amount we withdraw steadily increases over time.

So, how much can we withdraw? Well, the average initial withdrawal rate is 6%. The problem with the average, though, is that half the time, it runs out of money. What rate never ran out of money? 4%. Since 4% has worked in every scenario, we can call it the "safe withdrawal rate." This exact exercise was performed by financial advisor William Bengen in 1994, which led to the creation of the renowned "4% Rule." (With some slightly different assumptions, this figure has been revised to 4.5%.)

Alright, 4% is the highest initial withdrawal rate that worked in every scenario since 1928, but let's look at the numbers another way. How much money would we have had left if we withdrew 4% in every scenario? Figure 21-2 shows the results of strategies beginning from 1928-1990.[2]

FIGURE 21-2: Ending Balance When Following the 4% Rule

Figure based on a concept by Michael Kitces at Nerd's Eye View.

Notice that most of the time, there's *a lot* of money left over (and it never runs out). This means an initial withdrawal rate of 4% usually leaves an incredible amount of spending on the table. Relying on the 4% rule is like dressing for the coldest day on record all year round. If you don't experience the coldest day, you'll be overprepared. (But if you do experience it and don't prepare for it, you could "die.")

Most of the time, a higher withdrawal rate works, but is there a commonality linking when a higher amount doesn't work? Look at the years with the lowest withdrawal rates in Figure 21-1; the end of the 1920s, the mid-1960s, and the mid-1970s. I don't expect you to be a market historian, but here's what you should know: the market "crashed" in those periods. So the periods that began right before a crash had the lowest withdrawal rates. (Since these studies require 30 years of data, we cannot yet look at how a strategy that began before the crashes in the late 1990s or mid to late 2000s performed.)

If we recall the lesson of sequence of returns risk, these results make sense. When withdrawing money, losses in the early years, when your account balance is likely highest, has a greater effect than losses in later years, when your balance is likely lower. So, unless you retire right before a market crash, 4% is way too low of a withdrawal rate.

Again, the finance industry is aware of this. We know that the less we pay, the higher our expected return. We also know that when making withdrawals, losses in the early years hurt more than in later years. If we can combine these two concepts by beginning a withdrawal strategy at a time when prices are lower (and expected returns are higher), does this allow a higher withdrawal rate?

Based on history, the answer is yes. Figure 21-3 shows the CAPE ratio, the measure of how "expensive" the market is, as well as the highest 30-year withdrawal rate for that sequence of returns.[3] Notice the inverse relationship. The lower the CAPE (the cheaper the market), the higher the withdrawal rate. (This also means lower withdrawal rates when the CAPE is higher.)

FIGURE 21-3: Effect of Market Valuations on Withdrawal Rate

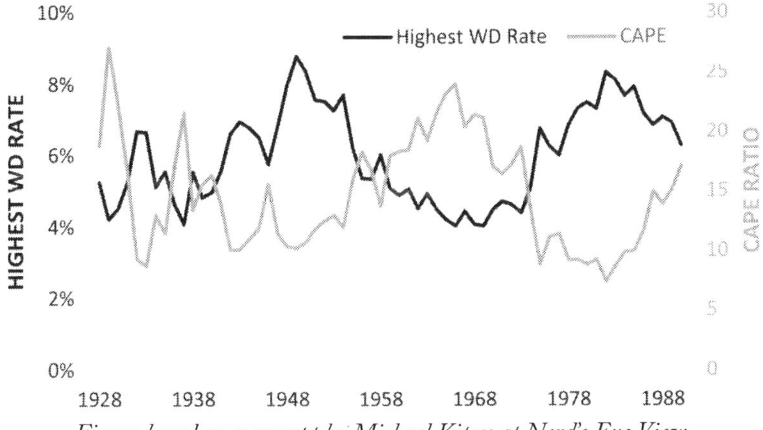

Figure based on a concept by Michael Kitces at Nerd's Eye View.

This method of considering valuations is our second approach to estimating how much we can withdraw, what we aptly call the historical approach accounting for valuations.

Okay, so adding stocks to our portfolio significantly increases the amount we can spend compared to cash and bonds. But we haven't found the magic bullet of retirement income. The first couple of reasons should be obvious.

These strategies are created and validated based on historical results. As we saw in Chapter 3, this can be problematic. For starters, the worst in history is constantly being replaced, so there could easily be an "even worse" 30-year sequence we've never seen before that could cause even the "safe" withdrawal rate to fail. The studies showing what our highest withdrawal rate "could have been," like what we see in Figure 21-1, aren't very practical either. To calculate such a number, we need to know in advance what our return sequence will be. This kind of exercise is great if you want to make yourself feel bad for not predicting the future, but it doesn't help the retiree in Year 0 figure out how much to withdraw. While it's nice to know that we can spend more if we avoid a negative return sequence, there still isn't a reliable way to predict when a negative return sequence is coming, despite the inroads made with the CAPE ratio. All of these reasons are part of the "you never know" factor we'll revisit in a minute.

The next few reasons require us to dig into the math a bit more.

The 4% rule is based on the historical returns of a portfolio of 60% stocks and 40% in bonds. Bond returns during the period used to calculate these withdrawal rates have been quite high, averaging around 6%. As we've touched on multiple times, bond yields are currently much lower, so whether your portfolio is 60/40, 50/50, 70/30, or some other combination, the bond portion of your portfolio will likely be earning much less than the historical average.

In a similar vein, an argument can be made that stock returns may not be as high in the future as they've been in the past. In the period these returns were measured, the U.S. was a relatively new country expanding and growing across undeveloped land. The argument is that this level of growth cannot be maintained in the next 100 years. Proponents point to safe withdrawal rate studies performed in more mature nations, such as Italy and France, and how withdrawal rates in those countries are far below the withdrawal rates found in studies of U.S. returns. Personally, I find this argument a little loose, and there is a strong counterargument I won't make here. However, this way of thinking is worth at least pondering. There's a reason we always say, "past performance is not an indication of future results."

Next, we must consider the inclusion—or exclusion—of fees. Most of these studies do not factor in fees. If we include fees, it can substantially lower our withdrawal rate as fees are essentially lowering our returns each year by around 1%. (Even with the lower fees available today, any fee greater than zero is going to have a negative effect on a withdrawal rate calculated with no fees.)

Another factor that will affect our withdrawal rate that is nearly impossible to model is the exact timing of withdrawals (or rebalancing, for that matter). Remember how we discussed intra-year price swings can be much wilder than year-end swings? If you are withdrawing in the middle of the year, or more than once a year, you introduce more or different return sequences to consider, and the returns could be much wilder than what we typically see on an annual basis. We can use stock returns in 2020 to demonstrate. If you are making year-end withdrawals, there is nothing to consider as the market was up 18% for the year. But, if you made a withdrawal early in the year when stocks were down nearly 40%, you would have had to sell at lows, leaving less money in the account to recover and thus dramatically altering the trajectory of your portfolio. (Recall our discussion of money-weighted returns in Chapter 3 to see how *your* return can be very different than the return of the underlying investment.) It's hard enough to project yearly returns, never mind monthly.

Assuming you are basing your spending need on an after-tax number, tax rates also matter. Two retirees in different tax brackets will have to withdraw different amounts to create the same after-tax spending. In addition, if tax rates increase, the amount you will have to withdraw will as well, which again changes the projection.

At this point, we need to make the distinction between the "laboratory," where we can run all of the hypothetical examples we have so far, and the "dinner table," where real humans make real decisions. Some strategies work in the lab but not at the dinner table. For example, some of the "successful" 4% sequences would have required the retiree to withdraw $50,000 when they had only $200,000 left in the account and no idea how much longer they'd live. While the ensuing return sequences were favorable enough for the account to recover, how many people would have stuck with the strategy?

This brings up the final reason withdrawal strategies are tricky; we are still making a longevity assumption. Even if we get all of the return, timing, and tax assumptions correct, we are still planning to deplete our accounts. If we live too long, what do we do? By the time it becomes clear that we might outlive our money, we have likely already spent most of our principal and will have very few options.

Season to taste

The 4% rule is based on a 60/40 portfolio and 30-year retirement. If we change either of these variables, our withdrawal rate will change as well.

Let's start with longevity. Shorter longevity leads to a higher withdrawal rate and vice versa. Table 21.1 shows the probability of success of different withdrawal rates for given retirement durations.[4] For example, for a 95% probability of success over a 30-year retirement, the retiree can withdraw 4.0%. If they want the same probability of success over a longer or shorter period, they simply move up or down the table. If they're willing to accept a lower chance of success (higher chance of failure), move left. Again, the exact numbers in this table are subject to debate and are also not the point. The point is that the longer and higher your withdrawals, the lower your chance of success.

TABLE 21.1: Withdrawal Rate Based on Probability of Success and Longevity

Duration	Probability of Success					
(Years)	70%	75%	80%	85%	90%	95%
10	11.5%	11.2%	10.8%	10.5%	10.0%	9.3%
15	8.4%	8.2%	7.9%	7.5%	7.1%	6.5%
20	7.0%	6.7%	6.4%	6.1%	5.7%	5.2%
25	6.1%	5.9%	5.6%	5.3%	5.0%	4.5%
30	5.6%	5.4%	5.1%	4.8%	4.5%	4.0%
35	5.2%	5.0%	4.8%	4.5%	4.1%	3.7%
40	5.0%	4.8%	4.5%	4.2%	3.9%	3.4%

The 60/40 portfolio is used partly out of tradition and partly because it strikes a good balance between upside and lower volatility. Still, it is not the only portfolio allocation we can use. Changing our allocation will affect our withdrawal rate; the more risk we take, the more income we can produce. Table 21.2 shows the probability of success employing different withdrawal rates and portfolio allocations with a 30-year horizon.[5] There is a subtle takeaway from this table. The relationship between risk and withdrawal rates is not linear, meaning more risk does not always produce more income. It's more of an arc. If you take too little risk, like in a 0/100 portfolio, you won't be able to generate much income, but if you take too much risk, like in a 100/0 portfolio, your chance of running out of money is much higher.

TABLE 21.2: Probability of Success Based on Allocation and WD Rate

WD Rate	Portfolio Allocation				
	0/100	25/75	50/50	75/25	100/0
3%	82%	100%	100%	100%	100%
4%	41%	87%	100%	98%	93%
5%	18%	42%	68%	77%	77%
6%	10%	17%	43%	57%	65%
7%	3%	10%	22%	45%	53%
8%	0%	3%	10%	33%	40%

Combining all of these reasons cools some of the confidence in the 4% rule, or more appropriately, the confidence in withdrawal rates much higher than 4%. We can attempt to factor all of this in with the "dynamic" approach, which utilizes a Monte Carlo simulation.

Remember what a Monte Carlo simulation does. It allows us to play with different variables—returns, allocations, fee amounts, tax rates, etc.—by generating random variables and running thousands of simulations to establish a "probability of success." It's dynamic because we can quickly see what happens if we have a 70/30 or 50/50 portfolio, if our withdrawals are inflation-adjusted or fixed, or if we withdraw for 20 or 40 years. The goal of the analysis is to determine an amount that we can withdraw that gives our portfolio an acceptable chance of failure. (Many advisors will tell you that there is no such thing as an acceptable chance of failure in retirement. We'll discuss the semantics of this statement in the "Retirement is not an airplane" box to follow.)

Monte Carlo simulations are incredibly powerful and useful, but we must remind ourselves of their limitations. First, the simulations are only as good as the inputs. Second, markets are not normally distributed, so the simulations understate the risk of outliers (e.g., market crashes) that are the usual reasons withdrawal strategies fail.

Monte Carlo simulations are the engine behind the majority of the planning software that advisors use today (and many of the calculators published on websites for retirees to play with). You must read the fine print. Some simulations may show a high chance of success with a higher than normal withdrawal rate, or vice versa, and the reason is usually the assumptions they are using. All else being equal, a higher return or lower standard deviation will increase the allowable withdrawal rate or raise the probability of success. One simulation may assume an 11% return for stocks, and an 18% standard deviation, while the other assumes a 10% return and 19% standard deviation. That might not sound like much, but it is.

While writing this, I researched what various companies are currently saying the "safe withdrawal rate" is. The first two results were as follows. Company A showed a 4.5% safe withdrawal rate. The fine print showed they assumed a 28-year retirement (instead of the usual 30). Company B published a 3.5% safe withdrawal rate. The fine print showed two peculiarities. 1) The portfolio was 25/75, and 2) they never let the account dip below 25% of its initial value (which means instead of depleting the account using 100% of the available funds, there must always be a 25% cushion, meaning we can use only 75% of the initial funds for income. Obviously, this will require lower spending). These differences aren't an accident. Why? Incentives. Company A is an investment company, and Company B offers insurance solutions. If that reasoning isn't clear, it will be after the coming chapters.

We can spend as much time and computing power as we want trying to determine the best withdrawal rate, but in the end, it's all about returns in the early years. See the following extreme example.

Three brothers each have $1,000,000 and retire one year apart from each other. They have seen the research and decide to use a 5% withdrawal rate on their 60/40 portfolio. The oldest brother, Sam, retires in 1973, the middle brother, Pete, in 1974, and the youngest brother, Matt, in 1975. How'd they do? (If you don't know, the market was down significantly in 1973 and 1974.)

FIGURE 21-4: A Tale of Three Brothers – Starting WD Strategy 1 Year Apart

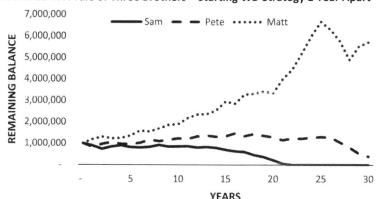

Despite implementing the same strategy just one year apart, their results are wildly different. While one takeaway from this example is how sensitive these strategies are to the early years, we need to think about this a little more practically. Sam's no dummy; he wouldn't keep withdrawing even though he's clearly going to run out. Matt isn't a dummy either, and he'll probably want to spend more. Pete's decision is easier since he's stuck in the middle, not quite able to raise his withdrawal amount, and not at serious risk of running out. This raises an important point. No retirement strategy, but especially not a withdrawal strategy, is a "set it and forget it" process. You can and should adjust. There are three ways to adjust a withdrawal strategy.

1. **Change your allocation.** There are many ways to do this, but the most common is to increase your risk based on valuations. For example, if the market is "cheap," increase your allocation to stocks. If it is "expensive," decrease it. The idea is to capture the potential upside when the market is cheap and lower your exposure when it's expensive.

2. **Change your withdrawal amount**. This is the most popular and arguably most valid adjustment. Since the success of a withdrawal strategy is really all about the early years, it holds that if you have a favorable sequence in the early years, you can "ratchet up" your withdrawal amount later. While this strategy again looks good on the spreadsheet, it comes with a heavy dose of "you never know." You never know if the market will turn against you as soon as you crank up your withdrawals. There are more formal guidelines for how to execute this strategy that we won't get into here.

3. **Change where you withdraw from**. This one is tricky, and it's all about how it's presented. The most prominent variation of strategy works like this: after a down year in the market, pull money from a different "non-correlated" account (so that it won't also be down). The math is pretty incredible if you do so. Forgoing a withdrawal after a down year drastically changes how much money you'll have left in the account and usually greatly increases how much you can withdraw. There is nothing wrong with this version of the strategy, but it's not quite as fantastical as some make it out to be.

I'm intentionally trying to avoid using numbers, so let's just think logically about what is happening. If you don't withdraw money, you are essentially "leaving money" in the account or making a withdrawal and then making a deposit of the same amount back into the account. Either way, it should be evident that putting more money in the account will increase how much is left.

Unfortunately, the financial planning industry likes to abuse cool math tricks to sell products. I cannot dedicate the amount of space required to fully discuss (and dismantle) one particularly heinous version of this strategy that goes by several aliases, such as the volatility buffer, sequence defense, and distribution straddle technique. This strategy posits that the alternate source of funds you *should* pull from is cash value life insurance (that you likely need to buy, and you can probably guess from whom.) I'll just say this, pulling money from somewhere else can absolutely increase how much you can withdraw from a portfolio of stocks and bonds, and cash value life insurance is one viable source. But in no way whatsoever is that a good enough reason to buy or create a cash value life insurance policy.

Since I just brought up life insurance, I should briefly mention the other way of generating income using insurance, annuities (the subject of Chapter 23). For centuries, annuities and pensions (which are effectively an annuity) were the tools retirees used to generate income. That's partly because the stock market as we know it wasn't around until the last 150 years or so. It's also partly because stocks are not designed to generate income. Remember, we buy stocks as long-term investments that we know will be volatile. Nothing about how stocks work suggests we should sell them frequently and rely on them during the most vulnerable period of our lives. Somewhere along the way, the investment companies saw how much money retirees had and combined that with the fact that strategies relying on the market for income looked good on the spreadsheet and decided they should start offering retirement income strategies. This has led to, in my opinion, an unnecessary "holy war" of sorts between the investment and insurance industries. (It also explains why the previously mentioned Company A and B published the safe withdrawal rates that they did.)

Here's where I stand on this. How you choose to generate income is not a "one or the other" either-or decision. Most tools work better together. As we'll see, the value of the insurance strategies is their guarantees. The value of the withdrawal strategy is its flexibility and higher upside. There is no reason they cannot be used together. The 4% rule is neither the 8th wonder of the world that some claim it is nor the witchcraft that others accuse it of being.

Retirement is not an airplane

Probability-based strategies such as the 4% Rule or a Monte Carlo simulation establish a probability of success, which also implies a probability of failure. For example, if you have a 90% chance of success, you have a 10% chance of failure. A variation of the word picture below is used by advisors to explain this 10% chance of failure that I find to be deceptive:

If you boarded a plane and the captain came over the loudspeaker and said, "Thank you for boarding... we have a 10% chance of crashing this evening..." would you stay on that plane?

While this story certainly connects on an emotional level, it has several flaws. The implication is that you die in a plane crash, and if your probability-based plan fails, you will experience the financial equivalent of a plane crash. Usually, this story is told to expound the value of a guaranteed strategy with a 0% chance of failure (just FYI, annuities are guaranteed). I have two issues with this story.

First is the use of "failure." In the context of probability-based strategies, "failing" means that what you originally set out to accomplish did not materialize. If a safe withdrawal plan "fails," it can mean one of two things happened: 1) you depleted your accounts (i.e., $0 remaining) or 2) you had to "cut back" your spending and produce less income (e.g., had to withdraw $35,000 instead of $40,000). It doesn't say anything about the *severity* of the failure. Sometimes the plan ran out in the 28th year or worked with a 3.9% withdrawal rate. While both scenarios qualify as "running out of money," and you should hope to avoid them, comparing them to a plane crash feels a bit hyperbolic.

This dovetails into my second issue with this analogy. In retirement (and not unlike many plane rides), we have time to react when trouble appears. If you experience a bad sequence of returns, and it looks like your plan will fail if you continue on the same trajectory, you can adjust your withdrawals to help prolong your account. This is not unlike a plane that flies around a storm that pops up on the radar. It makes for a longer trip, but it's better than flying straight into it just because that was on the original flight plan.

While cutting back is not ideal and fits our definition of "running out of money" from Chapter 1, I feel that this story bends the meaning of failure to imply something more catastrophic than it is. A more accurate version of the story is:

If you boarded a plane and the captain came over the loudspeaker and said, "Thank you for boarding, we have a 10% chance of not making it to our destination, but we have a parachute attached to the plane and multiple runways we can land on along the way to get you close"... would you stay on that plane?

While this is still not ideal, and you may still decide not to get on that plane, this version of the story communicates something very different than the original.

Rather than mixing stocks and bonds, some investors prefer to invest in stocks that provide income in the form of dividends. We'll discuss this strategy next.

Dividends

Dividend investing is incredibly popular amongst retirees. The opportunity to generate income without having to sell any investments can seem like a perfect fit. However, dividend investing is often misunderstood. The following will explain how dividends work and clear up many of these misconceptions.

Dividends are distributions of excess cash made to shareholders of a company. The payments are made at the company's discretion, and unlike a bond, are not contractually guaranteed. Companies can and do cut dividends. There are countless examples of companies cutting dividends that at one time seemed inconceivable, such as GM, Ford, Citigroup, AIG, and Kodak.

When a company pays a dividend, all else being equal, the stock price will drop by the amount of the dividend. If we value a business based on the amount of cash we expect to get out of it, then this makes sense. For example, if you expect the total future cash flows you receive from a company to be $100, the company's price will be $100. If the company pays a $5 dividend, you no longer expect to receive those cash flows in the future, and the price will drop to $95. As an investor, your net position has not changed; you own stock worth $95, and you have the $5 you received from the dividend for a total of $100.

Let's understand the implications of this. If a company pays a dividend and the price drops by the dividend amount, you are no better off. For your wealth to increase, the price of the stock must also appreciate. The total return of a stock is calculated as the change in price plus the dividend yield. (Dividend yield = dividend ÷ share price). If the stock price increases by 2% and pays a 5% dividend, then your total return is 7%.

Some think that dividend stocks let you have the best of both worlds, income and price appreciation. This can happen, but dividend-paying stocks do not outperform other stocks for two reasons. Remember, all else being equal, dividends alone do not add anything to your wealth. The price must still appreciate. There is no reason for a stock to increase more than others just because it pays a dividend. Second, the self-correcting nature of markets will apply. If a stock is paying a high dividend and the price is increasing, it will attract new investors. As demand increases, so will the stock price, eventually to the point that the dividend yield is lower, as is the expected return of the stock. (Stock prices are also a reflection of expected dividends, so if a stock pays a high dividend, the stock price will already reflect that.)

Historical data seems to agree with this point. A popular index, the S&P 500 Dividend Aristocrats, which only includes stocks that have paid an increasing dividend for 25 years, has underperformed the broader market over the last year, 3, 5, and 10 years.[6]

Dividend-paying stocks are commonly thought to be more stable than other stocks. We think that if a company is able to return excess cash to shareholders, they must feel confident that they won't need it in the future. While that makes sense in theory and is true to a point, dividend-paying stocks are just as subject to decreases in price as other stocks. The previously mentioned S&P 500 Dividend Aristocrats index offered no more downside protection in falling markets than the broad index funds. Additionally, if conditions get too bad, companies may cut their dividend, which can be considered a sign of trouble and often causes the price to fall even further. If you attempt to sell your shares after a dividend cut, you will be selling in the face of a (possibly temporarily) declining share price.

Perhaps the biggest misconception surrounding dividends is the value of generating income without touching your principal. Once again, it sounds great on the surface, but it can miss the bigger picture, as there is often no difference between generating income from dividend-paying stocks and from non-dividend-paying stocks. Remember, stock returns in a given year are made up of dividends and changes in price. Consider the following example.

A share of XYZ stock trades for $100. During the year, the company pays a $5 dividend, and the price of the stock increases to $105. Your total return for the year was 10% ($5 of price appreciation + $5 dividend = $10 return. $10 return ÷ $100 initial price = 10%).

Let's now see where investors get confused. John is a retiree who needs $5 per year to live. John invested $100 into XYZ stock at the beginning of last year. During the year, John receives the $5 dividend, which gives him the income he needs, allowing him not to touch his principal, which is now worth $105.

His brother Joe also needs $5 per year to live on, but Joe invests $100 into shares of ABC stock. ABC stock ended the year worth $110 but did not pay a dividend. Joe will need to touch his principal in order to create the income he needs. Joe sells $5 worth of his ABC stock and is now left with his principal, which is $105 worth of stock.

Is John better off than Joe? No, they're the exact same! While John didn't have to touch his principal, Joe earned the same total return even though he didn't receive any dividends. The idea of not touching your principal sounds nice but misses the point of total returns.

Dividend investing is a sound strategy but has flaws as a standalone strategy. The retiree who invests solely in dividend-paying stocks is considerably less diversified than one who buys a broader index. Not all stocks pay dividends, and even fewer pay a dividend of any real size, meaning the dividend investor has a much more concentrated position than the broad index investor.

Despite all this, dividend-paying stocks are still viable investments and will be part of a diversified portfolio. Just don't be fooled into thinking dividend stocks allow you to have your cake and eat it too.

SUMMARY

Compared to cash and bonds, adding stocks to the mix may allow us to generate significantly more income. The tradeoff, of course, is uncertainty.

This uncertainty comes from two places, 1) we don't know how long we'll live, and 2) we don't know what returns will be. This makes answering the questions "How much can I spend?" and "How long will it last?" a real challenge.

History is a good place to start, but it's not without limitations. At the end of the day, if we can survive the early years, a withdrawal strategy should work just fine. We may even be able to generate more. Unfortunately, there's always an element of "you never know," and we must perpetually err on the side of caution. This cautiousness may cause us to hold back from spending as much as we possibly could to make sure we leave a cushion, "just in case." In Chapter 23, we'll talk about the tools that allow us to spend without this worry, annuities. But first, we need to finish our discussion of stocks, examining the behavioral side of investing.

22

INVESTING IN STOCKS

Chapter 19 talked about how stocks work, but this chapter will focus on how to interact with them. That's because the biggest determinant of our success as an investor will be how we manage our emotions and behavior.

Stocks are polarizing. We all know that. They're the center of attention, and people either love them or hate them. But like I've said, tools are tools. They do what they do. In my opinion, any issues we have with stocks come from misusing or misunderstanding how they work. If we simply accepted them for what they are and used them for what they do, we wouldn't have any issues. But, we love efficiency, so we misuse and sometimes abuse them. I'll explain.

Remember what stocks are. Stocks are ownership interests in companies, the value of which is determined by emotions, cash flows, interest rates, and other factors that fluctuate constantly. Day-to-day, even year-to-year, these valuations are completely unpredictable. Individual stocks are especially volatile. While unpredictable in the short run, stocks as a whole move up over the long run. And move up considerably they do, providing the highest returns of any of the asset classes we have discussed so far. So, where or what is the problem?

There are two reasons we invest in stocks. 1) To grow our money, and 2) to generate income. Let's start by revisiting income.

We generate income from a portfolio of stocks by withdrawing a mixture of growth, dividends, and principal. If we experience big losses early on, we will deplete our accounts quicker. If we don't experience losses, our plan should work, and maybe we can withdraw more. The problem is, we never know for sure what returns will be, so we're constantly one bad return sequence away from disaster.

Does a tool that fluctuates unpredictably sound ideal for such a strategy? No. So why do we use it? Because we can possibly have more money if we do. It would be "inefficient" to only own bonds and give up all of that juicy potential upside. To be fair, and this is important, if your goal is *not* to have a steady, predictable income, then stocks are fantastic. You'll maintain tremendous upside; you just have to be willing to surf the downside. However, most people prefer a steadier income in retirement yet still demand to ride a bucking bronco (stocks) off into the sunset. So that's problem number one. We use them in a way they're really not designed to be used.

What about growth? If we put all our money in an individual stock, we can lose all of our money (we can also make a lot). However, if we diversify, the chance of losing all our money is quite low, and we still have pretty considerable upside. A diversified portfolio of the 500 largest stocks in the US (called the S&P 500) has returned around 11% per year. Again, what's the problem? Oh, that's right, in between, prices move around and may go down quite a bit. We don't like that. Remember, humans love gains and hate losses. As a result, we try to have both, all gains and no losses. That right there is where it starts. We are also competitive and compare to others, so we try to do better than everyone else. These two reasons—trying to avoid losses and beat the market—underpin nearly every issue people have with stocks.

Before I talk about what we do wrong, let me share my opinion on how we should view and interact with stocks.

First of all, I don't see the problem with the return stocks have given us, 11.6% simple average and 9.8% annualized average.[1] Yes, they go down sometimes, but what are we expecting, to never lose money and only gain 11% per year? That's like playing blackjack and saying, "Yes, Mr. Dealer, I'd like only to win and never lose, please." While we'd like to earn the average return every year, understand why we literally cannot: if riskier investments reliably produced higher returns, they wouldn't be riskier. So first, life is a lot easier if we accept and appreciate the returns that stocks offer as good enough rather than trying to squeeze a little more out of them.

It's easier to accept what stocks do when we know what to expect from them. A huge factor in determining how much to expect from stocks is your time horizon. Again, stocks go up over the long run but up and down in the short run. An incredibly helpful way to set expectations is to revisit Figure 22-1, previously shown in Chapter 19. Let's assume, purely for the sake of example, that this is how things will be in the future; you will receive somewhere between the returns shown over the period you're invested. For example, if you're investing for 25 years, you will earn between 8-17% per year.

FIGURE 22-1: S&P 500 Returns Over Various Holding Periods

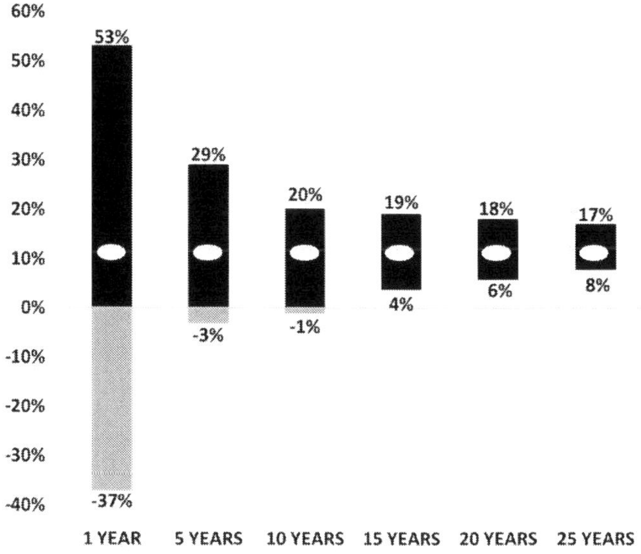

Remember what those long-term returns of 8-17% per year are made of; big ups and downs (like Figure 19-2 that showed how far returns were from the average over the best 30-year return sequence in market history). Do we care about these big ups and downs? Recall our discussion of temporary and permanent losses from Chapter 16. If we're not selling, then we shouldn't care. We may prefer our experience to be a "straight line up and to the right," but this volatility is the price of admission to receive the 8-17% per year return we will earn. In other words, don't worry about it.

What if you need to access your money (i.e., to sell) in a "few" years? Well, ask yourself, can I afford to lose 1% per year for the next 10 years? Or lose 3% per year for 5 years? (Notice, the question is not, "Can I afford to gain 20% or 29%?" You know you can afford that. We're worried about the downside, what we can't afford.) If you can't afford to lose money, it doesn't mean you invest in stocks and try to avoid losses. It means you don't invest in stocks…or, at the very least, lower your allocation to stocks.

So, where does this leave us? On the money invested for the long-term, we expect to earn pretty good returns. On the money invested in the short term, we realize we may lose money, but we only put money at risk that we can afford to lose, so that's okay. Under this mindset, what problems could we have?

Of course, people don't take this mindset. Why not? Remember the two reasons: we hate losses and want more. This means we try to 1) avoid losses and 2) beat the market (usually #2 is achieved by accomplishing #1). This usually results in us trying to "time" when we buy and sell, selling before drops, buying back in before rises, and trying to pick big winners, which leaves us less diversified.

We can look at this desire to time the market in three ways. First, why we try. Second, why it usually doesn't work. Third, the behavior this encourages (which also explains why it usually doesn't work).

There are several reasons we try to avoid losses, besides just wanting to. I may want to fly, but I know I can't, so I don't try. Since we try to time the market, we must somehow think it is possible.

One elementary reason we think it's possible is that past returns can look explicable. In hindsight, it can seem obvious what happened and that we *should have* bought and sold at certain times, which makes us think we'll know when to buy or sell the next time. Of course, in the moment, it's completely impossible to know. Think back to the market reactions in the first quarter of 2020. The perfect strategy would have sold stocks near the end of February and bought them back near the end of March. But remember what it was like then. How could you have known to sell in February? How could you know when the market began to rebound in March that it wasn't a "false bottom" and wouldn't soon go back down?

A second reason we try to time the market is that certain companies encourage us to. In the early 2000s, DIY trading began to proliferate, and their commercials told us how we could have "money coming out the wazoo," and a trash-talking baby bragged about his conquests in the market. (As far as I remember, we were never told it was so easy a caveman could do it.) But understand the incentive of DIY trading companies; they want you to trade. They don't necessarily care how good you are at it.

Not only do companies tell us, but the media does too. We see news stories of fund managers or hear stories of friends that properly timed a transaction and hit it big. But remember, it's the outliers that make the news.

The final and probably most confusing reason we think we can time the market is that professional money managers used to have a decent track record of doing so. The reasons it used to work also explains why it doesn't anymore. I'll explain.

There are two approaches to investing. *Active* management involves more trading and typically attempts to *outperform* a specific benchmark. *Passive* management involves less trading and usually attempts to *mimic* an index or benchmark. Active managers try to pick and choose what to own and for how long; passive managers take what the market gives them.

Years ago, active management was the way things were done. Fund managers from yesteryear were rockstars and wrote countless books extolling how you too could get "one up on Wall Street." Here's how they used to beat the market.

First, they had access to information quicker. One example shared with me by a prominent fund manager from the '80s and 90s explained how they used to send analysts to sit in courtrooms and relay the ruling back to the office in New York before it hit the news wires (this was completely legal). This gave them information before traditional media outlets could spread the news, which they could use to make buy and sell decisions. The quicker they had the information, the quicker they could trade on it. The quicker they could trade, the better the price they received, and the better their returns were.

Second, they had the ability to digest information quicker. These funds had teams of analysts working around the clock to assess and identify potential trading opportunities.

The final reason is they had less competition. Not only were they able to quickly identify trading opportunities and inefficiencies in the market, but when they did identify them, they stayed available longer because there were fewer participants in the market.

Let's think about things today. Information reaches nearly all corners of the earth instantaneously. A single computer or software program can perform the same analytical duties that used to require a large team. And finally, there are so many traders now that opportunities vanish in microseconds.

Here's an example of how an increase in market participants can make it harder to beat the market. For example, assume that you discover that the market always goes up 1% on Wednesday. Naturally, you'll be inclined to design a strategy that buys stocks late on Tuesday to participate in these gains on Wednesday. But guess what, so will other people. As you begin to buy on Tuesday afternoon, others will too. Eventually, enough people will buy on Tuesday that the price will increase and eliminate the gains available on Wednesday morning. This is part of why it is so hard to sustainably beat the market. You may identify inefficiencies that work momentarily, but the more participants in the market, the quicker these opportunities are discovered and eliminated.

So, beating the market through active management has become tougher as information spreads quicker and more people participate in the market. We can closer look at the other reasons we think timing the market works to see why it actually doesn't.

While the past may look explainable, the future doesn't have to repeat it. Patterns are often just coincidences, and they work until they don't. That means they're not *deterministic*. If you've flipped a coin and it has alternated between heads and tails the last five flips, the sixth flip still has a 50/50 chance of being heads or tails, despite what the pattern calls for. Likewise, if the market has gone up 1% the last six Wednesdays, it's not going to go up on the seventh Wednesday just because it's Wednesday.

As for those news stories, it is absolutely true that people successfully time and beat the market (people also win the lottery). What they usually don't show is how many people tried and failed to do so. This is the same concept as the 10 people who correctly predicted 10 coin flips in Chapter 3. Ten did it, but 1,014 did not.

Coin flips actually provide a helpful analog for the next reason timing doesn't consistently work. You have to be right *twice* in order to profit from it. You must not only correctly time when you *sell*, but you must also correctly time when you *buy* back in. It does no good to sell your investments and avoid a big drop, only to buy them back at a higher price than when you sold. You may be able to correctly time your trades once or twice, but the odds of doing it consistently are stacked against you. An example will explain.

Let's assume that you have a 50/50 chance of correctly timing when to sell, meaning there is a 50% chance the market will go up (bad timing) and a 50% chance it will go down (good timing) after you sell. You also have a 50/50 chance of correctly timing when to buy back in, meaning that the market again will either go up (good timing) or down (bad timing) after you buy. Getting both right is equivalent to correctly predicting two coin flips in a row, which you have a 25% chance of doing (50% x 50%). So, from the start, the odds are stacked against us.

You also have to outsmart a few million people to beat the market. Consider the two things it takes to beat the market, 1) be contrarian and 2) be correct. If you think the market is going up, and so does the market, that does you no good. You must think the market is going up *more* than the market does or going down when the market thinks it's going up (or vice versa). And then you must be right. If you think the same as the market, your returns will be the same as the market. Markets are also forward-looking, so you must be right before it's obvious you will be. You can't wait until a company announces great results to prove you were right and start to invest.

Let's now revisit those DIY tools. Years ago, very few people had access to stocks. These days, anyone with an internet connection can invest and trade (not the same thing).* On the surface, this seems like it would be a great thing, but in reality, this access can encourage some of the most detrimental investing behavior.

Just because the functions of trading (buying and selling) have become easier to execute does not mean investing successfully (making money) has too. Remember how you make money; you sell something for more than you paid for it. Having the ability to buy and sell does not endow you with the ability to buy low and sell high. Furthermore, there is usually an inverse relationship between trading frequency and performance. In other words, the more you trade, the worse you do. Famed economist Eugene Fama put it best, "Money is like soap; the more you handle it, the less you have."

While timing the market may be a losing strategy, the previously mentioned advances in technology make it all too easy to try. We can now check our investment accounts around the clock and trade from anywhere at any time (now that trading is mostly free, this problem is intensified). This access does two things. First, it makes us acutely aware of price changes, and second, it gives us the ability to do something about it instantaneously. Rather than calmly thinking things through, we can impulsively buy and sell on the spot. Regularly checking your performance and increasing the frequency you trade are two of the worst habits an investor can have.

When you check your investment account, you cannot help but feel emotions. Sometimes emotions sharpen our focus, but often they cloud it. If you see more money in your account, you might be happy

---

* Investing follows a longer term buy and hold strategy. Trading is a much shorter-term strategy. Speculating, an even wilder form of trading, is a bet on a short-term change in price, and is often compared to gambling.

and excited, and if you see less money, you may be angry or sad. When you see more money in your account, it can lead to what's called the *wealth effect*. Feeling wealthier as their account balances are higher, investors may be more willing to spend in other areas of their lives (like buying a boat because their 401(k) balance is high). The problem is, sometimes this wealth effect is temporary, and when prices fall, they are no longer as wealthy, and cannot "unspend" the money.

On the other side, when our account balances are down, we feel uncomfortable, and when we feel uncomfortable, we try to do something about it. If we're tired, we drink some coffee, or if we have a headache, we take Tylenol. When we are uncomfortable because our investments are down, sometimes we buy or sell to ease the pain, and often it is these interventions that prove costly (just like we can overdo it by taking too much Tylenol or drinking too much coffee).

The following thought exercise shows how *not* frequently checking your accounts can protect you from yourself. Imagine you invest $100,000, and whenever you check your account, all you see is a black box. Thirty years later, the black box goes away, and there is $1,000,000 in its place. Would you be happy? Of course, you would. What if you look back over your old account statements, and see in year three, your account only had $60,000 in it. Ten years later, it had $400,000 and, after 15 years, had only $300,000. If you're honest with yourself, you realize if you had seen your account balances along the way, you might have declared, "This strategy's not working," or you may have panicked and sold your investments. If you had sold, you probably wouldn't have bought back in and would have missed out on the gains. You certainly wouldn't have the $1,000,000 you have today.

Paying less attention may seem counterintuitive, but it also may protect us from ourselves. That's partly because our natural wiring doesn't align with what it takes to be a successful investor. Being a successful investor requires discipline and steadfastness, like the meme of the cartoon dog drinking coffee in a room that's on fire with the thought bubble "This is fine." When humans see fire, they flee, but successful investors often need to sit in the blaze to come out the other side. Of course, we don't normally sit there calmly. Instead, we do things like buying more as things get more expensive.

Imagine you are shopping for a home. You find a home you like that normally costs $500,000 but is currently listed at $350,000. You tell your friends, "I really like the house, but I'll be more comfortable buying it once the price goes back to $500,000 or maybe even higher." Sounds crazy, right? It is, yet, this is what many people do with stocks.

When the market drops, people want nothing to do with it when, in reality, that can be the best time to buy. As prices rise, your expected return falls, and the market becomes riskier, yet people gain confidence and often choose to buy more. The popular "Cycle of Market Emotions" shown in Figure 22-2 perfectly summarizes the emotional cycle most people go through when investing.

FIGURE 22-2: Cycle of Market Emotions

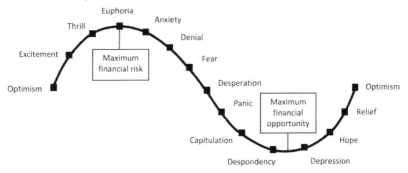

In May of 2020, I had a conversation with a friend who embodied this cycle. In her late 30s, my friend contemplated opening an investment account that she didn't plan on touching until she retires in 25 years. All of her savings were in cash. At that time, the market had begun to bounce off its lows, but there was still a lot of uncertainty about where it was going (as is always the case in the stock market). I explained that there was no guarantee that the market wouldn't go back down, but it's highly probable that over the next 25 years, stocks are going to perform better than cash. She decided she wanted to "wait until the market bounces "*all the way back*" before she buys. Unfortunately, this way of thinking is completely backward.

This graphic also explains why manias, panics, and crashes are an inherent part of markets. When the market's going up, no one wants to miss out, and when it goes down, everyone bails out. As long as human emotion is involved, these cycles will continue to happen. These emotions perpetuate the cardinal sin that so many investors make; they buy high and sell low.

But why does this keep happening? I briefly touched on it earlier. We've repeatedly seen that the market doesn't go up forever, and when it does crash, it usually bounces back. So why do people continue to buy into bubbles and sell out during crashes? Fear of missing out (FOMO) is one, but why do we ignore history? Because we think *this time might be different*. We say, "I know the bubble popped in '99 and '07, but this time might be different, so I better buy." Or, "I know the market bounced back in '02, '09, and '20, but this time might be different, so I had better sell." Here's the hard part; maybe this time will be different. So far, it hasn't been.

The paradox of price

In the last few chapters, we have been saying that the riskier an investment is, the higher your expected return should be. Well, often with stocks, your expected return is lower the riskier an investment is.

Suppose a stock worth $100 is selling for $50. If you buy it, your expected return is 100%. If the price rises to $75, your expected return is now 33%. But you also have more room for it to fall, making it riskier. So when the stock is $75, it is riskier *and* has a lower expected return than when it is $50.

To further the confusion, lower prices do not always mean higher returns. We need to look out for what are called *value traps*. While a cheap stock could mean higher returns, it could also signal future trouble and be on its way to a much lower level.

While the discussion so far has been about *not* selling, sometimes we do need to sell, especially in retirement. Here again, we can have trouble.

A great source of this trouble comes from the effects of *anchoring*. Anchoring occurs when a price has psychological significance to us but means little to the rest of the world.

There are several ways anchors can be dropped. The most common is the price you pay for an investment, but constantly checking your accounts is another way to create anchors, especially when prices are high, like during a bubble. Instead of seeing our position as it is, anchoring causes us to see it as "up from" or "down from." For example, if your investment peaks at $100 but is currently selling for $75, $75 may be a good price, but we will see it as "down from $100."

Many people can't bring themselves to sell until the market price reaches their anchor, which raises another point, *you don't have to make money back the same way you lost it.* See the following example.

Assume that you purchase XYZ stock for $100, and it soon falls to $80. You know there might be better investment opportunities elsewhere but cannot get yourself to sell at a loss. You patiently wait two years for the price to recover and sell it for $100 (up 25% from $80).

During this same period, ABC stock increased 50%. You could have sold your XYZ shares and bought ABC for $80 and ended up with $120 rather than the $100 you currently have. Since you weren't willing to sell XYZ before it reached your anchor, even though you didn't "lose money" on XYZ, you could have had more money if you'd been willing to cut the anchor loose and buy ABC.

Refusing to sell because a price hasn't reached its anchor is a little bit like refusing to take a working elevator because the one you *were* on broke. If there is a clear and better option, don't be afraid to take it. Chapter 29 will talk more about when to change and when to stick.

Aside from the issues of anchoring, people also have a hard time selling when prices are rising. It seems as if they always want to hold on "just a little longer." However, if they hold on too long and prices fall, they can end up riding the following cycle:

1. **Market is going up.** "I can't sell now; the market is going up."
2. **Market crashes.** "I can't sell now; I have to wait until it bounces back."
3. **Market bounces back.** "I can't sell now; the market is going up."
4. **Repeat.**

Many people can't bring themselves to sell because they don't want to miss out on the upside. If they sell and the market goes up a few percent, they are filled with regret. It's almost as if they want to wait until they sell at a point that the market will never go up again, ensuring that they didn't leave one penny on the table. Of course, the market always goes up or down and will continue to do so after you sell. If you sell and the market goes up, that doesn't mean you made a bad decision. The market will always be uncertain, and there will never be a time we know exactly what the market will do.

One way to make this decision is to sell when you've got what you need from the market. Once you have enough to accomplish your goals, why push for more? (We all know the answer, we want more money, but why risk snatching defeat from the jaws of victory?)

To help people get over this hurdle, a colleague of mine tells his clients who have enough to accomplish their goals, "Risk is for people trying to get to where you've gotten. You've already won; now just don't lose." If you've already won, that doesn't mean you should sit in cash forever. It just means not to throw away a sure victory by taking risk that won't materially improve your life. If the Kansas City Chiefs left Patrick Mahomes in the game when they're winning by four touchdowns with five minutes left, everyone watching would wonder what they were doing. There are three possible outcomes: 1) they score again and win by five touchdowns, 2) the game ends, and nothing changes, or 3) Patrick Mahomes gets hurt, and the rest of the season is in jeopardy. This is the same as staying overly invested in stocks once you have enough. You can either have more that you don't really need, stay the same, or lose and possibly have to cut back on your lifestyle.

Once again, if we don't put money at risk that we can't afford to lose, it's hard to get hurt by the market. I'm all for trying to get the most out of life. Just remember that we can all afford the upside, but you need first to be sure you can afford the downside.

The lesson so far is this. Use Figure 22-1 as a guide. When you're investing for the long run, temporary drops in value shouldn't bother you; it's part of the price you pay. If you can't afford the low end of the range for the period you are looking to invest, then don't invest it in stocks (at least not 100%). Panicking and trying to time the market won't work consistently. If you decide you need to sell, make the decision and don't worry what the market does after.

So, do you try to manage this all by yourself, or do you get help? There are three primary ways you can manage your money:

1. Do it yourself
2. Hire a professional
3. Automate it

Before we discuss these specifically, we must understand that there are two main tasks of investing. First, there is strategy design. This is the very involved process of determining what, when, and at what price you should buy and sell. Second, there is execution. This is the actual buying and selling of and access to investments. Years ago, the execution function was mostly limited to professionals and was a costly process. As discussed, technology has eroded these barriers, and nearly anyone can buy, sell, and perform the execution functions with ease.

But remember, just because you have access to the execution tools doesn't mean you know how to use them. We all can change our oil, but we still need to know how and which oil to use. The same is true of money management. There is a lot that goes into it. When you are accumulating for the long term, the process is fairly simple. If you are managing for income, the process is much more involved.

1. Do it yourself

If you know what you are doing, then there's no reason you can't manage your own money. The person who knows what they are doing must then ask, do I *want* to do it? Do you want to spend the time and energy not only designing your plan but monitoring and maintaining it? Just like cutting your grass requires continued maintenance, so does managing your investments.

If you don't know what you are doing, it should go without saying, but you shouldn't do it yourself. Money management is a little bit like playing with explosives. You can put on an incredible show, but you can also blow yourself up.

Don't fool yourself

I've met with many do-it-yourselfers who are quite proud of their investing prowess over the last decade (the 2010s). They point to the growth in their accounts as proof of their skills. Here's the thing: almost everything has gone up in value in the last decade. When everything is going up, your account better be going up too—when all tides are rising, it's easy to look good. Your true test will come when the storm hits, and you see how you come out on the other side.

It's also important to understand where your returns are coming from. In the 2010s, several stocks, Apple, Amazon, and Netflix, for example, each had incredible returns and were very popular amongst DIY investors. If you owned shares of these companies, you likely did quite well. However, as we've discussed, this may be due not to skill but to luck. Going forward, you should ask, will you be able to pick the next Apple, Amazon, or Netflix?

2. Hire a professional

In theory, hiring a professional is great, as you expect to receive "expert" advice. (We'll talk about the label of "expert" in Chapter 30.) Like any service you hire, though, you have to pay for it. The key is to make sure you are getting what you are paying for. (As Warren Buffett says, "Price is what you pay, value is what you get.")

Investment managers charge a fee for managing assets. The reasons to pay a professional to manage your money include:

A. *Expertise.* The advisor uses their professional expertise to select the optimal investment portfolio that fits your purpose and time horizon. They should also consider the timing of rebalancing and any relevant tax consequences.

B. *Service and ease of use.* They handle all of the execution aspects: monitoring, maintaining, and rebalancing as necessary. They should also provide performance data and update you on any changes.

C. *Behavioral management.* I've already said that your success as an investor is mostly determined by how you handle your emotions. A true investing professional can help improve your investing behavior. There's even some evidence of this.

Numerous studies have shown that the average mutual fund investor does worse than the average mutual fund performs. While this may sound like I'm saying the average airplane passenger flies at a different altitude than the average airplane, the reason is that investors get to choose when they get on and off the plane (when they buy and sell). Investors underperform because they try to time when they buy and sell, and usually, they don't get it right. Instead, they either buy too much when prices rise or sell too much and buy too little when prices fall. While hiring a professional to manage your money doesn't guarantee you will never mistime a purchase or sale, a competent manager may prevent you from making many of the costliest mistakes.

The DALBAR Myth

An incredibly popular report circulated amongst advisors and shown to prospective clients is the "Quantitative Analysis of Investor Behavior" (QAIB) report published by DALBAR. For years, this report has shown how the "average investor" has underperformed the market, somewhere in the neighborhood of 3-4% per year. The reason is attributed to investor behavior. Advisors are encouraged to use this report as proof that clients need their services. (It also not so subtly suggests that hiring a pro will boost your returns by 3-4% per year.)

While I won't argue that investors underperform the market, the spirit of DALBAR's report is misleading. In short, the methodology used to calculate the report is flawed, as has been illuminated by authors Harry Sit, Michael Kitces, and Dr. Wade Pfau. The underperformance isn't nearly as high as what is published. As Mr. Sit said, "The 4% a year number is so incredible that it makes the number not credible."[2]

The QAIB report can be purchased by advisors, personalized with their logo and information, and sent to clients and prospective investors. The entire premise makes me uncomfortable. As I said, I do not doubt for a second that investors cost themselves due to poor investing behavior, but reports like this abuse and exaggerate the point and use the illusion of empirical data to sell services.

All three of these reasons—expertise, service, and behavioral management—can be worth the fee. Notice the one thing I did not say: outperforming the market.

We've already talked about the challenges of beating the market, but I must revisit it in the context of paying someone to try to. The truth is, more fortunes have been built by those willing to charge people to try to beat the market than by those who actually do beat it.

Ironically, the fees managers charge to beat the market makes beating the market that much harder. Charging a fee and trying to beat the market is like running a sprint with a parachute attached; it's going to drag you down. Imagine you're a money manager who attracts clients with the goal of beating the market, and you charge a 1% management fee. This year, the market returned 10%, but your fund returned 10.5%, beating the market by a handy 0.50% (which is actually a lot). Your clients, however, did not beat the market. They paid you a 1% management fee, meaning their return was only 9.5%.

So, not only do active managers have to beat the market, but they have to beat it by more than their management fee to break even. That kind of outperformance is a tall task. While it is certainly possible to do it in any given year, doing so consistently over time has proven to be a highly improbable endeavor.

Staying with our discussion of fees, the adage "you get what you pay for" is usually reversed in investing. There are piles of evidence showing that investment fees and performance are negatively correlated. The higher the fee, the worse the performance.

While paying a money manager to beat the market may not be worth it, paying them to do better than *you can* is worth it.[3]

There are plenty of reasons to hire a professional to manage your money and plenty of value they provide. Long-term outperformance of the market is not one of them. If you're paying someone to "beat the market," you may need to reconsider.

The price is right?

Investment advisors perform a service and deserve to charge a fee, but the question is, how much? First, let's establish the impact of fees.

Management fees are charged as a percentage of assets on a quarterly or annual basis. The fee appears innocently small, typically around 1% per year, but adds up over time. For example, if you invest $100,000 and earn 6% per year, after 20 years, you would have $320,714. If you paid a fee of 1% at the beginning of each year, you would have $262,314, about 18% less than if you paid no fees.

Years ago, the process of managing money was very involved. Trades had to be phoned in and entered by hand into a trade blotter, and performance reports were calculated, printed on paper, and mailed. (Not to mention the teams of analysts, computer servers, and other things I previously mentioned.) Nowadays, this is all automated and takes seconds. This increased efficiency has drastically reduced managers' operating costs.

In my opinion, these reduced costs should be passed on to the investor. With that being said, there does remain a fair price for these services. As of this writing, I believe a 1% fee is as high as any advisor should be charging, and depending on the strategy, it should be even lower.

There are two justifications an advisor can give for higher fees. One is that their own costs are higher. If this is the case, this is the advisor's fault. Too many services are available to reduce the advisor's costs, and the investor should not pay for the advisor's incompetence. The second reason is higher performance. As we've discussed, this reason doesn't hold water anymore. I'll just say this; If your local investment advisor consistently outperforms the market enough to justify a higher fee, they're about to be really famous.

I'm embarrassed to admit another justification I hear from advisors as to why they charge fees higher than 1%: "Because my clients will pay it." I'll leave that comment to itself. If you pay more than 1% in management fees, you need to re-evaluate.

Despite my arguments above, it frustrates me when I see calculations of what fees do to an account like the one I showed. We need to remember that fees do exist—even the lowest cost index funds have some fees—and while we should try to minimize them, they cannot be eliminated (yet). Examples showing a 0% fee are unrealistic, misleading, and give people false expectations, which leads to frustrations and resentment later.

3. Automate it

Rather than hiring a human, there is an expanding automated option referred to as "robo-advisors." Many human advisors do not like robo-advisors... I wonder why. Upton Sinclair may have offered the best explanation when he said, "It is difficult to get a man to understand something when his salary depends on his not understanding it." While the name "robo-advisor" may be off-putting, the reality of it is far less scary. Let's take a step back to understand what "robo" means.

Robo simply means automated. Automated means it does something automatically, as it was programmed to do. A human still has to program the computer to tell it what to do. So in a way, robo is simply an automated human advisor.

What if, instead of a robot, I introduce you to my friend Rob. I say to you, "Hi, meet Rob. He knows all of the same things I know and considers the same information I consider; however, when he makes decisions, he will do the analysis in a fraction of the time and will not let his emotions get involved." Would you have a problem working with Rob?

Since robo-advisors have fewer people to pay, they can usually charge lower fees. Given our previous conversation about fees, all else being equal, lower fees are a good thing. As you can imagine, this upsets many human managers. Not only do robo-advisors threaten to replace them, but they also threaten to undercut them before doing so.

The common attack against robo-advisors is usually one of ignorance. It's easier to say, "Are you really going to trust a robot?" than it is to say, "Are you really going to trust a set of investment principles determined by professionals that are automated in execution so that their emotions don't affect their decisions?"

I wish it were that easy

A tremendous body of evidence suggests that automating our decisions (based on rules) leads to better decisions. I'll give two examples for this, a technical one and an analogous one.

First, the technical. Error in judgment is made up of two parts, 1) bias, a consistent tendency in judgment (e.g., we always pick red), and 2) noise, random variations in our own judgment (e.g., we judge the same thing differently depending on when we judge it). Automating our decisions reduces, even eliminates, noise, which serves to improve the accuracy of our judgments.

Here's another way to explain it. Have you ever gone to a restaurant with the intention of eating healthy, only to not? How much easier would it be if we could remove all emotion and predetermine what we'll eat? Well, that's what automating our decisions does. It removes the fluctuating emotions we feel in the moment to make sure we make decisions based on predetermined rules that we set.

Are automated decisions perfect? Absolutely not. But that is not the right question to ask. Our judgments aren't perfect as they are, so the more important question is, is automating decisions better than our current method? Right now, the evidence strongly points towards yes.

Understand that automation works alongside the advisor (you know, like R2-D2 and Luke Skywalker). Automation may replace some of the advisor's tasks, but machines have been doing that for centuries, allowing humans to pursue more meaningful work. In my experience, the only people truly against automated investing are those who stand to lose by automation's rise.

To be clear, working with a robo-advisor does not necessarily mean you never work with a human. For some companies, this is true, but for many, it simply means humans work alongside automation.

At the start of this chapter, I said two things. 1) How you manage your emotions will be the biggest determinant of your success as an investor. 2) If we accept and use stocks for what they do, we'll have very few problems. I've also said so many times that you're probably annoyed: stocks go up in the long run and up and down in the short run. If you truly grasp these statements, you'll see that how we invest in stocks is very simple.

First, if you can't afford to lose it, then don't invest it in stocks. I'm sorry. I know many people say, "But I can't find a return like that anywhere else." Tough. You also can't find losses like that anywhere else. Again, remember what Buffett said, "Reaching for yield is really stupid."

Second, if you aren't selling for a while, then stop worrying about temporary drops in value. It kills me when I hear stories of people who sold thinking the market would crash, only for it to double or triple in value.

There will always be stories of people who hit it big by successfully timing the market. While it's tempting to try, more people fail than succeed. The ability to try offered by easy access to buying and selling does not give you the ability to buy and sell well. We all want to avoid losses, but generally speaking, the harder you try (the more you trade), the worse you'll do.

The stock market is the epitome of uncertainty. Denying, resisting, or succumbing to it is not the answer. If you understand the paragraphs above, then you understand how to embrace it.

Stocks are the best tool we have for long-term growth. What they're not great for is safety. Let's talk about tools that provide safety next.

23

ANNUITIES

Remember the three variables we must consider when generating income from our investments: 1) how much we'll spend, 2) how long we need it, and 3) what rate of return we will earn. Since we never know #2 and have to guess #3 when investing in a blended portfolio, we run the risk of running out of money. Many people don't like this risk, and as with any risk we don't like or can't afford the outcome of, we can pool our risk with others. Such a risk-pooling tool exists to protect against the risk of running out of money, known as an annuity.

Before we go any further, let's acknowledge two things. First, there are many kinds and uses of annuities. They can be used for income or growth (or both), can be immediate or deferred, variable or fixed. The wide variety of annuities makes them difficult to discuss concisely, and we will not cover them all. *As a disclaimer, the point of this chapter is to understand the concepts, not the technical definitions. There are too many caveats to point out and explain every exception.*

Second, we must acknowledge the stigma surrounding annuities. Annuities are the most polarizing financial tool in the marketplace. I must remind you, there is nothing inherently "evil" about a tool—they simply do what they do. As we'll see, most people's problems with annuities are with how they are described (sold) rather than with what they do. We'll revisit the disdain towards annuities later, but let's first understand how they work, starting with income annuities.

At their core, income annuities protect against the risk of living a long time by providing lifetime income payments. Today they are offered by insurance companies, but the first annuities date back to the Roman Empire when citizens would make a single large payment into the *annua* in exchange for annual stipends received each year until their death. While annuities have evolved over time, the ability to create a lifetime income stream remains.

Because annuities pay as long as you are alive, how much income they will pay depends on how long you are expected to live. The longer you are expected to live, the lower the annual payment will be, and vice versa. This explains why, all else being equal, older people receive more than younger people, males receive more than females of the same age, and policies on a single person offer more income than a joint (two-person) policy.

Annuities also allow you to make tradeoffs—certainty for income. Referred to as *mortality risk,* the more certain you are to receive money from the annuity, the less per year you will receive. The following examples will walk through these tradeoffs showing the different variations of income annuities available today.

Imagine you are 65 years old, have $1,000,000 saved, and are retiring later this year. You know you will need income when you retire, but there's a problem—you have no idea how long you'll live. A company comes along and says, "If you give us and annuitize your $1,000,000, we'll pay you $63,000 every year for the rest of your life. The $1,000,000 belongs to us now, but we guarantee you won't run out of money." This is an example of a **life-only** traditional **immediate annuity** (also called a Single Premium Immediate Annuity or SPIA). Life-only means it will pay as long as you are alive and will stop when you die. Immediate means it begins paying immediately.

Is this a good deal or a bad deal? When you *annuitize*, you give up the rights to your principal. It's like choosing the pension payout versus the lump sum. You can't access your principal if you need more than your income payment, and if you die, the company keeps whatever money is left, but in exchange, you own an income stream. The longer you live, the better the deal for you.

Suppose you are also married, and you ask the company, "Will you guarantee these payments for as long as either my spouse or I am alive?" The company says, "Sure, but since there's two of you, your combined life expectancy is longer, so we'll pay you $48,000 per year instead." While the income is lower, it is nice to know that your spouse will still receive income if something happens to you. This describes an immediate annuity with a **joint payout**. (How much the decrease is for joint policies depends on the age of the spouse. Annuities base joint payouts off of the youngest spouse's age.)

While you know this is a good deal if you live a long time, if you (or if joint, you and your spouse) die early, the insurance company keeps all of your money. You worked hard to save that money and don't want all of it to go to the insurance company if you die. This leads you to ask the company, "If I (we) die, will you guarantee a payout to my beneficiaries for a certain number of years, so I can be sure we receive something?" The company replies, "We will guarantee to pay for a total of 20 years, whether you are alive or not, but instead of $63,000, we will pay you $52,000. If you choose the joint payout, we will lower your payment from $48,000 to $47,000."[1] This is called a **period certain annuity** which will pay as long as you are alive or for at least a certain period if you die before the period ends. (The exact length of the period can vary. The longer the period, the lower the income since you are taking less mortality risk.) This ensures you don't give away all of your money to the insurance company if you die.

While the period certain annuity eliminates some risk, to receive income from a traditional annuity, you still must annuitize, which means giving up control of your principal. This leads you to ask the annuity company for further changes. You tell them, "I really like this guaranteed lifetime income, but I don't like that I can't access my money anymore. If I give you my money, I want to be able to access it if I need it." The company responds, "Okay, we can do that too, but that's a different kind of annuity. To accomplish this, we will add what is called an *income rider*. We will allow you access to your principal, and if you die, we will pass on whatever is left. But, if you do access your principal, we will reduce your income proportional to the amount of principal you withdraw. For example, if you withdraw 10% of your principal, we will reduce your income payout by 10%. With this kind of annuity, we will pay you $57,000 per year, and if you choose the joint payout, we will pay you $52,000 per year." This is an example of an annuity with an **income rider.** An income rider allows you to receive income without giving up access to your principal. The annuity company may or may not charge a fee for the income rider.

Table 23.1 compares the different annuities so far. Notice the tradeoffs. Income for single policies is higher than for joint policies because two people are likely to live longer than one. The annuity that stops paying when you die and does not pass on anything after death (SPIA Life-Only) pays more than the annuities that either pay out for a guaranteed number of years (period certain) or the ones that pass on any unused money when you die (income riders).

TABLE 23.1: Different Payouts of $1,000,000 Based on Type of Annuity

Type of Annuity	Single	Joint
SPIA Life-Only	$63,000	$48,000
SPIA 20-year Certain	$52,000	$47,000
Income Rider	$57,000	$52,000

So far, you like the changes the insurance company has made. Since you still have access to your cash and the remaining balance is passed on when you die, you think it would be nice if your principal could grow as well. You go back to the insurance company and say, "I don't see why my cash shouldn't be able to grow while you hold it. I don't want the possibility of losing money, but can you offer something that still allows the account to grow?" Once again, the insurance company obliges, "We'll offer several growth options and guarantee you won't lose money. You can choose a fixed option (that credits a set interest rate) or a performance-based option (amount will depend on the performance of an underlying investment). We'll let you make this decision once a year. Please understand, since you cannot lose money, this is a low-risk instrument, so your potential return will not be as high as riskier investments, such as stocks."

Impressed by the insurance company's willingness to work with you, you decide to push for one more feature. You tell them, "While I plan on retiring this year, there is a chance that I might want to wait to begin receiving income. If I give you my money today, I would like the income you'll offer me to increase while I wait; otherwise, I have no reason to give you my money today." (This also works for people several years from retiring.) One last time, the insurance company agrees, "We will do two things for you. First, your money will still grow, just like we described a moment ago. Second, we will guarantee to increase your income payment until you decide it is time to begin receiving income. Depending on which option you pick, your income will increase by 6-10% every year you wait, similar to how Social Security works." The tool just described is a simplified explanation of how a **Fixed Indexed Annuity (FIA)** with an income rider works.

The variations could go on, but we must stop somewhere. We started with a tool that paid lifetime income, but the principal didn't grow, you couldn't access it, and the money is gone when you die. We ended with a tool that still pays lifetime income, your principal can grow conservatively, gives you access to it, and allows you to pass on any remaining money at death. The tradeoff for these features is slightly lower income.

Clearly, annuities can be a useful tool in a retirement plan, but no tool is perfect. If any part of this seems too good to be true, I assure you there is more you need to understand. There are several elements to be aware of when evaluating annuities.

1. Fees

Most annuities, except those you annuitize (e.g., a SPIA), charge a fee for certain features. The worst offenders that have earned annuities a bad name are the variable annuities we have yet to discuss.

Usually, but not always, you receive something in exchange for the fee, like higher income or growth potential. Some annuities may advertise "no-fee," but you are giving something up in exchange for having no fee. Sometimes this trade is worth it; other times, it is not.

Always be conscious of fees and evaluate what you receive in return. The existence of a fee does not automatically make an annuity bad, and the lack of a fee does not automatically make an annuity good. I like to say, "Annuities can have no fees, low fees, or fees so high the whole thing is worthless."

2. Surrender Charges

While some annuities allow you to access your money, annuities are designed to be a long-term tool, not a liquid investment you pull money in and out of. Many annuities have a "surrender charge," which reduces the amount of money you receive if you surrender the policy or withdraw more than is "allowed." (Surrender charges do not apply to income payouts, and many annuities allow you to withdraw around 10% of the policy value without paying a surrender charge.) Charges commonly start between 7-10% in the first year and decrease over time, going away after the 7th or 10th year. Typically, the higher the charge or longer the period, the higher the income it will pay. While frustrating, there are several reasons and defenses for this design.

First, surrender charges give a guaranteed liquidation value that investments cannot. For example, if your annuity has a 6% surrender charge in the second year, you are guaranteed to receive a minimum of 94% of your account's value in two years. No stock or bond investment can guarantee how much it will be worth in two years.

Second, while surrender charges primarily exist so the annuity company can recoup the upfront costs they incurred when selling the annuity (e.g., commissions), surrender charges can improve the quality of the annuity as well. Surrender charges allow the annuity company to buy bonds with a longer maturity, which provide higher yields than bonds with a shorter maturity. These higher yields give them more money to put towards the policy.

Surrender charges are a non-issue if you properly plan for how the annuity will fit in your plan. Any money put into an annuity should have a long-term purpose. If you think you will need access to your cash in the near future (other than in the form of income payments), an annuity is not the right tool for that money. A well-designed plan should leave plenty of other funds outside the annuity for emergencies.

3. Level income

Most annuity payouts are level or fixed, meaning they do not in-crease over time. Those sensitive to inflation strongly dislike this. Some annuities can be inflation-adjusted, but these come with a tradeoff; the starting income amounts are much lower than level in-come annuities. For example, a level income annuity may pay $50,000 per year, while an inflation-adjusted annuity may start at $40,000 per year and increase 2% per year. The question then becomes, "How long until they break even?"

Figure 23-1 illustrates an example of this comparison. Under the above assumptions, it will take the inflation-adjusted annuity (solid black line) 13 years to equal the $50,000 income of the level-income annuity (dashed line). It will take 23 years for the cumulative payments received (solid gray line) to break even.

FIGURE 23-1: Level Income vs. Inflation-Adjusted Annuity

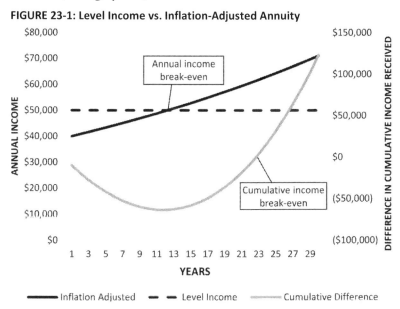

While this is just one example, and actual results will vary, if you live a long time, an inflation-adjusted annuity is likely preferable to a level income annuity. However, if your spending is flat or higher in the early years, as is the case for many retirees like we discussed in Chapter 6, then a level payout may not be problematic at all.

4. Understand what a payout factor is (and is not)

Annuities use the term "payout factor" to calculate how much income it will pay. For example, if you have $1,000,000 and a 5% payout factor, the annuity will pay $50,000 per year of income. While that seems simple enough, conversations about payout factors can be tricky.

First, comparing payout factors across different annuities is not always helpful. That's because the number the payout factor is multiplied against may not be the same across annuities. This provides another marketing lever for the insurance company that we won't get into here. Just know that a 4% payout factor at one company can sometimes create more income than a 5% payout factor at another.

Second, it's important to understand what a payout factor is *not*. A payout factor is not the same as the yield on a bond. If an annuity has a 5% payout factor and you hear someone say it has a "5% yield," this is a mistake. If a bond yields 5%, that means it is paying interest of 5%, and the principal is not being touched. An annuity with a 5% payout factor is spending principal, so this is a massive misstatement.

Finally, comparing payout factors to safe withdrawal rates is also tricky. Recall from our discussion on safe withdrawal rates that withdrawal strategies usually adjust for inflation while annuity payouts are level. Therefore, a 4% withdrawal rate that adjusts for inflation is not the same as a 5% payout factor that pays a level income. I cringe when I hear advisors say, "This annuity will provide you 25% higher income than the 4% rule will... and it's guaranteed!" It's simply not true. They're not the same calculation. Refer back to the discussion in #3 to understand the difference between level and inflation-adjusted payout. A level payout is not necessarily worse; it's just comparing two different things, like highway and city gas mileage on a car.

If annuities are so great, then why are they so polarizing?

Always remember the battle between insurance and investment companies and know that annuities are at the center of it. Decisions involving annuities typically involve large sums of money, and how you manage your savings for income in retirement is crucial to both of their businesses. This battle drives much of the messaging surrounding annuities. Predictably, annuity companies will try to scare you about the stock market, reminding you of how it crashes, is unpredictable, and that you can run out of money. Investment companies will tout the value of staying invested over the long run and how you can earn higher returns and have more money left over. Once again, it's greed and fear. Neither is necessarily wrong, but you must understand the incentives each company has.

While the above explains most of the polarization of annuities, there are three more reasons we must understand.

1. There are many kinds. You may hate one annuity and love another. Some may be really bad, while others are really good. We can't let our opinion of one type taint our assessment of another because they can be very, if not entirely, different tools.

2. They can be complicated and therefore misrepresented. This can lead to overpromises and misunderstandings of what the annuity will or will not actually do. Because both often rely on projections, we can get into a game of hypotheticals and who is willing to "illustrate better." I remind you of the importance of expectations. If you have faulty expectations of what an annuity will do, you will eventually be disappointed. Sometimes this misrepresentation is accidental; other times, it's intentional, which is usually a result of the third reason.

3. They can pay a high commission. Anything that pays a high commission will gain a lot of attention and has the potential to be abused and explained in a manner that bends the truth.

It is crucial to understand how annuities *should* be viewed. Annuities are much more similar in structure and risk to bonds than stocks, and comparing annuity returns to stock returns is misguided. Over the long run, stocks should outperform annuities since they carry much higher risk. But that doesn't mean stocks are necessarily better. When it comes to creating income, rate of return is only part of the equation; the sequence of returns is just as important.

As I've mentioned, the reason most people do not invest 100% of their money in stocks when generating income is that the volatility and resulting sequence of returns risk make the strategy too unreliable and risky. As a result, they add bonds to their portfolio to try to level out this volatility and dampen the sequence of returns risk.

Understandably, people inevitably compare annuities to withdrawal strategies. This is another exercise in hypotheticals that will ultimately come down to 1) how long you live, 2) how much you spend, 3) what rate of return you earn, and 4) what order the returns occur in. We've done this exercise a few times already in this book, so you should know the drill. We can look at which outcomes lead to which tool being better, but at the time you have to make the decision, you won't know what your outcome will be. That being said, let's look at the outcomes.

Table 23.2 defines which strategy is better quantitatively based on certain return sequences and longevities. An unfavorable return sequence consists of losses in earlier years, and a favorable sequence consists of losses in later years. We compare these sequences to how long you live, whether short of, equal to, or longer than life expectancy.

TABLE 23.2: Comparing Market-Based Strategies to Annuities Based on Return Sequence and Longevity

Compared to Life Expectancy	Unfavorable Return Sequence	Neutral Return Sequence	Favorable Return Sequence
Short of	Depends	Market	Market
Equal to	Annuity	Either	Market
Longer than	Annuity	Annuity	Depends

Two principles explain most of the results. Annuities are better the longer you live, and market-based strategies are better when returns are higher. If you live to your life expectancy and returns are neutral, then there will not be much difference in the strategies.

Where it says "Depends," the analysis will swing based on just how bad returns are and just how long you live. If returns are bad enough, an annuity may still be better even if you don't live a long time. Conversely, even if returns are good, the annuity may still be preferable if you live long enough.

Annuities and market-based strategies also differ considerably in what risks the owner takes on. The risk of owning an income annuity is that you will miss out on the upside. The risk of owning stocks is that you will participate in the downside. If you own an annuity and the market goes up 20% every year for 10 years, you still won't run out of money, but you missed out on a lot of upside. Conversely, if the market goes down 20% for 10 years, you were protected with the annuity but participated fully if you own stocks. Annuities narrow the range of outcomes, lowering the ceiling and raising the floor.

As I noted before, calculating both the risk and return of an annuity isn't always straightforward. Annuity payouts are guaranteed by the claims-paying ability of the insurance company and can have additional protections if the company runs into trouble, such as state guaranty funds.* If we can rely on these protections, the risk of principal loss is very low. Calculating the rate of return on an annuity is difficult, as it changes over time and is ultimately unknowable until you die. The longer you live, the higher your return.

Perhaps the greatest value of income annuities is behavioral, as they allow you to spend your money without the worry of running out. Remember, annuities continue to pay you even if you deplete the account. When you're taking withdrawals from a blended portfolio, there is always the "what if." What if the market tanks? What if we live to 100? What if I need this money later? You always leave money on the table because you'll never spend your last dollar on your death bed. Annuities eliminate the "what if." Spending the money an annuity pays today does not threaten your ability to spend tomorrow. An annuity may lag if the market soars, but there is value in the peace of mind knowing you won't run out. Only after we know what the market does and how long you live can we determine which was "best."

While it's nice to compare the strategies, comparison does not mean they are mutually exclusive. Annuities and withdrawal strategies usually work better together than separate. The guaranteed income of

---

* The rules of state guaranty funds vary by state and should be reviewed carefully when considering an annuity. While it is helpful to know they exist, the state guaranty fund is not a reason to purchase an annuity.

the annuity can take some of the withdrawal pressure off of your other investment dollars, possibly allowing you to take more risk and potentially ending up with more money than you would have if you had to manage an entire portfolio of stocks and bonds conservatively.

Is it liquid?

A common knock against annuities is that they are illiquid, meaning you cannot access the funds. This can be completely true. People often use this as a reason to implement a withdrawal strategy instead.

However, we need to ask, how liquid is a withdrawal strategy? If your investments are being used to generate income, the money is liquid in the sense that you can technically access it, but it's illiquid in the sense that accessing it will have consequences. If you withdraw 10% of your investment account, you will hamper the ability of the account to generate income. This illustrates the difference between what Dr. Wade Pfau calls *technical liquidity* and *true liquidity*.[2]

While annuities have been used to generate income for thousands of years, using annuities for accumulation (i.e., growth) has steadily gained in popularity in the recent past. We will discuss these kinds of annuities next.

ACCUMULATION ANNUITIES

You can think of the different features of an annuity as a spectrum. On one end is growth potential, and on the other is income production. The more growth potential the annuity has, the less income it will produce, and vice versa. If an annuity has more growth potential, it is considered an accumulation annuity.

For years, variable annuities have been the most popular type of accumulation annuity. Annuities allow money to be tax-deferred, and the brilliance of variable annuities was that you could hold mutual funds inside of this tax-deferred vehicle. When these were created, they were revolutionary, and there are still some benefits to this structure. However, there are also more costs (literally) that outweigh the benefits. The high fees, proliferation of investment alternatives, and improvements in other annuities have caused variable annuities to begin to fall out of favor. Gaining in popularity as a tool for accumulation are the same fixed indexed annuities (FIA) we discussed earlier.

FIAs used for accumulation are structured the same way as those used for income, except they slide across the spectrum, exchanging lower income production for higher growth potential. Before we talk about how they work, let's see where they work in your plan.

We know that when investing for the long-term, stocks provide the highest return and are likely to continue to do so given the self-regulating nature of the risk and return relationship. However, when investing for a short or intermediate term, the volatility of stocks makes them less favorable, and when you cannot afford to lose money, they are flat-out inappropriate. For years, bonds have been the preferred investment for these situations, but when yields are low, they offer little return and an increased chance of loss. This is where accumulation annuities can be a fit.

Most accumulation FIAs are considered intermediate-term instruments and are structured as 5 to 10-year contracts. Most can't lose money, and returns usually fit somewhere between stock and bonds. They allow you to access your money, and many will not charge a fee. For the money you'll need in a few years, can't afford to lose, and would like to earn a higher return than a checking account or bonds can offer, accumulation annuities are a great tool.

As it seems to be with all insurance products, accumulation annuities can be misrepresented. The general mechanics of how accumulation FIAs work is straightforward, but the specifics can get confusing. Understanding how they work will allow you to properly set your expectations for what they will do.

The friendly way to describe accumulation FIAs is that they receive part of the upside and none of the downside of some underlying index. That means they can't lose money due to market performance, but they can still grow. Since they grow by receiving part of the growth of an underlying index, this raises two questions. 1) What index? 2) How much is "part?"

The most popular index is the S&P 500, but there are many other indexes the annuity can track. Some are well known, and some are "proprietary." I will revisit the topic of proprietary indexes shortly.

Determining how much growth of the index the FIA receives requires a brief explanation. FIAs are never actually invested *in* anything. Instead, the insurance company purchases an option on an index. If the index goes up, they exercise the option and "credit" a portion of the index's performance to your account. If the index loses value, the option expires worthless, and your account is credited zero, which is how it can guarantee not to lose money. How much of the index's growth you receive depends on the "crediting method" used.

Examples of crediting methods include participation rates, caps, and spreads. *Participation rates* will credit a certain percentage of an index, for example, 50%. *Caps* will credit all of an index's performance up to a defined cap, for example, 5%. Finally, *spreads* will credit the performance of an index minus a certain percentage, for example, 4%. A simple example can be found in Table 23.3:

TABLE 23.3: How Much FIA Will Credit Based on Crediting Method

	Index loses 10%	Index gains 5%	Index gains 10%
50% Participation Rate	0%	2.5%	5%
5% Cap	0%	5%	5%
4% Spread	0%	1%	6%

That's how accumulation FIAs work. Typically, once a year, you choose an index and a crediting method. After the year, if the index increases in value, you receive a portion of the growth. If the index decreases, you receive zero rather than participating in the losses. There are also options to receive a fixed interest rate, much like a CD. The contract usually lasts 5-10 years, and the longer the contract, the higher the crediting rates. You can access your money if you need it, typically subject to the 10% free withdrawal provisions, and many accumulation FIAs do not charge a fee.

Would you like 2 nickels or 1 dime?

While some people spend a tremendous amount of time trying to determine which crediting method is best, it's mostly in vain. That's because, over the long run, there will be almost no difference between the different crediting methods. This isn't an accident. The full reasoning is beyond the scope of this book, but essentially, the insurance company only has so many dollars to put to work, and an option on an investment with higher return potential will cost more than an option on an investment with lower return potential. Here's a simple example.

Let's say the insurance company can only afford a 40% participation rate on an index that averages a 10% return. Conversely, let's say they can afford a 100% participation rate on an index that averages a 4% return. Both options over the long run are expected to average a 4% return.

Some strategies will capture higher returns but less frequently. Others will capture lower returns more frequently. When you tally them up over the long run, they're going to be very close. You can try to bounce around and pick which one will have the higher return that year, but often, you're better off just sticking with one or two. As we'll see, crediting methods are another area for insurance companies to play marketing games.

Based on the above discussion, accumulation FIAs sound pretty great. So what is there to look out for? Let's start by revisiting the concept of proprietary indexes.

Many of these proprietary indexes are created based on "backtested" results. Backtested means to simulate a strategy using historical returns, "as if" it had been in place. (A further discussion of backtesting will be held in Chapter 29.) Put it this way; nobody's seen a bad backtest. If it didn't look good in hindsight, they wouldn't create it. Companies love to tout their latest proprietary index that is going to do great things. The strategy goes like this. 1) Create an index that will look incredible if you simulate it based on historical results. 2) Market it like crazy and gather money. 3) If the index doesn't perform well in the future, oh well, as the money is already in their hands.

There used to be something like 30 indexes, but now the number is around 10,000. While some of these indexes have value, the majority are nothing more than marketing fluff. All will look good on an illustration, but there is no guarantee how they'll perform in the future.

We also need to revisit the marketing games companies can play with crediting rates. First, crediting rates can change throughout the life of the contract. What may have started out with a 50% participation rate could have a 20% participation rate just a few years later. Second, we must consider the net result of these rates. Here's what I mean. Some annuities may advertise "no-fee" but have lower crediting rates to make up for it. As a result, the difference between annuities with and without fees can be negligible. We also cannot directly compare crediting rates without considering what index it applies to. A 50% participation rate on the S&P 500 index could be more valuable than a 150% participation rate on some lower risk index. Nevertheless, unsuspecting consumers fall for these tricks all the time.

Next, we must discuss the "power of zero," meaning the value of not taking losses. Let me say this, 1) it's probably more powerful than you think, and 2) it's not as powerful as the insurance company wants you to think. I will use the same example to prove both points.

An FIA offers none of the losses and some or most of the gains. If there are no market losses, then the annuity will underperform. But if there are losses, the annuity will be more valuable. Therefore, the more losses the index takes, the better the FIA will look.

Well, fortunately for the insurance companies, the 2000s provided a great set of return sequences to show the power of zero. Big losses from 2000-2002 and the financial crisis in 2008 made the value of taking a zero shine. In fact, if you invested $100 in the S&P 500 and $100 in an FIA with 50% of the gains and no losses, the FIA would be worth $143 after 2009, and the S&P worth $91. We can stretch this out further. After 2016, both the FIA and S&P strategies would have $210. Clearly, there is value in eliminating losses. The insurance companies pounced on this and started spreading the message that these annuities allowed you to "Get market returns without the risk!"

Here's where things go sideways. That return sequence is a bit of an anomaly. Obviously, an FIA *can* outperform the underlying index, but it should not be *expected to*. If you ran the same strategies from 2010-2019, the S&P dwarfed the FIA, $353 to $183. The 2000s provided an amazing example of the value of zero, four years with sizable losses, but they skew expectations of what these tools will do.

Despite this misdirection, there is absolutely value in a strategy that eliminates losses and receives half of the gains. Over the long term, such a strategy has averaged around a 6-7% return. That is fantastic. The S&P, as we've discussed, has averaged around 10-12%. One eliminates losses; the other participates in them. For the record, if your problem with accumulation annuities is that they don't beat the stock market, then you were looking at them wrong the whole time. They're not supposed to or designed to.

Accumulation FIAs are an excellent intermediate tool for safe money that can earn a higher return than bonds. If they outperform stocks, then fantastic, but do not expect that to happen. They are especially great as a bond alternative in low-interest-rate environments.

Don't forget about MYGA

Another type of annuity that can be used for accumulation is called a Multi-Year Guaranteed Annuity (MYGA). MYGAs are often compared to Certificates of Deposit and work very similarly. MYGAs offer a fixed interest rate for a defined period, such as one, three, or five years. Typically, the longer the period, the higher the interest rate. MYGAs usually offer higher interest rates than CDs and should be considered as a safe alternative that provides a fixed return.

Let's remember the value of annuities. They are a form of insurance, so they limit your range of outcomes. Income annuities eliminate sequence of returns risk and the risk of running out of money and give you permission to spend your assets. In addition to those features, FIAs with income riders allow you to still have access to your money and pass on any remaining money at death. Accumulation FIAs provide steady returns without the risk of losing money. As a tool to combat uncertainty, both are phenomenal.

But that doesn't mean that they are the perfect solution. People tend to take an either/or approach to annuities, thinking it's investments or insurance rather than investments *and* insurance. As I've said all along, these tools work best together. For example, income annuities take the withdrawal pressure off of your remaining investments, which can allow you to take more risk with your remaining investments. Accumulation annuities are an intriguing bond alternative to complement a blended portfolio with a conservative return over an intermediate term.

While annuities certainly have their favorable features, they are not for everyone. They deserve a look, but they are just one part of a well-designed plan. Another tool that serves a purpose but is not for everyone is life insurance, which we'll discuss next.

24

LIFE INSURANCE

If you want to start a heated conversation, ask a group of financial advisors how much life insurance you should have in retirement.

While we won't be settling that debate, we will look at how life insurance works, what its original purpose was, some of the ways it is used today, and why it can be controversial.

Once again, there are a lot of intricacies and technicalities with life insurance policies. The purpose of this discussion is to understand the general functionalities, not to point out and explain every exception.

Life insurance provides a payment (death benefit) in the event of the insured's death. There are two purposes for this death benefit. 1) To replace wages lost as a result of premature death. 2) To replace the value of an estate spent down in retirement.

How much death benefit you *can* buy depends on the purpose of it. (Can buy and *should* buy might be different numbers.) Let's begin with the purpose of replacing lost wages. Since life insurance is meant to *replace* wages, not give you more than you would have earned, you must approximate how much earning potential you have left in your life. This amount is known as your *economic life value*, and the calculation is admittedly flawed. Generally speaking, it is calculated by multiplying your current income by how many working years you have left. For example, if you are 30 years old and make $100,000 per year, you can reasonably expect to work until age 65, meaning you have 35 working years left. Making $100,000 for 35 years gives you an economic life value of $3,500,000. This is roughly the maximum amount of death benefit that you can buy.

Notice that life insurance is not designed to be profited from; it exists to replace a loss. While life insurance can appear to be a windfall for beneficiaries, in theory, it is simply replacing what they would have received had the insured not passed away. Also, note that, in our example, you could not buy $10,000,000 worth of death benefit, as that is more than you are expected to earn. (That would be like receiving a check for $100,000 when you total your $35,000 car.)

For the retiree no longer concerned about lost wages, the death benefit is used to replace assets spent while retired. The general rule to determine how much you can buy is approximately 1.5 times your assets. So, if you have $1,000,000 in assets, you would be eligible for up to $1,500,000 in death benefit.

Death benefits come in two forms, temporary and permanent. The most common form of temporary death benefit is *term insurance*, which provides a death benefit for a set "term." The length of the term can range from less than a year to 30 or more years. At the end of the term, the death benefit goes away. Permanent death benefits, on the other hand, pay a death benefit as long as the policy is not surrendered or lapsed (e.g., you quit paying premiums).

Just like any kind of insurance, how much the premiums depend on how likely the policy is to pay a claim (death benefit). So, in this case, premiums depend on how likely the insured is to die while the policy is in force. The more likely you are to die, the higher the premiums. This means two variables drive the equation. First, the age and health of the insured have a lot to do with how likely they are to die. All else being equal, premiums for a 60-year old will be higher than premiums for a 30-year old, and premiums for a healthy 60-year old will be lower than premiums for a less healthy 60-year old.

The second variable is whether the death benefit is temporary or permanent. The statistics vary, but industry sources say that somewhere between 95-99% of term policies never pay a death benefit. Permanent policies payout 100% of the time unless you drop the policy, so it is understandable that, all else being equal, premiums for term insurance will be lower than premiums for permanent insurance.

An important difference between the different types of policies is what happens to your premiums if you don't die.

One of the downsides of term insurance is that the only way to receive any money from the policy is to die. If you don't die, any premiums paid are lost. It's like car insurance. If you don't use it, you lose it. Alternatively, assuming you do not surrender the policy, you are at least guaranteed to receive some money (the death benefit) from a permanent policy. (Technically, if you are the insured, "you" do not receive anything, your beneficiaries do.)

In addition to the death benefit, many permanent policies have *living benefits*. The most popular living benefit is *cash value* that allows you to access some of the premiums you have paid while you are alive. Cash value can be one of the most attractive and misunderstood features of life insurance. Let's first understand how cash value is created before discussing what we can do with it.

To fully understand how cash value is created requires a conversation outside the scope of this book. A good enough understanding can be gained with a high-level review.

Cash value builds as a result of excess premiums paid on permanent policies. A portion of every premium dollar paid goes towards building cash value. As a result, the cash value balance will increase over time. These set increases are guaranteed.

Cash values may also increase beyond the guaranteed amounts if the policy pays a dividend. A dividend is a return of excess premium and typically results from either positive 1) mortality experience or 2) investment performance.

Mortality experience refers to how many people die. Recall our discussion from the chapter on insurance. If fewer people die during the year, then fewer death benefits will be paid, and more money remains in the pool. This means more money can be returned to policyholders in the form of a dividend.

As for investment performance, your cash value will be invested in something, and what exactly that is will depend on the type of policy. *Whole life* policies are typically invested in safe bonds and high-quality real estate. *Indexed Universal Life* policies are similar to indexed annuities in that they will track and receive a portion of the performance of an underlying index with no risk of loss. *Variable Life* policies invest in mutual funds. In general, the better the performance of the investment, the more the cash value can grow. This also means interest rates play an important role in determining the amount of dividends.

Which lever do you pull?

There is tremendous flexibility in the design of cash value policies. Some can be geared towards higher guaranteed values, some towards higher dividends. This can make comparing policies a bit of a challenge.

Comparing dividend rates across policies is also a challenge. Dividend rates are not like dividends on stocks in that they are not directly comparable. For example, a 4% dividend rate on one policy may pay higher dividends than a 5% dividend rate at another. Keep this in mind when you see companies advertise a high dividend rate.

Unfortunately, not all consumers understand all the complexities of the policies and equate "dividends" with being good, and thus think "higher dividends" must mean a better policy. One very popular carrier advertises the highest dividend rates in the industry. They also generally have the highest premium rates. (Remember, dividends are a return of excess premium, so it makes sense that higher premium policies also pay higher dividends.) There can be legitimate reasons for this design, but in reality, it's usually used to attract policyholders who don't understand the connection.

It's important to understand what happens to cash values when you die. Cash values are "inside" the policy, so you have access to them while you are alive, but they "die with the policy," meaning you don't pass on both the death benefit and cash value when you die (with the exception of some Universal Life policies). For example, if you have $100,000 of cash value and a $1,000,000 death benefit while you are alive, you have access to the $100,000 cash value, and when you die, you pass on the $1,000,000 death benefit. You don't pass on $1,100,000.

Okay, so what can we do with cash value? Let's first think of *why* we would want to access our money.

There are two main reasons to access cash value. The first is for more "one-off" needs, like a liquidity crunch or to take advantage of an investment opportunity. Many entrepreneurs use their cash value as seed capital for new businesses. The second reason is for more prolonged spending in retirement. Why we need the money will often determine *how* we access it.

Think of cash value as having two parts, 1) the existing cash value and 2) the periodic dividends received. Let's start with what we can do with these ongoing dividends.

You have three choices of what to do with dividends. First, you can simply receive the cash payment and spend or save it as you wish outside of the policy. Second, you can use dividends to offset future premiums, reducing your out-of-pocket costs. The third option is to purchase more death benefit. These are called "paid-up additions," and the effect is similar to reinvesting dividends. It allows both the cash value and death benefit to grow exponentially.

I must point out that dividends are not guaranteed. While many companies have paid dividends for 100+ years, dividends are very dependent on interest rates, and dividends can be cut. This can lead to *illustration risk,* the risk that illustrated values don't materialize. We'll revisit this risk later.

We can also access the existing cash value. There are two ways to do so, by taking 1) withdrawals *from* the cash value and 2) loans *against* the cash value.

Withdrawals work similarly to how a withdrawal of principal in an investment account works. Withdrawals reduce your death benefit roughly dollar for dollar (it could reduce the death benefit more if paid-up additions are withdrawn), and you'll no longer earn dividends on cash value that is withdrawn. This is like pulling cash out of a savings account and no longer earning interest on the money withdrawn.

Withdrawals are received tax-free up to your basis (remember, you don't pay tax on the money you've already paid tax on). Your basis is approximately equal to your premiums paid minus dividends received. Let's assume you have a $1,000,000 death benefit, basis of $150,000, and cash value of $200,000. Conceivably, you could withdraw $150,000 (the amount of your basis) tax-free. Your death benefit would be reduced to $850,000. (Exact amounts will vary.)

You can also take loans *against* the cash value. Interestingly, the loans do not have to be paid back; you can allow the interest to compound over time. Any outstanding loan amount, including any interest accrued, will be paid off at death by the death benefit, which decreases how much of the death benefit your beneficiaries receive. As long as the cash value remains greater than the loan balance, the loan proceeds are received tax-free. Some types of policies allow you to still earn dividends on the money loaned.

Recognize what's going on

A popular selling point of cash value life insurance is that dividends can still be paid even if a loan is taken against it. (This is true of *non-direct recognition* policies. *Direct recognition* policies pay a reduced dividend on money loaned.) On the surface, this sounds great. Where else can you make money on the money you borrow! Upon further review, however, this may not be all that it appears.

Assume you have $100,000 in the bank and $100,000 of cash value in a non-direct recognition life insurance policy (meaning full dividends are still paid on loaned money). You have a need for $10,000 and are deciding whether you should take a loan against the cash value in your policy or withdraw cash from the bank.

For simplicity, we will assume that you earn 0% interest on your cash at the bank, cash value increases 4% per year, and the interest rate on the loan against your cash value is 4%.

Table 24.1 compares the two. In this example, the $10,000 loan against the cash value compounds and effectively decreases the death benefit. The cash value will still grow while the loan is outstanding. Alternatively, when you withdraw cash from the bank, there is no loan to charge interest, cash value will continue to increase, and the death benefit will not be decreased as there is no loan against it.

Remember, cash value is not passed on at death. While you are alive, you have access to your cash value and cash in the bank (equal to the "Net Cash Available"). When you die, your heirs receive the death benefit and cash in the bank (equal to the "Net Worth at Death").

TABLE 24.1: Cash Value Loan vs. Bank Withdrawal

	Cash Value Loan	Bank Withdrawal
Balances Today		
Cash in Bank	$100,000	$100,000
Cash Value	$100,000	$100,000
Death Benefit	$1,000,000	$1,000,000
Net Worth at Death	$1,100,000	$1,100,000
Net Cash Available	$200,000	$200,000
Access Cash		
Cash Value Loan	$10,000	$0
Bank Withdrawal	$0	$10,000
Balances 10 Years Later		
Cash in Bank (0% interest)	$100,000	$90,000
Cash Value (4% growth)	$148,024	$148,024
Death Benefit	$1,000,000	$1,000,000
Loan (@ 4% interest)	($14,802)	$0
Net Worth at Death	$1,085,198	$1,090,000
Net Cash Available	$233,222	$238,024

Notice that both the cash available while you're alive and net worth at death are greater when using cash in the bank (under these assumptions).

Taking a loan against the cash value and still earning dividends is one of those situations where a feature sounds great, but when you stop and think about it, it's not exactly what it seems. The ability to take loans against the cash value is nice, but it's no different than other types of loan (other than possibly a slightly lower interest rate), and it may be inferior to spending cash that does not charge interest.

So far, there is nothing controversial. Life insurance is a tool that protects your family from an early death while working and replaces money you spend in retirement after you die. Why then, is life insurance so controversial?

Some of the controversies arise from *legitimate* differences in beliefs about how much death benefit you need. Consider how personal of a decision it is. When you're working, the death benefit exists to replace wages lost from premature death. When people are relying on your income, such as a spouse and children, this is invaluable. But even if you agree that a death benefit is necessary, how much death benefit you need is less easy to agree on. Do you leave enough so that those relying on you are okay for a few years, 10 years, 20 years? While we could argue there are some wrong answers (if you have a spouse and four young children, leaving one year's salary behind is probably not the best), there are plenty of right answers. Who am I to tell you?

The same debate exists when we look at this from a legacy or inheritance perspective. For some, leaving behind a chunk of money to people and organizations they care about is important. For others, they believe they've passed on enough while they're alive and would like to enjoy their savings. To each their own.

Some of the controversies can also arise from *illegitimate* differences in beliefs of how much you should have. Here I am referring to how policies are sold. Before we start bashing life insurance salespeople, let's recognize the position they are in. Many salespeople are well-meaning, and many consumers do not recognize the value of life insurance and the many valid ways it can be used in a plan. I do believe that most people underestimate how much life insurance they need. That being said, the incentives of life insurance salespeople are to sell as much as possible. This can lead to some of the less honorable sales practices that paint the industry and product in a poor light.

The insurance companies themselves are not absolved. I believe much of their actions are in response to the battle they are in with investment companies. Let's think through how the battle between investment and insurance companies has evolved to where it is today.

Assume you need a death benefit. You start with a simple term policy. You don't like the idea of losing all of those premiums if you never die, so you look at a permanent policy. With a permanent policy, you know that your beneficiaries will receive something if you die, and you will have access to your cash value while you're alive.

The investment industry sees the sizable commitment you've made to paying premiums and says, "Hey, why not buy a term policy, and instead of paying the higher premiums for a permanent policy, you save and invest those premiums with us. Because of the market's high returns, you'll likely have more money in your investment account than you will in cash value, and when the term ends, the amount you saved will likely be as high as the death benefit you would have had."

This proposal is known as *buy term and invest the difference.* As we've discussed several times, whether this type of strategy is "better" depends on four factors: 1) the spread between premiums and benefit, 2) when you die, 3) what your rate of return will be, 4) what order the returns come in. And of course, it assumes you actually save and invest.

So how do you, the consumer, make your choice? Since you don't know what the future will hold, meaning you can't answer the four factors listed above, you have to rely on projections. The insurance company, wanting to attract your premium dollars, may begin to illustrate higher dividends. And from there, the illustration battle is on.

Illustration wars

If you are buying a policy based on the prospect of cash value growth, you are relying on dividends to make this happen. Since dividends are not guaranteed, any future dividend amounts are projected.

So, what is the insurance company's incentive? To make the illustration look as good as possible. If a company cannot meet its illustration, this usually happens many years down the road. By this point, they have made their money, and there is often very little you, the policyholder, can do.

Insurance is designed to make you whole after a loss. Anytime insurance tries to cross over into the world of returns and start going head-to-head with investments, you need to be careful. Remember that insurance illustrations are nothing more than projections.

If you have a one-time or short-term need for accessing the cash value, then the illustrations being slightly off won't have much of an effect. But if you are planning on using your cash value to generate income, it can completely alter the outcome. Let's walk through the options you have to generate income from the cash value.

Your first option is to simply surrender the policy and take the cash value with you. If you do, a gain equal to the difference between your cash value and basis will be recognized in the year you surrender and will be taxed at your ordinary income rates.

When you surrender the policy, you also surrender the death benefit. If you would like to maintain the death benefit and access the cash value, then you can take withdrawals of or loans against the cash value.

Like any income plan, you must make an estimate of 1) how long you're withdrawing for, 2) how much you'll withdraw, and 3) what return you will earn (in this case, dividend amounts.) Since dividends are projected by the company, that leaves the policyholder with two assumptions. They can either assume how long they are withdrawing to solve for how much they can spend or assume how much to spend to solve for how long it will last.

As long as things go as planned, this can be a great strategy, and you'll receive loan proceeds tax-free (just as you receive any loan proceeds tax-free). But if things don't go according to plan, a proverbial "tax bomb" can explode.

If the loan balance exceeds the cash value in the policy, then retroactively, all of the money you have received in excess of your basis becomes a taxable gain. Depending on how long the strategy has been in place and the size of the policy, this amount can be in the hundreds of thousands of dollars. This gain is recognized in the year the tax bomb goes off, which can lead to an extremely high tax bill. Compounding the problem is the fact that you likely spent most of the money you received and may struggle with the wherewithal to pay (finding the funds to pay the tax bill).

What can detonate this tax bomb? Like always, when reality differs from our expectations. Recall our two assumptions. First, if you live longer than originally anticipated, the loan balance can grow larger than the cash value.

Second, dividends can be less than illustrated (what we previously called illustration risk). If dividends are less than projected, your cash value will increase slower, which means the loan balance can catch up to it quicker. (The overall effect is really no different than an investment account, and how building a plan based on the assumption of a 4% rate of return will be threatened if your actual return is 2%.)

This puts a tremendous amount of pressure on the illustration. Consumers who make purchasing decisions based on illustrated values are making a serious commitment of trust to the insurance company. Remember, insurance companies have an incentive to illustrate as well as possible. Following through on that commitment comes second.

Caveat emptor (buyer beware)

Currently, one of the most popular life insurance strategies involves the use of Indexed Universal Life (IUL). These policies allow the cash value to *potentially* grow significantly more than other cash value policies such as whole life insurance. The danger here once again is in the word "potentially." Illustrations of IUL policies almost always look amazing. At least two things must be considered when reviewing IUL policies. First, investment performance may vary significantly from what is illustrated. Second, fees may be considerably higher than what is illustrated.

IUL illustrations can be run under ideal and normal assumptions. It is not uncommon for the difference between these illustrations to be as high as 80%, meaning one illustration may show $50,000 of income, and another using more realistic assumptions shows $10,000 of income. I came across one illustration showing how a $16,000 premium being paid for 10 years would generate $24,000 per year of income forever. When we looked at the "normal" conditions, the illustration showed $5,000 per year of income.

When it comes to insurance, it is always safest to trust the guarantees. Relying on illustrations is a dangerous game.

Fit for a rebel

Cash value life insurance has a bit of a cult following in certain realms of the financial planning world. Some of this is due to the favorable features of life insurance (tax-free, flexibility, steady and safe return, etc.). Some of it is due to human nature. These "cults" tend to prey on the same three vulnerabilities in people. 1) Fear of higher taxes. 2) Fear of market crashes. 3) Desire to be different.

So many of the "pitches" I hear start with a discussion of the national debt and declare tax rates are going to skyrocket in the future. They recount horror stories of the tech wreck in the early 2000s and the financial crisis in 2008. They also tease you with "What Wall Street doesn't want you to know." There's always a wrinkle of truth to these pitches, but underneath is a canyon of misdirection.

Recall some of the valuable features of life insurance. Cash value grows and can usually be accessed tax-free, so it is valuable if tax rates rise. Most cash values cannot take losses, so they grow steadily and are immune to market volatility. They also are not part of the Wall Street cabal, so they run counterculture to traditional financial advice. These features, plus human psychology, combined with a good illustration, can make life insurance very appealing.

Here's the thing. Life insurance isn't a secret, it's not hiding, and access to it is not restricted (other than being healthy enough to be insured). If life insurance really were the silver bullet some claim that it is, there are enough savvy investors out there that they would gobble it up.

Everyone loves to feel like they know something others don't. But, for every visionary trailblazer, there can be many delusional followers. Sometimes the contrarians know something you don't; other times, they're just out of touch.

Okay, we get it. The way life insurance is designed is not the problem. The problem is with how it is sold. Usually, the problem comes down to blurring the line between what a policy *can* do and what the policy *will* do. Unfortunately, we won't know the answer until later.

While life insurance can be misrepresented, it can also be a valuable part of your plan. It's fairly irrefutable that some death benefit is necessary if people are relying on your income while you are working. But what about when retired? There are two primary uses of a death benefit in retirement.

First, if you have a desire to leave money behind to individuals or organizations you care about, life insurance is obviously useful for that.

Second, the death benefit can be used to create higher income while you are alive, especially for couples. Having a death benefit can allow you to spend your assets more aggressively while both spouses are alive, knowing that death benefit proceeds will replenish your pool of assets when one spouse passes. It is also valuable when an income stream, such as Social Security, a pension, or a single-life annuity ends at one spouse's death. However, if you won't experience this drop in income, or have no desire to leave money behind, then you probably don't need a (or as much) death benefit in retirement.

How much death benefit should you have? In theory, we may all want to be insured for our full economic life value, but in reality, a death benefit of that size can be unaffordable for many people. You have to decide what is right for your situation. For couples, identifying the loss of income when one spouse passes and how much income needs to be replaced can help determine how much of a death benefit to have. If you have charitable inclinations, you can also target a certain amount. For those to whom the estate tax will apply, life insurance proceeds can be a great way of paying those bills.

Another challenge retirees face when buying life insurance is affordability. The older you are, the more expensive premiums get. Term premiums may no longer be the deal they once were, and it may not be worth the risk of paying premiums for years only for the term to end, and you and your beneficiaries receive nothing from the policy. Premiums for permanent policies may be so high that they are completely out of the question. This is where a tool I call "termanent" insurance can be useful. Technically called Guaranteed Universal Life (GUL), the structure is a blend of term and permanent insurance. The death benefit can be guaranteed until age 120, effectively becoming permanent, and the policy does not build a cash value. As a result, the premiums are lower than permanent policies, yet the death benefit lasts longer than temporary policies.

"If you were to die tomorrow…"

Here's a neat life insurance sales trick. When prospects are waffling on how much life insurance they need, the advisor can ask, "If you knew you were going to die tomorrow, how much death benefit would you want?" You're supposed to answer, "As much as I can get." Armed with your own words to use against you, the advisor can say, "Well, you're going to die someday, so why not get as much as you can."

Here's how I would answer. I would say, "You're right. If I did indeed know I was going to die tomorrow, I would indeed buy as much as I can (this whole exercise assumes the insurance company doesn't know you'll be dying tomorrow because they won't underwrite you if they do). However, I do not know that I will die tomorrow, so it's irresponsible to plan for this all-in scenario. I need to plan for other scenarios, such as living a long time and increased cost of living."

Forgoing the all-in strategy and preparing for a range of outcomes is an example of embracing uncertainty. But this tactic works both ways. If you need to leave some money behind, either for a spouse or some other reason, you may believe you have many years to save and invest. But the truth is, you may not live a long time, and it may be true that some amount of death benefit is necessary.

Some of the discussions in this chapter may give the idea that I am anti-life insurance. This is not true. Several years ago, we bought my wife a whole life policy. We bought it because it offers a permanent death benefit that increases over time, guaranteed cash value with conservative and steady growth, flexibility in paying premiums, and the ability to stop paying premiums and maintain a death benefit if we want. She can also access the death benefit while she's still alive if she needs certain kinds of long-term care, and the insurance company will pay her premiums if she gets disabled (this is the result of an additional "waiver of premium" rider.) In other words, the policy gives us optionality by allowing us to be flexible with future payments. It diversifies us from the traditional asset classes of stocks, bonds, and real estate. And it builds in a cushion (redundancy) in the case of an emergency. We didn't buy it because we think it will outperform our stock investments. We didn't buy it because we think tax rates are going to double.

With all these different features (and there are many more I did not mention), it is important to remember what life insurance is. Life insurance provides protection in the event of premature death and replaces the assets you spend down in retirement. It may also be used to create an income stream or to protect against long-term care in certain scenarios, and overall it can provide tremendous peace of mind. Cash value policies can provide a safe and steady return, are typically not correlated with the market, and can offer incredible flexibility. Because insurance is lower risk, over the long run, it will not outperform stocks, and that is okay! Not everything in life has to chase the highest return.

There is a place for life insurance in your plan the same way there is a place for bonds or other asset classes. Life insurance is another tool in a diversified toolbox and is a good enough tool as is. It doesn't need to rely on the tricks that have soiled its reputation.

25

REAL ESTATE

When writing a book such as this, it is impossible to cover every tool and strategy at the level of detail needed to fully understand it. "Real Estate" is a broad topic that deserves far more room than I will give it here. We will briefly discuss the two most common ways people generate income from real estate in retirement, 1) rental income and 2) accessing the equity in their own home.

These are obviously very different strategies with mostly different risks. We'll start with rental income.

There are few investments better than a rented (or leased) piece of leveraged real estate. The benefits are clear. Rental payments are usually high enough to cover the property's carrying costs (mortgage, insurance, taxes, maintenance), which essentially means your tenants are buying the property for you. If the rental payments exceed the carrying costs or the property is paid off, this can provide a nice income. It's hard to beat when it's all working.

There are a few things that can make the strategy stop working. For starters, the property itself can stop working, which may require large maintenance bills. If unexpected, these can put you in a crunch. Insurance covers a lot of things, but not all things.

The biggest risk, though, is vacancy or default. A nice cash flow can quickly turn into a cash drain if your tenant moves out or stops paying. You must be sure you have the funds to survive a lengthy vacancy period (especially if the maintenance precipitates the vacancy). If you cannot afford to weather this vacancy period, you may be forced to sell the property, and if you have to sell in a rush, you might have to sell at a price below market value. If you still have a debt on the property, you may even have to sell for less than you owe (called being "underwater"), which compounds the problem.

The retiree must also consider their own level of involvement required to generate the rental income. I meet a lot of 60-year-old retirees who plan to count on the rental properties they manage themselves. You must think of your future self and whether finding renters, responding to service calls, etc., is something you will be willing and able to do at an advanced age, and if not, if you can afford to pay a management company to do it for you.

The other common way to generate income from real estate is by accessing the equity in your own home—the difference between what the home is worth and how much you owe.

There can be many reasons why you might want to access the equity in your home. For example, you may have depleted your other savings and need an additional source of income, or you might just need cash for a different investment, project, or short-term need and don't want to liquidate your other investments.

One option you always have to access the equity is to sell. Of course, if you still need a place to live, you probably need to use the funds for your next residence.

Fortunately, there are ways to access this cash without having to sell or move. Which tool is best depends on what you need the money for and how long you need it. (All of these tools are soaked in minutiae, which I will not be explaining. There are also technical terms which I will not always use appropriately. I trust that no one will decide to pursue any of these tools based on the following descriptions.)

Reverse mortgages, as they are most commonly thought of, can be used to create an "income" stream that lasts as long as you are alive. How much you receive depends on your age. Payments are "tax-free" since the IRS considers it a loan advance, rather than income. The money received from the reverse mortgage creates a loan, and the loan balance compounds over time. If you pass away, or move out of the house, the loan comes due. If the value of your home is greater than the loan balance, any remaining equity is kept by you if you're alive or your heirs if you're dead. Reverse mortgages are usually structured as "non-recourse loans," which means, if the loan balance is greater than the value of your home, then you or your heirs are not liable for the balance.

There are other ways to structure reverse mortgages besides the lifetime income option (which is technically called a "tenure reverse mortgage"). These other structures have their own risks to be aware of. One of the biggest catches with reverse mortgages is that the loan can come due if you don't live in the house for a year, even if that's because you're receiving long-term care in a facility. If you do not have the funds to pay off the loan balance, this may force you to sell the house to pay off the loan when you don't want to.

Other tools allow you to access your home equity through more traditional credit methods. Home equity *loans* are lump-sum loans that will charge interest on the entire loan amount, whether or not the funds are used. Home equity *lines of credit* can be thought of like a credit card, with the amount of equity representing your credit limit, and only the amount you put on the line of credit is subject to interest. Both are useful for shorter or intermediate-term cash needs that you plan on repaying.

The things to look out for with all of these options are the usual suspects. Fees can be excessive, and interest rate terms can change and be unfavorable. Reverse mortgages, like rental income, can be great when they work, but disastrous when they don't.

There's a reason that just as many fortunes have been lost as have been built using real estate. For the right person, they are an incredible tool. The big takeaway here is that the equity in your home can be accessed and used without selling your home. It may be a primary source but is likely a supplementary or last-resort source.

More generally, real estate is usually a great inflation hedge.

However, if you lived through the Great Recession, then you're well aware that the value of your home does not always increase indefinitely. The biggest risks with any real estate transaction are 1) the value dropping, 2) illiquidity, and 3) carrying costs. If all goes as planned, it can be the best investment you'll ever make, but it can also kick you out on the streets as fast as any other investment.

26

SUMMARY OF
RISK AND RETURN

When you save money, it must be held somewhere, and as long as it's not stashed under a mattress or buried in your backyard, your money will earn some rate of return. It could be positive, or it could be negative.

Conventional wisdom says the amount of return you can potentially earn depends on how much risk you're willing to take. This is mostly true, but what "risk" is will vary from person to person. Finance uses volatility, as measured by standard deviation, to quantify risk. While that's a useful measure, we ultimately care about the value of our investment when we need to sell it. If you don't need your money for many years, then an investment that temporarily loses value in the short-term but gains value in the long term isn't risky at all.

From a planning perspective, volatility when making withdrawals or deposits introduces sequence of returns risk that makes projections less reliable. This emphasizes once again the importance of planning for a range of outcomes.

As for what return you can expect, we'll never know for sure. Historical averages can be helpful, but if conditions have changed (like they have for bonds), then historical returns may be misleading. We'll never know the absolute returns different investments will earn, but we can be confident that returns relative to each other will stay mostly the same (over the long run). Anything can happen in a given year.

Insurance is difficult to plot on the risk and return charts like the ones we saw in Chapter 16. First, "risk" is different for most insurance policies. They are not volatile like traditional investments and instead face two different kinds of risk. 1) Company risk, the risk that the company will stay in business and meet any claims made, and 2) projection risk, the risk that any projections or illustrations will come true. The second reason insurance is difficult to plot on the risk and return chart is that calculating the rate of return often depends on when the insurable event happens (e.g., when you die for life insurance and annuities), so there is tremendous variation in returns.

Calculating rates of return on insurance can miss the point. The primary purpose of insurance is to eliminate the downside, not pursue the upside. We don't use insurance to become rich; we use it to keep from becoming poor. Some tools like cash value life insurance and annuities can blur this line, but even then, the value is in their safety, not their growth.

Again, we will never know what our rate of return will be. Many times, rate of return is just part of the puzzle, and the sequence of returns is most important. If predicting our rate of return is a nearly impossible task, then predicting our sequence of returns is a completely impossible task.

Sophisticated statistical software can be used to provide a probability distribution of outcomes, but we must remember at least two limitations. First, the analysis is only as good as the inputs used. Second, while these analyses are great for multiple attempts, your life is still a sample size of one.

Accepting that we cannot know for sure what our return will be and, therefore, cannot completely rely on our projections can be disheartening. We want to feel in control and not knowing what the future holds is uncomfortable. Once again, this is an opportunity to embrace uncertainty. Rather than work tirelessly trying to predict an exact rate of return that will only be wrong, instead plan for a range of possible outcomes. While less precise, this will be more accurate and leave you better prepared when reality doesn't work out as you hoped.

27

SUMMARY OF INFLOWS

As the preceding pages have shown, the "inflows" column in our model is quite comprehensive. As I've said before, our inflows can be a function of our outflows, meaning how much we need to spend will determine how much income we need to create, or our outflows can be a function of our inflows, meaning how much income we'll have determines how much we'll spend.

Inflows can come from sources inside and outside your plan and can be guaranteed and non-guaranteed. Outside sources of income include Social Security and pensions. If your spending needs are greater than these outside sources, you must fill the gap with inside sources (i.e., your savings.) Inside sources of income can come from spending your principal, interest earned on your principal, growth of your principal, and any combination in between.

When it comes to creating income from your savings, many tools are available. What tools are right for you will depend on the facts of your situation, such as how much you have in savings, how much income you need, the mix of non-discretionary and discretionary spending needs, etc. It also will depend on your appetite for risk. There is no "right" answer.

At the end of the day, when it comes to creating income, we want to know the answer to two questions, 1) how much can I spend? and 2) how long will it last? What level of certainty you want to be able to answer those questions with will determine what tools you choose. By now, you understand the tradeoff for certainty is upside.

You will also have to balance the tradeoff between maximizing what you have now and making sure you don't run out in the future. A market-based strategy using stocks and bonds has more upside, but it may fail. If you rely on the market for income and the market cooperates, your kids will someday thank you for leaving more money behind. But if the market doesn't cooperate and you experience losses, especially in the early years, you may end up relying on your kids instead. The use of insurance, such as annuities, provides safety and guarantees, but it also limits your upside. You must choose which is more important to you: making sure you don't run out of money or potentially being able to spend more if the market cooperates (which implies a willingness to spend less if the market *doesn't* cooperate).

Deciding which tools to use is not an all-or-nothing or one-time decision. Remember, just like building a house requires multiple tools, so does building a financial plan. You do not have to choose between all stocks and bonds or all insurance. You can use a blend. They are complements, not substitutes, and they work better together than they do separately.

Only in hindsight will you know which tool you "should have" used. Just like how we diversify our investments because we don't know which will go up and which will go down, we diversify the tools in our plan because we don't know which ones we'll need for what jobs in the future. As with any form of diversification, you guarantee you'll do worse than the best outcome, but you'll also do better than the worst outcome. Some people understand and appreciate the value of diversification; others would rather pursue the biggest winner. This is yet another tradeoff you will have to make as you create your plan.

28

SUMMARY OF THE DEEP DIVE

In Part I, we introduced the seven assumptions inherent in every financial plan, and in Part II, we took a deep dive into each of them. The seven assumptions are:

1. How long we will live
2. How much we need to spend
3. What inflation will be
4. Whether we will face any unexpected expenses
5. What our tax rate will be
6. What our rate of return will be
7. What order (sequence) our returns will be in

Notice, we also covered how to populate the framework introduced in Chapter 2. Chapter 4 talked about time, Chapters 5-11 about outflows, Chapters 12-15, 21, 23-25 about inflows, and the others about return. We can summarize our findings as follows:

1. *Life expectancy statistics can be misleading as they represent the midpoint of when you are expected to die.* This means half the people are expected to live past their life expectancy, so if you plan to deplete your accounts at life expectancy, there's a 50% chance you'll still be alive when you do. Additionally, most measures are calculated for the population as a whole using historical information. To be more accurate, you must adjust for your unique demographics and improvements in technology and medicine. Finally, the combined life expectancy of a couple is far greater than their individual life expectancies.

2. *Your total spending is a function of quantity and price.* Most retirees purchase less in terms of quantity as they age, which reduces the effects of price inflation. Discretionary expenses often decrease more than non-discretionary expenses. Calculating your Retirement Adjusted Spending Amount (RASA) can help you picture what is likely to change and plan accordingly.

3. *You have your own inflation rate.* While the CPI is a useful measure, your inflation rate (CPI-YOU) will be different. Only changes in the price of goods and services you consume will affect your spending.

4. *Certain unexpected expenses are more probable than others.* A prudent plan must do one of two things: 1) create a pool of money by setting aside funds each year or reserving a portion of your existing savings to cover these costs, or 2) insure against them if you cannot afford the consequences if they occur.

5. *What is considered taxable and the rate it is taxed at is what matters.* Both of these will change, and it's important to know how you'll be affected when they do. We don't pay taxes on the money we've already paid taxes on.

6. a) *Low interest rates are challenging traditional planning methods.* Using historical averages can sometimes be more harmful than helpful. Future returns of cash and bonds are expected to be below their historical averages. This leads many people to increase their allocation to stocks and take more risk than is otherwise advisable.

6. b) *It is nearly impossible to predict what your rate of return will be, and it is completely impossible to predict the order your returns will occur.* Be prepared to experience a range of possible returns rather than a fixed or linear return.

7. *Volatility introduces sequence of returns risk.* While it is nice to have the highest rate of return, when creating income, the sequence of returns is just as important. Losses experienced when your accounts are at their highest can significantly alter the outcome of your plan.

PART III
DECISION TIME

B y now we understand that every retirement plan requires us to make unknowable assumptions that will play out over an unknowable length of time. We know it is important to understand the range of possible outcomes of each assumption, and when planning, it is likely prudent to be slightly conservative as the outcome of running out of money is much worse than dying with more money.

While Part I laid the groundwork of what retirement is and what assumptions we make, Part II looked at the tools we can use. Much of Part II was technical in nature, like a tutorial or "how it works" manual. Part III will be about how we decide to put it all together.

How we make decisions is affected by both internal and external forces. Outwardly we receive advice, some of which is good and some of which is bad. Inwardly, we are still human, and humans are flawed, and so are our decisions. First, we will look inward at how we get in our own way when making decisions by falling victim to the biases and fallacies that come with being human. Then we will look outward and discuss where to go for help by having an honest look at the state of the financial planning industry and the challenges of working with an advisor.

29

GET OUT OF MY (OWN) WAY!

We know that planning for the future in many ways requires us to try to predict the future. Inherent in this process is the requirement for us to make decisions. We discussed the challenge and process of prediction in Chapter 3, so in this chapter, we'll focus on how and why we make decisions the way we do.

Throughout this book, we've talked about how a flawed understanding of the past or present can result in both flawed projections of and decisions in the future. For years, the field of economics (and by extension, finance) operated on a flawed understanding of human nature to project future behavior; it assumed that individuals are *rational*. As a result, much of the financial advice given on these topics did too.

The definition of rational relies on two terms: *consumption*, purchasing and using something, and *utility,* a measure of enjoyment or usefulness. It is said that a rational consumer always makes the choice that *maximizes utility*. This means a truly rational person will only consume something up to the point that consuming more causes a decrease in utility—until consuming more makes things worse. For the rational person, having more choices and the option of more is always better—if they don't need more, they won't consume more. A rational person would never knowingly do something harmful to themselves and would never be affected by the choices others make.

Clearly, we're not rational. This fact infiltrated academic economic thinking when Dr. Richard Thaler hosted a dinner party, and his guests asked that a bowl of nuts be removed so they wouldn't spoil their appetite for dinner. A seemingly innocent request was a revelation for the host. His guests, whom economics assumed were "rational," were deliberately asking for *less choice*. Were they not rational? If so, where else were they not rational? The answers to these questions snowballed into the fledgling movement and field of study known as behavioral economics, which is the study of economics while attempting to consider real human emotions and behavior.[1] (This always makes me wonder what traditional economics tries to consider.)

In addition to Thaler, two psychologists, Daniel Kahneman and Amos Tversky (1937-1996) laid much of the bedrock of this now flourishing field. Kahneman's truly seminal book *Thinking Fast and Slow* is requisite reading on the topic. I do not intend for this chapter to be a cheap summary of their work but rather a synthesis of the main concepts as they relate to financial planning.

Another note about this chapter. At times we will be discussing biases, and for most people, the word "bias" has a negative connotation. In a clinical sense, a bias is a tendency in behavior or judgment and is as natural as breathing. Biases can stem from the "human-level"—biases all humans share—or at the "person-level"—biases unique to an individual based on their life experiences and perspectives. I can assure you that we all have biases, so please do not feel like I am accusing you of being uniquely unwitting.

In Chapter 1, I shared the two basic instincts of every species, to survive, and pass on their genes. The drive to survive results in several principles of human behavior that also affect our decision-making.[2]

One such principle is that we are *cautious*. This cautiousness manifests itself as loss aversion, which is our recognition that it's more beneficial to our survival to avoid threats than to pursue opportunities.

The second principle is that we are *social beings*. It is beneficial to our survival to find harmony with the group, and as a result, we often rely on and follow others.

Relying on others is, in a way, a *shortcut*, which introduces our third principle: that we need and rely on shortcuts. This isn't because we're lazy, it's because it is impossible to consciously think through every decision we make, so we use representations, substitutes, and heuristics to craft our interpretation of reality. (Especially in an unfamiliar situation or when we don't know what will happen, in other words, when faced with uncertainty.) Shortcuts trade speed for accuracy and can result in biases and "less than perfect" decisions.

It's helpful to understand *when* we rely on shortcuts. As detailed in Kahneman's book *Thinking Fast and Slow*, humans have two modes of thinking, System 1 (faster and more automated) and System 2 (slower and more intentional).[3]

System 1 is our default way of thinking. We go about our day largely on autopilot, not consciously thinking through everything that is happening to us. System 1 is engaged when we're driving down an open highway or calculating 2 + 2. It's also engaged when we have "instinctual" snap reactions that aid in our survival, like swerving to miss a deer in the road or jumping when we see a snake. When the situation calls for it, System 2, the more deliberate and slow thinking is activated. System 2 is engaged when parallel parking on a crowded street or calculating 17 x 63.

We predominantly rely on shortcuts when System 1 is engaged. System 1 is also the source of our "biases" as we don't take the time to think through everything and thus rely on representations to react. Sometimes, the representation isn't right. When we make financial decisions using the wrong representations, our decisions suffer.

So, we want to survive, and to survive, we are 1) driven by fear, 2) don't consider everything, and 3) follow the lead of others. These principles explain much of why and how we make decisions.

A speck in the eye

It's important to understand that these principles are strengths as they are essential to keeping us alive. But like any strength, in certain situations, they can be a weakness.

If we don't know where our strengths are weaknesses, they can become blind spots. We all have blind spots. Literally speaking, when it comes to our eyesight. Figuratively speaking, when it comes to our decision-making. The existence of blind spots is problematic enough, but ignorance or denial of our blind spots is doubly troubling.

A prime example of these principles affecting our decision-making occurred recently in the city I live in. At a crowded mall on a holiday weekend, there was a loud "bang." A few people began to flee for the exits. Soon after, others began to flee. Panic ensued, with people hiding in dressing rooms and police swarming the area.

Given the above description, no one would question this behavior. Consider what all happened. 1) The loud bang resembled a gunshot (shortcut). 2) Those who heard the bang fled after deciding it was better to get out of there than be stuck inside with a gunman (cautious). 3) More people fled because they saw others fleeing (social beings).

Here's why this example is so interesting. The loud bang was caused by a man slamming a skateboard on the ground.[4] While the crowd's behavior was "logical" (even rational), *it was not the proper behavior once all the information was known.* (But you could strongly argue it was still the best decision given what they knew.)

This example is a perfect microcosm of our financial lives. We have to make decisions with incomplete information, and we can easily see what others are doing. We evaluate incomplete information by determining what it resembles, using shortcuts, and relying on other people's interpretations of it. We then opt for the decision that keeps us alive, which, in a financial context, usually means preventing losses and lowering the chance of running out of money.

Our reactions and decisions are part of a "cue-reaction" cycle. There's a stimulus (cue), and we react. How we react depends on our interpretation of the cue. Sometimes this reaction is automatic (System 1), and sometimes it is deliberate (System 2).

We build our understanding and interpretation of cues in a similar

"1-2" manner—something happens, and we assess. We 1) gather evidence and 2) assess or synthesize evidence. Flaws in our understanding of what happened will cause flaws in our reaction. These flaws can occur at either step in the process; by not gathering the right evidence or by not assessing or interpreting the evidence correctly.

Let's spend some time understanding how these flaws can happen.

The whole process starts with gathering information and evidence. Recall from Chapter 3 the problem with evidence. It shows us what happened, but not what didn't happen or what evidence is no longer around, which leads to (**survivorship bias**).

When trying to explain what happened (how the evidence came to be), we often rely on our memory. The easier something is to recall, the more likely we are to use it as an explanation (**availability bias**). Usually, the more recently something happened, the easier it is to remember, which leads to **recency bias**. For example, if there have been a lot of shootings recently, then a loud bang will call up memories of gunshots rather than skateboards. Likewise, if the market has recently crashed, a drop in prices will call up memories of further losses rather than a potential buying opportunity.

It's important to understand that it isn't always things that happened most recently that are easier to recall. Some experiences stick in the front of our minds forever. The fact is, and this is a fact we'll constantly revisit in this chapter, our own experiences shape many of our views and opinions about money. For example, a strong personal memory of the market crashing when you first started out investing may cause memories of market crashes to pop up any time there's turbulence in the market. In contrast, someone who went 10 years without seeing a crash may be less attuned to crashes and may think of temporary blips as a buying opportunity. (This also starts to explain why investors can have such different views; because we all have different experiences (memories) we draw on.)

Ease of recall, whether from a recent or long-ago event, also affects our assessment of how likely things are to happen in the future. We saw this after 9/11 and how people feared flying. We also see it after market crashes and how people are hesitant to get back in. As a result, we end up protecting against the things that did happen, which isn't necessarily bad, but we're still left exposed to what *could* happen. (This is part of why regulations designed in response to the last crisis rarely prevent or protect against the next crisis.)

One of our favorite ways to make sense of the past (gather and assess information) is to search for patterns. Patterns can be helpful but also deceptive. Concluding that you have a food allergy if your face swells up every time you eat shellfish is a proper use of pattern recognition. Thinking that standing on one leg helps your favorite team score because those two events coincided a few times is less useful. The difference between a pattern being informative or misleading is determined by whether the pattern (**correlation**) can also explain the reason (**causation**) something happens. History is littered with examples of people mistakenly blurring the line between correlation and causation and is one of the easiest ways we are "fooled by randomness."[5]

Our passion for finding patterns can betray us when the patterns don't mean anything. This is seen in the **gambler's fallacy**, the tendency to erroneously believe a random event is more or less likely given a series of previous events. If you've ever watched or played roulette at a casino, you've seen two versions of the gambler's fallacy at work.

Suppose you walk by a roulette table that has landed on red four spins in a row. One camp will be betting that red is "hot," and the trend will continue. The other camp will be betting that black is "due," and the trend must reverse. In American roulette, the odds of the ball landing on a red or black is each 18/38 (two greens make up the other two possibilities). If there have been four reds in a row, what are the odds of the table turning up red again? 18/38. As much as we want to believe otherwise, previous spins have no bearing on the next one.

Those who think black is "due" are making the mistake of thinking that probabilities are *deterministic*. Probabilities and the law of large numbers tell us what to expect over many tries but do not affect what will happen on an individual try. For example, if you've flipped a coin nine times, and it's landed on heads four times, you may think that the next flip is more likely to turn up heads since that would mean it has five out of ten times (which would be 50% of the time and what we expect of a "fair" coin). But the odds of the coin turning up heads are 50/50, whether you've flipped four heads or four tails.

Here's a "fun" thought experiment that captures the challenge of deciphering randomness. Suppose a coin has landed on heads 20 times in a row. What are the odds of the next flip being heads? There are two ways of thinking. If the coin is fair, the odds should still be 50/50. But is the coin fair if it's turned up heads 20 times in a row, or is the coin "biased" (weighted)? That's the challenge! How do you know?

We can commit the gambler's fallacy while investing when we see a stock that appears to be following a pattern. Coincidentally (or not), so often, just after we decide to buy or sell the stock to exploit this pattern, the pattern ends. This practice of scouring the past for patterns to exploit is an example of **data mining**. With increases in computing power, this practice has become easier and more widespread.

In an investment context, data mining involves reviewing data for patterns and devising investment strategies based on historical results. Recall the example from Chapter 22 of the market going up 1% on Wednesday morning. The enterprising investor might design a strategy that buys stocks on Tuesday evenings. If they were to test this strategy against historical results (called **backtesting**), they'd likely see that they would have beaten the market.

As also explained in Chapter 22, these strategies do not find sustained success going forward due to the self-correcting nature of markets. Other participants would also identify this pattern, and any gains available on Wednesday mornings will be eliminated in the future.

Back to the Future

The topic of backtesting is tricky. Some of the most successful investment strategies in history have come from studying past data, but for most people, it's a fool's game. Here's why.

Not to get too sci-fi on you, but backtesting brings up some of the same issues that the concept of time travel does; it violates the *principle of causality*. If you go back in time and change something, doesn't everything after change as well? For an extreme example, consider the scenario of going back in time and killing your mother before you were born. If you kill your mother, you wouldn't be born, so how can you go back in time to kill her.

Here's the parallel in investing. If we identify a trading strategy that "would have" worked for the last 10 years, it probably would have worked because nobody identified it in the last 10 years. Once somebody does identify it, it likely won't work much longer due to the self-correcting nature of markets we just discussed. (This also means that if someone had identified it 10 years ago, the opportunity you discovered 10 years later wouldn't have existed. It's all very circular.) It's easy to lament "what could have been" if we had made a decision differently, but we must realize that everything after that would be different too.

While *testing* your strategy against historical data is not a bad idea, *developing* your strategy based solely on how it would have performed in the past usually is. The scientific method tells us to make a hypothesis, collect data, then evaluate the results, not to come up with a hypothesis from data already collected.[6] Backtesting is great for identifying relationships, but whether the results are useful or not going forward depends on whether the relationships will continue.

The practice of backtesting is rampant in the investing world today. Sometimes these backtested strategies work for a short amount of time. This "success" allows an investment fund to show impressive results (remember, nobody publishes a bad backtest). Since investors use past performance to decide what funds to invest in (due to what is called matching—the belief that what *is* good or bad will *stay* good or bad),[7] a history of good results brings in lots of new money.

Read the fine print

Historical performance can always be misleading, but especially if it isn't real. Many investment strategies will show results going back 5, 10, even 20 years. However, not all of these funds have been "live" (had real money invested) for that long. Sometimes the results they show are based on backtesting, which means all they've accomplished so far is discover a pattern and exploit it in historical simulations. Backtested results are required to be disclosed, but like most disclosures, they can be hard to find and translate. (Unfortunately, live data can be misleading too, as we saw when we discussed mutual fund incubation in Chapter 3.)

One reason that backtested strategies stop working and why high-performing funds in general struggle to find sustained success is **reversion toward the mean**. Reversion toward the mean states that the greater the deviation of a random variable from its mean, the greater the probability that the next measured variable will deviate less far. In other words, you'll be closer to normal after a big outlier.

Imagine a baseball player that averages 25 home runs per year. If he hits 50 home runs one season, no one is surprised if he hits 20 home runs the following season, as he "reverted towards the mean." But be careful. Reversion toward the mean is often misunderstood. If you have an *above*-average performance, it doesn't mean you'll have a *below*-average performance next. It just means that your next performance is more likely to be "closer to the average" or "less above average." In our baseball example, if he hits 49 home runs the next season, he is still reverting *towards* the mean.

Investors can be fooled by reversion toward the mean in two ways. First, they might *ignore* reversion. For example, they might see a fund have high returns, expect it to continue (ignoring reversion), and be disappointed when it subsequently reverts. Second, they may *over-rely* on reversion, for example, seeing a fund underperform, expecting it to revert (relying on reversion), and be disappointed when it reverts less than expected.

There is ample proof of reversion toward the mean in the investment world. For example, Morningstar publishes their list of "Five-Star Funds," which attempts to identify funds they expect to be top performers. Multiple studies, including an extensive one performed by the Wall Street Journal in 2017, have shown hardly any difference in performance between funds rated five-stars and funds rated one-stars, with many of the five-star funds underperforming.[8]

Remember that high performance comes from having high returns, and high returns come from selling investments for more than you paid for them. Sometimes, high returns result from astute decision-making; other times, it is due to flat-out luck. We often see this cycle: 1) Investment fund hits on a lucky bet and shows high performance. 2) Investors see high returns and pile money in. 3) Future returns underperform as their luck runs out.

Investors who always chase last year's hot manager or stock will likely find their returns lacking as they missed out on the outlier and subsequently participated in the reversion toward the mean.

I've mentioned several times that humans like to feel in control, and "intervening" gives us that feeling of control. Reversion toward the mean can also make it challenging to evaluate the effectiveness of our interventions. Here's an example. Does criticism or praise change future performance?

When a person does well at something involving an element of randomness (e.g., hitting a baseball or investing in the market), we often praise them, and when they do poorly, we often criticize (or put more delicately, "coach" them). If we had them try again, it wouldn't be unusual for those who did well (the ones we praised) to do worse and those who did poorly (the ones we criticized) to do better.[9]

When this happens, it's easy to think that our criticism (intervention) helped and encourages the idea that our interventions have an impact. This belief feeds the *illusion of control* that we'll discuss shortly. Surely our interventions have some effect, but most of the change in performance is likely due to reversion towards the mean—they would have done better or worse regardless of whether or not we praised them.

The financial lesson is that sometimes, doing nothing is better. Overreacting to an outlier is rarely the right decision. The challenge is determining whether the outlier represents the beginning of a "new normal" or if it is simply an anomaly.

It is harder to make that distinction when we have a shorter track record to evaluate an outlier against. If a 10-year veteran that averages 25 home runs per year hits 50 home runs, we recognize that it was a good year but will be cautious about proclaiming newfound greatness. However, if a rookie hits 50 home runs, we may think we have found the next Babe Ruth. The same goes for investing. When a new fund has a big year, investors will be eager to pile money in, thinking they have found the next big thing, when in reality, the fund might just be having their outlier early. (Another benefit of having a big year early on is that "past returns" will look good for the next several years, which of course, will continue to attract further investment.)

The discussion of track records is really just a discussion of sample sizes. Chapter 3 talked about the perils of drawing conclusions from smaller sample sizes and how our life is a sample of one amongst the population of human experiences. Earlier in this chapter, I mentioned how our own experiences affect our assessment of what happened and how likely things are to happen. Author Morgan Housel explains it this way, "Your personal experiences with money make up maybe 0.00000001% of what's happened in the world, but maybe 80% of how you think the world works."[10] This means even the "smartest" of us all walks around with a limited set of knowledge and experiences when compared to the totality of knowledge and experience in the world.

There's a concrete reason for this limitation. Knowledge is either first-hand or second-hand, meaning you learned it from your own experience, or it was passed on from someone else. There is no third-hand knowledge through osmosis; I can't know what you know just from knowing you. That means if you haven't been exposed to it in some way, you literally can't know it. The best you can do is recognize that there is a limit to what you know, and no matter how much your experiences seem to confirm it, you could be wrong.

Recognizing this limitation should encourage us to keep an open mind. Drawing conclusions from our small sample can blind us to the other possible outcomes.

The poem *Blind Men and the Elephant*, written by John Godfrey (1816-1887), is an artful story of drawing conclusions from an incomplete sample. We can summarize the poem as follows: Six blind men come upon an elephant, each encountering a different part of the elephant's body. The man who touches the elephant's horns thinks it's a spear. The man who touches its trunk thinks it's a snake, its legs a tree, its ears a fan, its body a wall, and its tail a rope. All the blind men draw conclusions from their incomplete sample. The poem ends with:

And so these men of Indostan
Disputed loud and long
Each in his own opinion
Exceeding stiff and strong,
Though each was partly in the right,
And all were in the wrong!

If we're honest with ourselves, we aren't much different from the blind men in this poem. We are adamant (confident) in our opinions and beliefs based on what we experience. This confidence can turn into arrogance, and arrogance can lead to ignorance (not to mention overconfidence). Capturing this relationship between arrogance, ignorance, and actual knowledge is the **Dunning-Kruger effect**.

The Dunning-Kruger effect suggests that the less we know about something, the more confident we are, and the more we know about something, the less confident we are. Eventually, we reach a point where our actual knowledge and our confidence align. Figure 29-1 illustrates the progression of the Dunning-Kruger effect.

FIGURE 29-1: Dunning-Kruger Effect

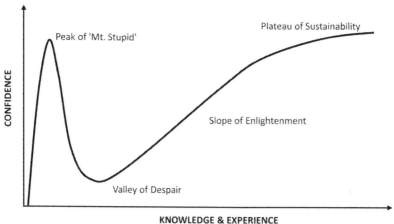

Those who summit Mt. Stupid typically know just enough to be dangerous (like the person who read a book on stocks and has now opened a trading account). On the backside of Mt. Stupid is the Valley of Despair—the place where people realize they don't really know anything after all (likely after getting burned in their trading account). Slowly over time, knowledge increases until they become a true expert (although at this point, they may hesitate to claim this expertise.)

The internet has built a high-speed chairlift to the peak of Mt. Stupid. A few minutes on Google can make anyone feel as if they're an expert. Just as WebMD has made us all doctors, we think we are ready to go toe-to-toe with investing professionals because we read a book on investing or an article in the Wall Street Journal. The Valley of Despair is littered with people who have learned, and are still learning, their lessons the hard way.

Two biases, in particular, extend our stay on the peak of Mt. Stupid. When we look at evidence, we can "see what we expect to see" (**confirmation bias**), and we can also "see what we want to see" (**desirability bias**). If we really like (or dislike) an investment or tool, we have no trouble "supporting" our feelings and justifying our decisions, and if we really want (desire) for something to happen, we seek out support that favors this belief. We also quickly dismiss information that says otherwise.

Perhaps more than any other bias, confirmation bias can be the most destructive. It is the source of so much conflict, pain, and despair, not to mention some of our worst decisions.

The truth is, when faced with evidence, most people do not evaluate the evidence for what it is. They evaluate it in reference to their current beliefs. Similar to the effects of anchoring, when presented with new information, they see it as agreeing or disagreeing with their existing views.

Why does this happen? Several reasons. First, beliefs provide order. It's not fun to think that your conception of the world might be wrong. Second, there's this attitude that being wrong is shameful (the same attitude exists towards failure.) We see this attitude as early as grade school and the shame kids feel for giving the wrong answer after bravely raising their hand. The third reason is that our ego and identity can become wrapped up in or synonymous with our beliefs. As a result, we think that if our belief is wrong, then something about us is wrong.

We also shouldn't ignore that some people have an incentive for their belief to be right. The obvious parallel in this context is advisors, but this is true of many other professions as well.

Hopefully, it's clear why confirmation bias is a problem. A key to making good decisions is having accurate information and dealing with the world as it is. If you willfully shut out information to protect an existing view, then that's probably not going to work out well. This is why the real flaw with resisting to update your views isn't that you "were wrong," it's that you're going to *stay* wrong if you don't change.

I can't help but take this a level deeper. I think most people want to know the truth and how things really work; I don't know many people who actually want to be wrong. So why then do so many of us protect our beliefs? Let's go back to the school example of raising your hand and being wrong. Why is it shameful? If you were taking an anonymous quiz online, you'd probably have no problem guessing the wrong answer. That means it must be shameful because your classmates will know that you didn't know something. So really, many times, we don't want to be wrong to protect others' opinions of us. We think that if people know that I'm wrong, then they'll think less of me. (I'm touching on the difference between a *fixed* and *growth* mindset, as described in Carol Dweck's fantastic book, *Mindset*.) But by this age, you should know, most of the people in the room didn't know the right answer either, and they're thankful for the person willing to speak up. For some reason, so many of us assume that "everyone else" has everything figured out and is always right. It's just not true.

One last semi-related point before I get off my pulpit. Sometimes we can feel so confident in our opinions that we can't imagine there's another way. But just remember, there is a limit to how much you can possibly know. If you see someone with a different opinion, realize the incredible opportunity in front of you; to discover how this opinion is true in their mind. That doesn't mean you'll end up agreeing, but understand this, most people aren't actually crazy, and there is a reason they have the opinion they do. Something about their life experiences up to that point has led them to think, feel, say, do, or believe what they do.

Taking this approach is how I personally try to combat confirmation bias. For example, if I want to buy a share of stock, I ask why someone is willing to sell it to me? Understanding why the other party no longer wants something that do I want helps me see both sides and either reinforce or change my existing view. Sometimes you find out you had it backward.

Searching for and evaluating disconfirming information is one of the best ways to improve the quality of your decisions. Keep in mind, blindly confirming your existing views is only costing you. The sooner you find out you're wrong, the quicker you can become "right."

Relying too much on our own experience can be problematic, but so can relying on and comparing with others. As social beings, we have a desire to belong and a fear of missing out (**FOMO**). Finding the exit when someone yells "FIRE!" is helpful, but this **herd mentality** can also make us follow each other off a cliff. When **groupthink** (when the desire for consensus trumps critical evaluation) takes over, no one speaks up because we all think "someone else would if something was wrong." The **wisdom of crowds** (the idea that large groups of people are collectively smarter than individuals at making judgments) is real, but judgments must be independent. If everyone is basing their opinion on other people's opinions, then group judgments often become self-confirming. These ways of thinking form the **information cascades** that result from confirming each other's thoughts and behavior and is why bubbles and panics remain an inherent part of markets. All of this is fed by the **illusory truth effect**, where the more things are mentioned, the more we believe them to be true. Media companies can fall for the illusory truth effect too. One outlet runs a story, then another picks it up, and next thing you know, it's everywhere. It must be true if it's everywhere, right?

Not only do we follow others, but we compare ourselves to others, and this too affects our decisions. The discussion of **relative versus absolute wealth** in Chapter 1 showed how we can make decisions that make us worse off overall if it means we're better off relative to those around us. We have to remember that every person's circumstance is different, and what works for them may not work for you, and what is safe for them may be risky for you. If you are okay and accomplishing your goals, why does it matter what someone across the street is doing?

Since we compare to others, we protect our ego when we reflect on our lives. It's very typical for us to attribute our successes to our intellect and skill and our failures to bad luck. Interestingly, the reverse may apply in how we evaluate others. **Illusory optimism** explains how we overestimate our own abilities and underestimate others. For example, we clearly see that others are guilty of biases, but not ourselves.

The preceding are ways we misinterpret information, but we can still struggle to make decisions even with a proper interpretation.

Some of this struggle comes from the pressure we feel to make the *best* decision. This pressure comes from, amongst other reasons, a glorification of efficiency, the innate desire to elevate our social status, and how easy technology has made it to compare ourselves to others.

This pressure to always make the best decision was captured in 1956 by Herbert Simon (1916-2001). Simon posits that when making decisions, people fall into one of two camps, **maximizers**, who want to make the "best" choice, and **satisficers**, who want to make the "good enough" choice. (Simon also noted that all of us are maximizers and satisficers in certain areas.) Based solely on these definitions, most of us will think that being a maximizer is preferable, but that isn't always the case.[11]

Maximizers may be more confident about their decisions but spend so much time thinking about what they turned down that they are often less satisfied. The reason is due to basic psychology and loss aversion. If you evaluate ten options and choose only one, you gain the features of the one item you chose but take the psychological equivalent of nine small losses by giving up the features of the other nine. Rather than enjoying what you have, you see what you lack.

Both approaches have healthy and unhealthy ranges. A healthy maximizer pragmatically thinks things through, while an unhealthy maximizer obsesses over frivolous details. An unhealthy satisficer borders on carelessness, while a healthy satisficer focuses on what they can control and doesn't worry about the rest. We want to find that balance. Think things through, recognize what we can control, do the best we can with what we can control, and not worry about the rest.

Besides not enjoying decisions, some maximizers struggle to make a decision at all. This is known as the "paradox of choice." If we don't choose at all, we fall back on our defaults. The problem is, sometimes our defaults aren't appropriate.

The situation usually gets worse the "bigger" the decision. The bigger the decision, the higher the stakes, and the more fearful we are of making the wrong choice. Decisions related to your retirement qualify as "big" decisions, and as we have discussed, they are made in the face of considerable uncertainty. They also represent change, and humans are wired to resist change—we prefer the familiar. Uncertainty, along with the presence of too many choices, often leads to decision paralysis. Since humans are loss averse, **status quo bias** sets in, meaning people prefer to stay where they are rather than change. This reasoning is understandable and, at times, can even be the right choice.

Trying new things is risky. If you're hiking in the forest, you're probably safer sticking to what you know than you are trying a new species of mushroom or berry you've never seen before.

Illusion of Control

Sometimes doing nothing is best. The following classic survival test, adapted from an article written by Nir Eyal, offers a wonderful demonstration.[12]

Imagine that your plane crashes in the desert. Several items survive, of which you can choose five: a pistol, jugs of water, a book on plants, a mirror, a map, a compass, a flashlight, a knife, a raincoat, etc. Which items do you choose?

What items you choose depends on what you plan on doing next. If you plan on trekking through the desert, the gun, map, compass, knife, and book on plants will be helpful. If you choose to stay where you are, items that allow you to signal for help, like a mirror, will be helpful.

Which is the best choice? In this example, staying where you are is. Search-and-rescue teams will look for your last known position, so the closer you are to that position, the more likely you are to be found.

Unsurprisingly, when given this choice in an experiment, most people do not choose to stay where they are. The **illusion of control** causes people to believe they have more control over outcomes than they actually do. Doing something (e.g., trekking through the desert) makes people *feel* like they are in control, however illusory that feeling is.

People make this mistake with money all the time, especially during market crashes. There just seems no way that doing nothing could be best. But sometimes (not always), it is.

Financial advisors can fall for (and use) the illusion of control. During the market crash in the spring of 2020, I heard many advisors proclaiming that "doing something is better than nothing." (After you read the chapter on advisors, you'll see why this "advice" is so common. Hint: doing something usually involves moving money.)

We're especially resistant to changing the status quo because we have **regret aversion**. When we choose *not to do* something, and a poor outcome follows, we feel less regret than when we choose *to do* something, and a poor outcome follows. Consider the following example, from the book *Why Smart People Make Big Money Mistakes*:

> Fred currently owns $1,000 worth of stock in Toyota. A trusted friend suggests that Fred sell it and buy $1,000 of Ford stock. Fred does not sell, and over the next year, Toyota's share price drops 30%, turning his $1,000 investment into $700.
>
> Now suppose Wilma currently owns $1,000 worth of stock in Ford. A trusted friend suggests that Wilma sell it and buy $1,000 of Toyota stock. Wilma does sell, and over the next year, Toyota's share price drops 30%, turning her $1,000 investment into a $700 stake in Toyota.
>
> Who do you think feels worse, Fred or Wilma?[13]

Both Fred and Wilma turned their $1,000 into $700. Even though they are left in the same position, it is fair to say that Wilma will be filled with more regret than Fred. Wilma chose to act, and decisions to act—to change the status quo—impart a higher level of responsibility than decisions to do nothing.[14] When we choose to do nothing, we are often protecting our future selves by attempting to prevent future regret. One of the best ways to combat this indecision is to remember that *choosing not to make a choice is itself a choice*. Whether we make changes or not, a decision is made. (Interestingly, in the long run, it is often the things we don't do that we end up regretting most, like taking a trip, starting a business, etc.)[15]

In addition to our trouble evaluating new options, our future decisions are also affected by the decisions we've already made. Sometimes we keep doing something simply because "we've already been doing it." This mindset can result from what is called **escalation of**

commitment and the separate but related **sunk cost fallacy**, which essentially says, if we've spent considerable time or money on a project or item, we are less likely to give it up or stop using it, even if it is not the best option. As Morgan Housel says, "Sunk costs make us prisoners to our past selves."[16]

We see governments, companies, sports teams, and individuals all fall victim to these two fallacies. A company realizes that a product they've worked on for two years won't work, but they don't want to "waste the time they spent," so they push on with development, even though they will waste more money by doing so. A football team doesn't want to bench their high-priced quarterback because they pay him a high salary, even though they're paying the same salary whether he plays poorly on the field or sits on the bench. A retiree doesn't want to surrender an old insurance policy for a better one because they've already paid premiums for so many years.

Once again, the flip side of this is a strength. There is value in perseverance and not quitting. But we also must understand that time or money already spent is gone, and we can't get it back. The only thing that matters is what you do next. It can be incredibly difficult to grasp the idea of sunk costs, but when you do, you'll free yourself from your past decisions, which allows you to improve your future ones.

We can also struggle to let go of things we own because, frankly, we can overvalue them. The **endowment effect** describes our tendency to retain an object we own that we would not otherwise acquire if we didn't already own it. It causes us to overvalue what we currently own and undervalue what we could own. There are numerous examples and applications of the endowment effect, but the following classic experiment describes it best.

In the experiment, half the students in a classroom were given a small item of value, in this case, a coffee mug. Those that received the mug were asked how much they would sell it for, and those who did not receive one were asked how much they would pay to buy one. The asking price of those who received the mug was twice as high as the price those who didn't receive one were willing to pay. Ownership of the item resulted in a belief that it was worth more.[17]

The best way to combat the sunk cost fallacy or endowment effect is to ask yourself, "If I didn't already own this item (or was already working on this project), how much would I pay for it (or how much time would I spend)?" Asking this can help you identify what you would do with your money or time instead.

We should also remember the effects of **anchoring** discussed in Chapter 22. Getting stuck on a number that means something to us and no one else can keep us from taking advantage of opportunities and is another example of past decisions hindering future ones.

All of this can lead to inertia and unwillingness to change. We further entrench ourselves as we tend to view people who change their minds as weak. Politicians who do so are labeled "flip-floppers," and there is pressure to "stick to our guns." This is incredibly flawed. As new information becomes available, we should always evaluate our current courses of action, and if a better way exists, we should assess the merits of making a change.

Much of this resistance comes from the idea that making a change is an admission of being wrong. Sometimes that is true, but sometimes a better way becomes available. As we discussed earlier, if you used to do something 20 years ago, and there is a better way now, it doesn't mean you were wrong for doing it the way you did. You're only wrong if you refuse to change when there's clearly a better way. It's unrealistic to think that things won't change. Remember, it's better to admit you were wrong now, and be right, than deny that you were wrong and continue to be wrong.

In *The Dip*, Seth Godin provided a tidy analogy for thinking about when we should change and when we should stick. Imagine three types of people in line at a grocery store. One picks a line and stays in it, never changing. A second person looks for the shortest line, then switches to one that moves faster and switches again when another lane moves even quicker. The third person picks a lane, and only after it becomes clear there is a better option makes a change.[18]

Of the three people, the third is what we want to be like. We don't want to never change out of stubbornness, and we don't want to jump around flippantly. We want to change when it becomes clear and obvious there is a better way.

If you resist making a change simply because you don't want to admit you were wrong, you're only hurting yourself. If you're worried about what people will say if you change your mind, I urge you to internalize a quote (questionably) attributed to John Maynard Keynes, "When the facts change, I change my mind. What do you do, sir?"

You may have noticed that many of the concepts in this chapter contradict themselves. "Don't be afraid to make a change," but "staying where you are and not overreacting can be better." "Don't be fooled by outliers in the news," but "update your views sometimes based on what is in the news." These contradictions underscore the challenge of making decisions.

One of the criticisms of discussing cognitive biases such as these is that they're not great at preventing them. Even Kahneman himself has essentially said, "I'm still going to make mistakes."[19] So, what was the point of this chapter if we're still going to make mistakes?

Remember, very few people are crazy. We all have a reason for making decisions the way that we do. The good news is, if we update our reasons, we can improve the quality of our decisions.

The authors of the book *Noise* (of which Kahneman is one) have a concept they call *decision hygiene*, which involves using decision rules to improve decision making. They compare it to washing your hands, and it is an especially apt comparison for several reasons. First, when you wash your hands, you don't know specifically what germ you are protecting against, but you know it is a good practice. Second, you will still get sick and be tempted to say it doesn't work. Since the benefits are not immediately (or ever) obvious, compliance is difficult.[20] (Remember, victory over an invisible enemy creates an invisible victory.)

We can improve the reasons we make decisions by practicing good hygiene—using decision rules, maintaining an open mind, learning from others, arguing the other side, and embracing uncertainty.

To practice good decision hygiene, start by grasping the key takeaways from this chapter. Understand our nature—cautious social beings who rely on shortcuts. Recognize the inherent limit of your knowledge and constantly update your views and seek disconfirming information. Don't be afraid to change when new information shows a clear and better way is available. Understand that confidence might feel good, but it can also blind you to what is possible. I know we like to have an established set of beliefs about the world that we can count on, and when this is disrupted, we feel a lack of control, but remember, it's better to be unsure and end up in the right place than to be confident and wrong.

A good place to start is to use the power of the question "why?" Ask, why am I making this decision? Why do I want to sell after this drop? Why do I want to buy after it's going up? Why do I think the loud bang is a gunshot? Why do I think I won't need long-term care?

Remember also; you're not always going to make the best decision. That doesn't mean you shouldn't try to, but recognizing this limitation allows you to cut yourself some slack and embrace the uncertainty. In the end, define the outcome you want to prevent or attain, recognize what you can and cannot control, make the best decision you can with the things you can control, and let the rest ride.

When making these decisions, is it better to make them on your own, or should you find someone to give you advice? Let's discuss that next.

An uncomfortable truth

An uncomfortable fact of life is that as we age, our physical and mental abilities decline. Never pleasant to think about, this fact cannot and should not be ignored. We should, however, recognize that it is natural and not something to be ashamed of.

There are two forms of intelligence. *Crystallized* intelligence refers to the accumulation of knowledge, facts, and skills acquired throughout life. *Fluid* intelligence is the ability to reason, problem-solve, and think flexibly. Both abilities peak at different points of life, and both will decline during typical retirement ages.

Keep this in mind as you plan for retirement. Declining cognitive abilities can exacerbate many of the biases we discussed. As your ability to digest information decreases, your decisions may suffer as a result. Planning who you want to help you make decisions *before* you experience any declines is crucial to protecting yourself later on.

30

ADVISORS

D o you need a financial advisor? Consider what all is involved in retirement planning. You must answer questions like: How much will I need to spend? How will my spending change? How long will my money last? What should I invest in? How often should I rebalance? How much will I pay in taxes? When should I begin receiving Social Security? Which Medicare programs should I enroll in? How should I prepare for long-term care? How much will my RMDs be? What happens to my money when I die?

Think also about what a good advisor can potentially do for you. Help answer the questions listed above. Ask questions you didn't even know to ask. Help reduce inefficiencies and save money. Boost investment returns by avoiding basic mistakes.

When you consider all of that, it seems silly to suggest you don't need some help. But, of course, there is a general distrust of advisors that leads many people to resist working with one.

I touched on some of this in the introduction. The lack of trust of advisors has created an inefficient standoff of sorts. Advisors must qualify and defend every word they utter. Retirees are either left to fend for themselves or double-check the advisor's work, both of which throw them into the sea of misinformation where for every article they find saying one thing, they can find ten more saying the other.

We know that the most common retort towards advisors is "they're just trying to sell me something." While it's easy to jump to blaming greed and poor morals, I believe most of the poor reputation results from two structural problems within the industry.

Here's the first problem. There is no clear definition of what a "financial advisor" is. Remember the gap between expectations and reality. It's easy to be disappointed if you don't know what to expect.

In a literal sense, a financial advisor is someone who gives financial advice. This broad definition includes bankers, brokers, realtors, accountants, attorneys, etc. But what most people think of as a financial advisor falls more into the "financial planning" realm. More specifically, one of the following roles:

1. **Investment Advisors** – offer investment advice and management
2. **Insurance Agents** – offer access to insurance products (e.g., life insurance and annuities)
3. **Financial Planners** – create "financial plans" (an ambiguous term we'll discuss)

Adding to the confusion is that the same advisor could wear one, several, or all of these hats. For example, one financial advisor may create financial plans and offer investment advice but isn't licensed to offer insurance, while a different advisor may offer investment advice and insurance but doesn't create financial plans. In some cases, the advisor creates financial plans but sends clients elsewhere to actually implement them. So sometimes, a bad experience working with an advisor can result from simply working with the wrong kind of advisor.

Furthermore, compared to other industries, there is no standard designation marking someone as a financial advisor. Designations like CPA, J.D., and M.D. provide a reliable signal of competence. Advisors don't have that luxury. There is a slew of designations the advisor can acquire; some are meaningful (most are not), but very few are required. To become licensed to provide investment advice, a relatively simple multiple-choice test must be passed, and an even simpler multiple-choice test must be passed to sell insurance. (Both require proper licensing with regulatory bodies, but that too is an easy process.) This low barrier to entry invites some of the bad actors who really are just there to sell you something and subsequently tarnish the reputation of the many well-meaning advisors.

So that's the first "structural" problem; there isn't structure.

We can now talk about the other problem. As I explained in the introduction, there is a difference between what people want from advisors and what advisors are incentivized to give. People want advice, but most advisors are incentivized to *move money*. This creates a murky roundabout situation where the advisor's advice is part of why they're paid, but they're only paid if their advice results in money being moved.

Take investment advisors, for example. As discussed in Chapter 22, most investment advisors charge an ongoing management fee, around 1% per year. The fee itself is not the problem; there is value in the service they provide. But here's our first roundabout. Yes, they are being paid to "advise" and manage and monitor the money, but there is no compensation until the money is moved. How about the insurance agent? The insurance agent is usually paid a commission by the company whose products they sell. Again, the commission itself is not the problem, assuming the product is a good fit for the client, but it brings us to our second roundabout. If you buy an insurance policy from an agent, yes, they did "advise" you on what kind and amount to buy, but again, there is no compensation until the policy is purchased and the money is moved.

Since advisors aren't just paid to give advice, that means ultimately, their job isn't just to give advice; it's also to convince. I believe this incentive structure is at the root of all the other angst people have towards advisors.

That being said, being convincing or persuasive isn't necessarily a bad thing. With good intentions, it can be the decent thing to do. Sometimes people need help when making a decision and may even need a "wake-up call." Just as your doctor may need to persuade you to take that blood pressure medication, your financial advisor may need to persuade you to save a little more or purchase insurance to protect against a risk you can't afford to take or don't understand exists. As long as you are being persuaded to do what is in your best interest, this persuasion is helpful. Problems arise when you are influenced to do something that is not in your best interest. The problem becomes especially sinister when the persuasion benefits the persuader more than it does the persuadee (e.g., if a doctor persuades you to take a medicine you don't really need but gets paid by the pharmaceutical company to prescribe it to you). This form of persuasion I consider manipulation. *The advisor must walk a fine line between persuasion and manipulation.*

Unless you are stashing all your money under a mattress, you will have to deal with advisors in some capacity. This chapter will look at how helpful convincing can turn into harmful manipulation, the problems that follow, and what we can do about it.

Before we get into the specifics, we must first recognize the broader problem with this incentive structure: it encourages *intervention bias*. Intervention bias occurs when a professional feels the need to do "something" (intervene) to prove their worth. For example, a doctor may feel pressure to provide treatment, or an advisor may feel pressure to move money. Some advisors might fall for intervention bias to keep up appearances and make it look like they're doing their job. But some might fall for it to protect their livelihood. Consider the following example.

Amy visits a financial advisor and asks the advisor to review her plan. The advisor reviews her plan and finds that it is perfect—it is designed exactly the way the advisor would design it, and there is nothing to change. The advisor tells Amy that she is in great shape and moves on. The advisor doesn't make any money but knows there will be other people to help. Now, imagine that 50 more people, just like Amy, visit the advisor with equally "perfect" plans. The advisor is in a tough spot. The absolute best advice they can give is to do nothing, but if they do that, they'll never make any money.

Do you see how the advisor is incentivized to "find something" to change? Even if people don't need "treatment," the advisor's livelihood depends on treating people.

The September 2020 cover of *Financial Planning* magazine succinctly captured the incentive to intervene. In an article questioning the practices of a very large and well-known company in the industry, the quote from one of the company's advisors read, "My advice, if I was going to feed my family, had to lead to some sort of sale."[1]

If the intervention or treatment isn't necessary, it can cause harm, resulting in what is called *iatrogenesis*.[2] Like a doctor performing unnecessary surgery or prescribing medicine that causes further health defects, a financial advisor can provide advice or sell financial products that destroy or detract from a client's wealth.

Financial planning companies themselves do nothing to alleviate this problem, often setting sales quotas for their employees to meet, which ratchets up the pressure to intervene. The thing is, there's a difference between setting a sales quota for t-shirts or cars and setting a quota for back surgeries or life insurance sales. (This is an important concept for the rest of the chapter. Advisors and financial companies don't do anything that any other company doesn't do. But personal finance is an intimate topic that affects all aspects of our lives, so we rightly hold the industry to a higher standard.)

So, unnecessary treatment can cause harm, but why would we get treatment if it's not necessary? Perhaps, because we're convinced to.

How are we convinced to do something? There are two parts to it. We like to think we're only convinced when the recommendation (*message*) itself is valid and will make our lives better (or "less bad"), but the truth is, sometimes we're convinced based solely on who is recommending it (*messenger*). That means both the *message* and the *messenger* can influence our decisions.

What kind of message convinces us to move money? Bear in mind that when we talk about moving money, we're really talking about selling. Selling is the process of moving someone to make a decision. Because of *status quo bias*, often people's default position is to do nothing. To make a change, we need to be persuaded. To be persuaded, we evaluate things logically and/or emotionally. Logically, we need to believe that the benefits of changing outweigh the costs. Again, this could mean "better," like gaining more, or "less bad," like preventing a loss. Emotionally, we need to imagine or experience an uncomfortable feeling we wish to avoid or a pleasurable feeling we wish to attain (which is a subtle manifestation of greed and fear). To keep it simple, we're convinced to act when we believe our lives will be better because of our action.

Let's talk about what makes a message convincing. For some, numbers carry a special level of validity; it's not true until the spreadsheet confirms it. So to appeal to our logic, explicitly quantifying how much better or worse off we'll be can be very convincing. The problem is, when projecting financial numbers, we usually make assumptions, and assumptions can be massaged. A few small tweaks can drastically change the conclusion.

Contributing to this problem is the fact that there is no standard way to present financial numbers, such as investment returns. You can slice and dice them any which way. There are multiple ways to calculate averages, multiple time periods you can use, and even multiple definitions of the "stock market" or "bond market." It can be a little bit like saying that a Ford F-150 gets 26 mpg and a Toyota Camry gets 28 mpg. Sure, I'm quoting highway mileage of one and city mileage of the other, but who needs to know?

This squishiness is why I dislike using projections when meeting with clients and why I did not include any case studies in this book; because I know how subjective the entire exercise is. An unscrupulous advisor can essentially shape whatever conclusion or outcome they want. For example, if they want an investment to look worse, they can choose a slightly different time period to calculate the average return. If they want it to look better, they can use the simple average rather than the compound average return. These small changes can seem innocent and may be imperceptible to the client, but as we saw in Chapter 2, just 1% per year can drastically change the outcome.

Many times, who wins the client's business (does the best job of convincing) comes down to who's willing to show better numbers, which incites the "Illustration Wars" I've previously mentioned. This is why advisors hate giving away their proposals for clients to shop around with; because they know the next advisor just needs to show a better outcome than they did to win your business. Sadly, deciding to illustrate well can be a lucrative business strategy. Like the adage, "It's easier to ask for forgiveness than permission," it can be profitable to overpromise and underdeliver. If things don't work out, the advisor can say sorry but still gets paid.

Some people aren't interested in numbers, so stories are the way to communicate. Stories are obviously powerful communication tools, but just like numbers, they can be edited for production. As we'll see shortly, the best convincers are usually the best storytellers.

No matter how good the numbers look or stories sound, they won't convince us unless they are plausible. We tend to equate plausibility with believability due to what is known as *processing fluency*—the easier a thought is to picture, the more it makes sense, the less our brain has to work, and the more drawn to the idea we become.[3] So, the more plausible and believable the message, the more convincing it is. The best (most persuasive) messages link the consequence or outcome to your action or inaction.

This may all seem obvious; that our brains prefer the path of least resistance, and believable stories are convincing. But there is something deeper going on. When we make decisions on our own, the areas of our brain involving critical thinking, like probability weighting, are active. But when we receive advice, these areas are inactive—even if the advice is bad. This inactivity is called "cognitive offloading." Interestingly, these effects were found to be especially applicable under two conditions. 1) When dealing with uncertainty. 2) When the advice-giver (messenger) is considered an "expert."[4] Since these happen to be the most common conditions under which retirees meet with advisors, the retiree is especially vulnerable to the messenger.

Let's now talk about the messenger. It's a fact of life that it doesn't just matter what was said; it also matters who said it. You've probably experienced a fairly innocent example of this with a child or spouse.

Someone else can tell them the same thing you've said 100 times, and they finally listen. Whether or not we follow financial advice also depends on who gives it.

What we're really looking for is someone we can trust. When it comes to what makes a messenger convincing and trustworthy, there are *hard* factors and *soft* factors.[5]

Soft factors include things like appearances and personality. There's a reason that almost every financial advisor you see in a commercial or advertisement is wearing a suit. It's the same reason pharmaceutical companies put actors in white coats in their commercials; it creates a signal of competence. Advisors can play into this, and the danger, of course, is that these soft factors can easily be faked.

It's also true that we often trust people we like. Very often, the reason someone chooses to work with an advisor is that they "liked him or her." It's easy to see why someone who is likable and a good storyteller can be quite convincing. While this is understandable and not necessarily bad, simply liking someone is not reason enough to listen to their financial advice. There's an old saying that sadly is fairly accurate, "to be a successful financial advisor, you need a good personality and a deep Rolodex."

Hard factors are supposed to be more tangible, like competence. We know that one of the easiest ways to signal competence is with confidence. In the introduction, the example of the two pilots showed how confidence could be used to create the illusion of competence.

As we just learned, when we're less familiar with a topic or uncertain of what will happen, we are especially drawn to confidence. Whether it is a doctor, a politician, or an advisor, we want to hear, "You *will* be okay," not "You *might* be okay." We want to hear, "You *will* get 8% per year," not "You *might* get 8% per year." Imagine two candidates running for political office. Candidate A says emphatically, "I will cut your taxes!" while Candidate B offers, "I will try to cut your taxes, but with a split Congress, I'll likely get shot down, and it will take several years to pass." Who are you more likely to vote for? Which candidate was more accurate?

There is a difference between precision and accuracy. A precise number, 8.24%, sounds better than a range, 7-9%, but the range is more accurate. We are drawn to the certainty of a precise number but are lying to ourselves if we think we possess that level of foresight in the topics financial planning deals with.

Sometimes even a range is inaccurate, as the possible outcomes may be unknown. In that case, "I don't know" may be the most accurate answer. But we don't like that answer and often punish someone willing to give it, considering it a sign of weakness that undermines their authority. Even if it is the honest and correct answer, people (i.e., advisors) shy away from those words and are incentivized to proclaim something as fact even when they know it's nothing more than a guess.

We can learn a lot about a person from the language they use. Shane Parrish, the founder of the brilliant blog Farnam Street, perfectly describes this.

"Generally, the people who know the most about something talk in terms that involve uncertainty (e.g., generally, if, but, yet, possible, unlikely). People that know the least tend to talk in absolutes (e.g., always, will, never). The language you read and hear, be it online or in person, is a proxy for quality. While we have a tendency to seek out certainty, nuance is generally more accurate."[6]

In the book *Noise*, the authors say something similar when talking about what personality traits we should look for in people we listen to:

> The personality of people with excellent judgment may not fit the generally accepted stereotype of a decisive leader….if the goal is to reduce error, it is better for leaders (and others) to remain open to counterarguments and to know that they might be wrong. If they end up being decisive, it is at the end of a process, not at the start.[7]

That description sounds like someone who embraces uncertainty. I have a personal test for confidence. Ask someone, "What do you think the market will do?" The more specific the answer, the more red flags should be raised.

Since we know that confidence can create the illusion of

competence, are there more concrete factors we can use to gauge an advisor's competence? What about investment returns? The number of clients they work with? How much money they manage?

If you were unfamiliar with an industry and wanted to know who the top performers were, you would probably start by finding out who is the highest paid. But this can lead to some flawed conclusions when we do the same thing with advisors. Here's why.

Advisors are paid to move money, and the more money they move, the more money they make. If an advisor moves (and therefore, makes) a lot of money, this usually means either one of two things. First, it could mean that they work with "big" accounts, which signals that wealthy people trust them. This can be taken as a further signal of competence due to the *halo effect* often applied to wealthy people. (We think wealthy people are good with money, so if a person who is good with money chooses to work with an advisor, then we think the advisor must be good). Second, if an advisor makes a lot of money, it could mean that they work with a lot of people, which is usually a reliable signal of *social proof*. Social proof effectively means the more people we see doing/buying/using something, the more valid it must be. So we think the more people who trust, follow, or work with the advisor, the more competent the advisor must be. Advisors can encourage this perception by sharing pictures of client events, making reference to the size of their client base, etc.

Within the industry, the attitude of equating production and competence is perpetuated. (Instead of calling it "moving money," the industry calls it "production," so advisors are often measured by their "level of production," e.g., premium sold or assets under management.) Companies hand out awards to their "top producers," prestigious groups exist that can only be joined by meeting certain production thresholds, and exotic trips are reserved for the biggest producers.

But if we're trying to measure the quality of an advisor's advice, production may not be the best measure. Why? Think about how an advisor "produces," by moving money. They move money by making sales. So really, a top producer is a top salesperson. This leads to my climactic point: *giving good advice and making a sale is not the same thing.* Sometimes the top salesperson also gives the best advice, but it would be naïve to think this is always the case.[8] I can think of no better example to illustrate the discrepancy between giving good advice and making a sale than the following true story (names changed).

In February 2020, Jan was considering selling $1M of her $3M investment account to fund an annuity. Before she sold, her investments dropped by almost 40%, to $1.8M. Concerned about further losses, Jan still wanted to fund the annuity, which would require her to sell her investments at depressed prices. The advisor recommended she wait, and her account recovered nicely (above the original $3M).

By not selling, her investments recovered over a million dollars in value. The advisor would have made a nice commission by selling her the annuity but made no money since he advised against it.

To me, this is a serious problem. The best advice (not selling at depressed prices) makes Jan a lot of money and the advisor none. The worst advice (selling at depressed prices) makes the advisor a lot of money and costs Jan dearly.

Guess who didn't qualify for the company trip that year? Remember, it's the advisors who move the most money that make the "top advisors" lists. *Companies don't give awards for talking people out of buying their products.*

Measuring advisors by their level of production is one way to judge competence and compare them. What other signals can we use? Remember, there is no clear designation marking someone as a financial advisor. However, there are other designations advisors can buy to expand the alphabet soup following their signature. As I mentioned earlier, some are meaningful, most are not, but all are valuable to the designation provider.

One particular designation growing in popularity due to a tremendous marketing budget on behalf of the designation provider is the Certified Financial Planner® (CFP).[9] The CFP is certainly one of the more rigorous designations an advisor can earn, but I find many people confuse it with how the CPA works for accountants. For accountants, being a CPA is often required to perform certain roles. The same is not true of the CFP and financial advisors. The CFP is an elective certification offered by a non-profit organization with no regulatory authority.

Certain sects of the financial planning industry deride the CFP with names like the "Certified Failure Planner." Anytime you hear comments like this, or even comments like mine in this chapter, you must ask why they feel that way? Is it a true disagreement or a way to disparage something they don't have? Personally, I understand the allure of these types of designations. It's a way for the advisor to show they care, and it's fun to learn. But I also recognize their limited value and that they're equal parts validity and vanity.

We need to see these designations for what they are, a signal that a person put in some work and invested in their career. They are not necessary and certainly don't mean the advisor will give "better" advice, but they do show a willingness to try.

Given the issues with designations, advisors may resort to other signals of competence. One such signal is to craft an image as an "authority figure." (Because, in theory, people listen to and take advice from "authority figures.") The most common way to do this is to leverage a longstanding human belief; that those published in newspapers/magazines/books, seen on TV, and heard on the radio, have a superior level of expertise or authority. Perhaps more games are played in this area than in any other we'll discuss.

Here's an example of how this works. When reading an advisor's bio, or evaluating their website, seeing the words "As seen on:" followed by a list of well-known media logos is a powerful tool. The implication is that if these media companies are willing to publish them, the advisor must have some knowledge, expertise, or authority.

This authority can sometimes be valid. But it's also true that advisors can pay to join groups that allow them to be published on these outlets. Very often, the advisor doesn't even create the content themselves.

This strategy also extends to radio. It's a surprisingly simple process to buy airtime and launch a radio show. Some advisors carefully create their content and put a lot into their show. I love that. But there are also "radio farms" that buy the airtime, write your scripts, schedule celebrity guests to buddy up with you, etc., all with the goal of exploiting the illusion of authority that radio provides.

Part of me thinks this is neat that advisors can share their messages through these channels. But you have to admit it feels a little different if you know they're paying to be there, and I lose all respect when I know they're not doing any of it themselves.

The area I'm especially sensitive to is books. Books are one of the greatest communicating tools in human history. It is an opportunity for the author and reader to spend an extended period together and provides a forum to more fully explain concepts not easily grasped in short meetings or over the airwaves. Some of the most applicable information on financial planning I've learned has come from books written by other advisors. However, some of the biggest loads of crap I've ever read have come from books "written" by advisors as well.

Here's the game that can be played. Before writing this book, I was offered to have a book written for me. I was told, "Just create the outline, and our ghostwriter will fill in the rest. Then we'll publish it, publicize it, and make you a local celebrity." Hmm.

If you think I'm kidding, see the following email I recently received. I thought it was a prank, but sadly, it is not. (I'm only showing the header of the email, but believe me, the body is even worse.)

FIGURE 30 1: Real offer to have a book written for you

"How to <u>Get Paid to Write</u> Your Own Best-Selling Financial Book without Ever Typing a Word"

"And Then Transform Your Best-Selling Book into a Powerful Client Attraction Mechanism that Magnetically Attracts Highly Qualified, Perfectly-Suited Clients"

Let me be clear with all of this. I have zero issues with an advisor wanting to advertise themselves or their message. In fact, I admire it. I have serious problems, though, with making a sham of the entire process and doing so only with the intent of creating an illusion of authority to increase compliance with their advice.

The takeaway is this: don't be fooled by an illusion of competence. A bio that says, "Published on *insert publication,* author of *insert book name,* and appeared on *insert TV station,*" may seem impressive, but ask yourself why you are impressed. After writing this entire book myself, I can tell you that writing a book is not proof of knowledge or authority. It is merely proof of the hardheadedness to finish a mind-numbing task. (However, writing a "good book" provides more evidence than simply completing a book.) As for being on TV, well, we should all know that competence is hardly a requirement to be on TV.

The incentive to be confident and brand themself as an "expert" or "authority figure" is not unique to advisors. But this raises an interesting question. Are advisors "experts?"

First, we should ask, what makes an expert? A simple definition is someone whose judgments can be trusted to be accurate. Some fields can have true experts, for example, weather forecasters. (Yes, I know they're wrong a lot, but they're also right way more often.) They are true experts because we can evaluate their judgments against actual results. In other fields, we cannot easily verify judgments. Financial advisors fall into this second category. It's true that we can verify the records of some economic and market forecasters, but in the domain of financial planning, where there are questions such as, when should I take Social Security, and do I need life insurance, we usually cannot. These unverifiable experts are called "respect-experts"—people who are revered as experts based on the respect they enjoy from peers rather than from verifiable proof of their judgments.[10] (Something to ponder: What makes an advisor respected? Is it production? Remember what leads to production.)

Here's an example of the dilemma of respect-experts. You could ask ten different investment "experts" what the market will do next year and receive ten different answers. Not only will they disagree, but we know at least nine, and probably all ten, will be wrong, yet we listen to them. Why? Because we respect their authority.

Nassim Taleb has shared similar thoughts on the expert problem, but the definition of "respect-experts" I found most applicable to financial advisors comes again from the book *Noise*. The following passage talks about a common attribute of respect-experts.

> Another characteristic of respect-experts is their ability to make and explain their judgments with confidence. We tend to put more trust in people who trust themselves than we do in those who show their doubts. The confidence heuristic points to the fact that in a group, confident people have more weight than others, even if they have no reason to be confident. Respect-experts excel at constructing coherent stories. Their experience enables them to recognize patterns, to reason by analogy with previous cases, and to form and confirm hypotheses quickly. They easily fit the facts they see into a coherent story that inspires confidence.[11]

Those are sobering words from several of the most revered minds in psychology that also sound a lot like the top advisors we've described.

Let's recap our discussion so far. Part of an advisor's job is to convince, and sometimes convincing can tip into manipulation. We can be convinced based on the message and the messenger. Convincing messengers are usually confident and convincing messages link your action or inaction to a better (less bad) or more pleasurable (less painful) outcome. If I had to summarize how to convince someone, it would be with this:

Confidently tell a **plausible** story that **appeals** to either **emotion** of fear or greed.

If you understand that sentence, then you'll begin to make sense of the advertising in the industry. Too much optimism sounds like a sales pitch, so most advisors and firms aren't so bold as to explicitly say, "you'll have more money if you work with me," but they can appeal to the other things people want, like safety and certainty. (In terms of greed and fear, safety is the "lack of fear.") I'm struck by some of the current slogans of large firms in the industry. Some include "Life well planned," "Retire with confidence," and "Talk to us today, feel comfortable about tomorrow." Another company talks about the "Planning Effect," and the commercial shows someone happily mediating and uses words like "zen." It's all about certainty. They know what people want, and they want people to know they can give it to them.

While it's absolutely true that working with an advisor, thinking things through, and putting a plan together, can provide a higher level of confidence and certainty, we must remember that financial planning involves projecting the future, and absolute certainty cannot be had. While confidence sells, it can also blind, and we must guard against manipulation. Once again, embracing uncertainty instead of denying or resisting it is the key.

So what can you do? Despite the issues of conflicting interests, marketing games, and illusions of competence and authority, there are a few steps you can take to protect yourself when dealing with the advising industry. In accounting, we recognize we cannot eliminate every mistake, but we can drastically reduce them by implementing "internal controls," which are, in a sense, guardrails and checks and balances to prevent obvious errors. We can implement our own internal controls by choosing an advisor with the following three attributes. (*Full disclosure, my firm and I share all three of these characteristics. To be clear, we built the firm this way because of the list; I didn't create the list because our firm is that way.*)

1. Fiduciaries

Fiduciaries are held to the fiduciary standard, which means they are legally bound to do what is in your best interest. Working with a fiduciary does not guarantee you will receive good advice, but it does give you legal recourse if you can prove the advice you were given was not in your best interest.

Many people are surprised to learn that not all advisors are held to this standard. The other standard that exists is the suitability standard, which requires the advisor to do what is *consistent* with your best interests. See the difference with this example.

Product A is best for you and pays the advisor $X. Product B is appropriate but not as good as Product A and pays the advisor 10% more. A fiduciary *must* recommend Product A since that is the best product for your needs. An advisor held to the suitability standard can recommend Product B since it is *consistent* with your best interests.

2. Independent

To understand the value of independence, let's use car shopping as an example. Imagine you are shopping for a vehicle, and you go to the Chevrolet dealership. You need a certain feature that isn't available on the Chevy but is available on the Ford model. Do you expect the Chevy salesperson to point this out to you? Just as not all cars and trucks are the same, neither are all investment or insurance products. A Chevy salesperson can't sell you a Ford, and a non-independent advisor can't offer you competing insurance or investment products.

While a lack of independence is not an immediate deal-breaker, this limitation should at least be disclosed and understood. I do not doubt that there are upstanding Chevy salespeople who are willing to send you to the Ford dealership; I just understand that more often than not, that won't happen.

There are also "degrees" of independence. Here's a true example. Owen was having a conversation with a dear friend and fellow advisor who works in the wealth management arm of a very large national bank. They were discussing the long-term care insurance products of a particular company when our friend mentioned, "Yeah, I offer both versions of their product." Owen asked, what do you mean, "both?" At the time, the insurance company they were discussing offered six very distinct versions of the product. Unbeknownst to our friend, his company only allowed employees to offer two versions of this product.

You might think this is no big deal. Aren't all insurance products pretty much the same? Well, no, but I can explain by continuing with our car dealership analogy. Suppose for a minute that the only pickup truck Ford offers is the Ranger (a much smaller version than the popular F-150). Ryan visits the Ford dealership needing a truck for his construction business. What is the Ford representative to do? He can offer Ryan a Ranger, which is indeed a pickup truck, but it has far less capacity than, say, a Chevy Silverado, which would better suit Ryan's needs. The representative's hands are tied, and he's in a tough position. In this (hypothetical) example, the Ford representative's company does not offer a product that solves Ryan's problem. He can offer the Ranger, which is suitable, but he can't really solve Ryan's problem, and it's very unlikely he'll recommend Ryan look at the Chevy.

Two other problems arise from this example. First, the Ford representative may not even know that Chevy has a truck that is better suited to Ryan's needs. The parallel with advisors is that they often know their own products extremely well but are less likely to be familiar with what else is out there. They may also honestly believe their product is the best, not just because it is to their benefit to sell them, but because of the effects of confirmation bias. If you surround yourself with people who also believe your product is best, like coworkers and fellow salespeople, it will be difficult to conclude anything to the contrary.

Second, if the representative does sell Ryan a Ranger, he can tell the regulators that he acted in Ryan's interest by selling him a pickup truck, even though it wasn't the best truck for his needs.

3. Strategy Agnostic

We've seen several times throughout this book how investments and insurance compete against each other. Some advisors are only licensed to offer one. Others may offer both but either choose to or are forced to focus on one. Working with someone who understands and uses both tools will help eliminate some of this conflict.

We can revisit the decision between annuities and withdrawal strategies to see an example. People often view annuities and withdrawal strategies as a "one or the other" decision. If an advisor is only licensed to sell insurance or only licensed to manage investments, then it truly is a "one or the other" decision for them. But an advisor who is licensed to offer both can serve you regardless of what you choose and will cut down on this conflict as much as possible. (But it cannot eliminate the conflict, as discussed next.)

Not all compensation is created equal

Even an advisor who is an independent fiduciary and strategy agnostic is not without conflict. Remember, "best interest" is still subjective, and there can be two right answers. It's also true that not all transactions compensate the advisor the same way. It would be ignorant to think this doesn't ever affect an advisors' advice. The following example highlights the potential conflicts an advisor faces when deciding whether to recommend investments or insurance.

Most investment managers charge a fee, for example, 1%, which can be charged annually. Insurance products, on the other hand, often front-load their compensation. Annuities, for instance, may pay 6% of the total premium in year one.

Let's assume you are contemplating how to generate income from your $1,000,000 of savings. If the advisor manages your money, they can charge 1%, $10,000, in fees every year. If they sell you an annuity, they'll be paid 6%, $60,000, in year one.

While the advisor can tell you, and mean it, that it is in *their* best interest long-term if they manage your money as they will be able to charge you a fee for longer, the temptation of a big upfront payday is a real thing.

It's not just the upfront payday that's attractive. An insurance sale is usually a one-time transaction, which makes for a lot less work than the ongoing process of managing an investment account. It also provides more certainty for the advisor. Investment balances change constantly, and if the retiree is spending down their account, then fee revenue is decreasing as well. There are also no guarantees you won't fire the advisor and move your money after a few years. All of these factors can incentivize the advisor to take the upfront payday that insurance offers.

I do not mean to imply these are the thoughts of every insurance agent. I'm simply laying out the factual conflicts that can exist between investment advisors and insurance agents, which can be the same person.

Again, working with someone with these three characteristics—fiduciary, independent, and strategy agnostic—does not guarantee you won't receive bad advice. Advisors are human and will get things wrong. However, these characteristics provide you with as much built-in protection as possible.

Let's suppose that you have chosen to work with an advisor. How much should you pay them? Below are the three most common ways advisors are compensated. Some are paid all three ways, some just one way, and some a combination of ways. Let's look at each a little closer.

1. Commissions
2. Management fees
3. Planning fees

1. Commissions

Commissions are most commonly associated with insurance products, although some investment products pay commissions as well (this is becoming much less common). Insurance commissions are submitted to, filed with, and approved by each state's Insurance Commission, meaning the advisor has no discretion over how much the commission is.* As a policyholder, there's little you can do about commissions other than to understand that they exist and that it's illegal for advisors to return any form of their commission to the policyholder (this is called rebating). Keep in mind you are always entitled to ask how much the commission is on any insurance sale.

(By the way, a rule was proposed that would have required

---

* Some companies will offer increases in compensation as the advisors sends them more business. In this case, the advisor has some discretion, but even these rates, the advisor cannot control.

disclosure of commissions on most insurance sales. Take a guess who fought and ultimately prevented the rule from passing?)

I know commissions are a dirty word but try to understand them from the company's perspective. Every company needs to distribute its product, and commissions are part of the distribution channel of a company. The company needs and wants to distribute as much of its product as possible (to a point) and thus must properly incentivize its distribution channel. If the incentive is too small, then no product is sold. If the incentive is too large, then abuse can happen. Yes, if they put less money towards the distribution channel, they could put more money towards the product, but this can also be said about the compensation of all company employees (e.g., actuaries, accountants, executives), the rent for the office, marketing costs, etc. We must draw the line somewhere.

While most can understand why commissions exist and agree that they are a necessary evil, a greater debate, and one we will not have here, is how much commissions should be.

2. Management fees

While commissions are highly regulated, and advisors have little say over them, investment management fees give the advisor considerably more discretion. Fees can range anywhere from a few basis points all the way up to 2.75% per year (1 basis point = 0.01%. 2.75% = 275 basis points), which is the statutory maximum. Most management fees are close to 1%. In my opinion, this is the most an advisor should charge, and in certain situations, this number may be too high. Technology has provided tremendous cost savings to the advisor, and there are simply too many other homogeneous options available to justify a fee much above the 1% threshold. As technology continues to make our jobs as advisors easier, these cost savings should be passed on to investors, continuing to lower fees into the future.

As discussed in Chapter 22, paying to outperform the market is no longer a valid rationalization for high investment management fees. However, they may be able to perform better than you could and can help increase your returns by improving your investing behavior, but there are limits to how much you should pay for this. The things that are worth paying for are A) expertise, B) service and ease of use, and C) behavioral management.

3. Planning fees

What constitutes a "financial plan" is extremely ambiguous. By nature, it will mean different things to different people at different stages of life and will also depend on what the planner is licensed to offer. As a result, planning fees are completely discretionary. They can be one-time or ongoing. They can be a hundred dollars or several thousand dollars.

There is some confusing terminology that surrounds financial planners and advisors. Some advisors are considered *fee-only,* which means they are not allowed to make a commission. That sounds nice, but it means if they recommend an investment or insurance product to you and it pays a commission, you will have to go elsewhere to purchase it. While fee-only advisors cannot earn commissions, they can charge investment management fees.

Fee-based advisors (different from fee-only advisors) are allowed to charge investment management fees and earn commissions. While at first, this may sound greedy, it can be more convenient. Rather than having to find another advisor to purchase a product from, as you would working with a fee-only advisor, a fee-based advisor can sell you the product you agreed to. In theory, a fee-based advisor could charge a planning fee *and* make a commission. In reality, most fee-based advisors either 1) do not charge a planning fee or 2) waive the planning fee if there are commissions or investment fees involved.

The increase in awareness of fees and advisor compensation in the financial services industry has mostly been a positive for society. A serious amount of fat has been trimmed, and I applaud that. Like all things, though, the pendulum can swing too far. Some people hear the word "fee" or "commission" and immediately close their minds, which may cause them to miss the bigger picture. A couple of points to keep in mind.

First, you must make sure you are comparing apples to apples. If I told you that Car A has a "fee" of $1,000 and Car B has a fee of $10,000, which car would you buy? It would probably help to know what kind of cars they are first. If Car A is a rusted-out 1975 Ford Pinto, $1,000 might be a rip-off. If Car B is a mint 1968 Ford Mustang GT (which recently sold at auction for $3.74M),[12] $10,000 might be the deal of a lifetime.

Second, you must make sure you are considering the net figures. Imagine Couple A sells their house without a realtor for $500,000 and saves themselves the 6% realtor commission. Couple B sells the identical house next door using a realtor for $550,000. Which couple is better off? Couple B is, who, after paying commissions, netted $517,000 compared to Couple A, who netted $500,000. Not paying a commission does not always mean you got the better deal. You must look at the net number (value).

Third, whether you are hiring a realtor, financial advisor, or anyone with a principal-agent relationship, *you have the most skin in the game.* We can again use an example of a realtor negotiating the sale of your home to explain.

Assume you have an offer on your home for $500,000, and your realtor stands to earn the standard 6% commission. If you could find a buyer for $520,000, you'll be happy as you'll be $18,800 better off (the increase in price minus realtor commissions). The realtor, who already stands to earn $30,000 with the current offer, will also be better off but by only $1,200. While this may still be motivating, you have far more skin in the game than the realtor, and your level of motivation to pursue the higher offer will be different. This same difference exists with investment advisors who charge a management fee. It's true they'll be better off if your account grows, but the difference may not be that impactful compared to how they're already doing by having you as a client.

People usually view commissions as something to be avoided, and as a result, there is an expanding offering of "commission-free" insurance products available today. It may come as a surprise, but many of these are actually inferior (in terms of the features and benefits they offer to the policyholder) to commissioned products. (Partly because there is no knowledgeable agent to point out these inferiorities.) Again, always evaluate what you are receiving before immediately closing your mind to something just because a fee or commission exists.

I do not mean to suggest in these examples that you will be better off if you pay a fee. My point is simply to be sure you always evaluate what you are receiving for the fee. If there is an equal exchange of value for the price being paid, both parties should be happy or, at the very least, feel like the transaction was fair.

Some people have a problem with advisor compensation because they claim they can do the same things themselves. While this can be true, there are plenty of examples of goods and services people pay for that they can either make or do themselves, such as mowing your yard, changing your oil, or cooking a meal. Remember the trade between time and money. Some things are worth paying for.

When choosing whether or not to work with an advisor, you must ask yourself two questions:

1. *Can I do what they do?* Do you have the skills and expertise to manage all of these moving parts? If you do not, then you probably need help. If you do, you must ask yourself the next question.

2. *Do I want to do what they do?* Do you have the time and mental energy? If you do, is that how you want to spend it? Just like the lawn mowing example, we all pay for things that we could do ourselves. Granted, the decision is different, given that the size of the expense is typically greater in financial planning than in lawn maintenance, but so is the size of the consequence if you mess something up.

There's actually a third question that needs to be asked. *Will* I be able to do what they do? As I touched on last chapter, cognitive decline is real. I encourage you to think through these questions before the effects of cognitive decline start to creep in. You can protect yourself by planning in advance who will help you, whether it is a family member, trusted friend, or a professional.

Your personality can also help determine if or what kind of advisor is best to work with. I find there are three personality types, each suited to working with a different kind of advisor. As always, there are pros and cons to each.

1. Do-it-yourselfer

DIYers rely on themselves. They change their own oil, mow their own yard, invest their own money, etc. The DIYer fluctuates between thrifty and greedy, practical and inefficient. The DIYer is best served by either a robo advisor or straight up using the infinite resources of the internet to find their way.

2. Delegator

Delegators are the masters of outsourcing and can be both efficient and naïve. They are efficient because they don't spend time doing something that someone who knows more can easily do for them. They can be naïve because they can easily be taken advantage of if they are unfamiliar with the task at hand. A delegator is best served by the full-service financial planning professional who manages their money for them.

3. Collaborator

The collaborator is a blend of the do-it-yourselfer and the delegator. They work alongside an advisor, seeking guidance, but typically still like to have the final say. They will consider advice rather than outright follow advice. Collaborators try to get the best of both worlds but often end up stuck between independence and dependence. The collaborator is best served by the advisor who charges for advice by the hour by the project. This gives them someone they can check in with but is cheaper than the full-service advisor whose work they'll end up doing a chunk of themselves.

Working with and choosing an advisor is not a decision to take lightly. It can be life-changing in both a good and bad way. While the financial advising industry is clearly far from perfect, the services it provides are still valuable and necessary. People still have questions and need help deciding what to do with their money. Since financial planning firms and advisors are unavoidable, you need to know how to deal with the industry.

I hope the spirit of this chapter came across properly. I recognize this was lengthy, but I feel it was important because it's not a fair fight. There is "asymmetry of information" between advisor and client, no different than the asymmetry between doctor and patient. You can Google all you want, but they're still going to know more, and if they really want to, they can use that asymmetry to their advantage. This chapter aimed to point out some of the ways this happens and how to guard against it.

I started this chapter by asking, "Do you need a financial advisor?" I think most people would agree that if they could find someone competent that they could trust and that charges a fair price, they would hire that person. The challenge is finding them. They are out there; you just need to know what to look for and where to find them.

BrokerCheck them out

Deciding who to accept advice from and help manage your life's savings is a big decision. One way to learn about investment advisors (but not all financial advisors) is through BrokerCheck, a database provided by FINRA (a regulatory body). Visit www.brokercheck.finra.org and enter the individual or firm's name to find background information on an advisor. You'll see a snapshot of an advisor's employment history, investment-related licensing information, as well their history of arbitration and complaints.

31

PARTING THOUGHTS

I n the introduction, I said this book is about making better financial decisions when we don't know what will happen next. I said it would be part technical and part conceptual. I also said it wouldn't be light on information. Since we covered quite a bit, let's review and summarize the main points.

We started by defining our basic needs and what money is, a tool we use to meet those needs. To acquire money, we usually trade our time for it by going to work. To make sure we can meet our needs in the future, we set aside some of the money we have today. This money we set aside, we want to grow. How much it can grow and how much it can shrink depends on where we put it. All through life, money comes in, goes out, and grows or shrinks in between. Once we think we'll have enough money to meet our future needs, we stop trading our time for it and retire.

Usually, our biggest fear in retirement is that we'll run out, which really means that we'll have to cut back on and change our lifestyle. Wanting to avoid this, we plan. When we plan, we make assumptions about what money will come in and out and what it will do in between over some length of time. Making these assumptions requires us to make choices, and making choices require us to make tradeoffs. We balance now with tomorrow, needs with wants, risk with return, and ultimately, greed with fear.

How we strike these balances determines what tools we use. Tools are places to put our money, like cash, bonds, stocks, insurance, and real estate. Nothing about a tool is good or bad; they simply do what they do. It's only bad when we use the wrong tool for the job. Most people's problem with financial tools isn't with how they are designed but with how they are described.

To keep track of the projections of our assumptions, we built a framework. We identified the five variables, 1) beginning balance, 2) spending (the net amount of our inflows and outflows), 3) rate of return, 4) time, and 5) ending balance. We also identified the seven key assumptions in a financial plan, 1) how long we'll live, 2) how much we'll spend, 3) what inflation will be, 4) what taxes will be, 5) what unexpected expenses we might encounter, 6) what rate of return we'll earn, and 7) what order the returns will be in.

Our goal for retirement determines which variable we solve for and which variables we assume. Ultimately, we really only have control over two of these variables, spending and return. Beginning balance is more of a fact, ending balance is a function of the other four, and time (how long we live) isn't easily controlled (at least ethically.) As a result, most of our plans come down to either assuming how much we'll spend to determine what return we need or assuming what return we'll earn to determine how much we can spend. The greatest unknown in any retirement plan is how long we will live.

We also saw how sensitive the outcome of our plan is to small changes in these assumptions. We run out of money when reality differs too much from our expectations which underscores how important our assumptions and predictions are.

Given this importance, we next looked closely at the process of prediction. Most people look at what has happened (history) to guess what will happen, but we saw how fickle history can be; it reveals much but conceals even more. It tells us what did happen but doesn't show us what all could have happened. While we look at history backward, we live life forward. We make decisions at the starting line, and retrospectively determining what we "should have" done only leads to resentment and regret. We saw again and again that the outcome does not determine the quality of a decision. Good decisions can have bad outcomes, and bad decisions can have good outcomes. A good decision is one that minimizes the possibility that stuff we don't want to happen happens.

We also took a look at the most common way to analyze history—using statistics. We saw that statistics, such as averages, are powerful when applied to large groups or multiple attempts but less helpful when dealing with a single instance, which is how we live life. The law of large numbers doesn't work so well when applied to small numbers.

Having built an understanding of what retirement is and a framework to analyze our decisions, we next took a deep dive into the different assumptions we make and the tools we use.

We looked at life expectancy and how it is calculated. We learned that life expectancy measures the midpoint when a group of people is expected to die, which means half the population lives longer. We also saw that certain factors like gender and education greatly affect how long you are expected to live, and the combined life expectancy of couples is much longer than the average of two individuals.

We then looked at our spending and how our total spending is a function of both quantity and price. While prices may increase, the quantity of our purchases may decrease, which quiets the effect of inflation. When it comes to inflation, we are mostly concerned about the price of the things we buy, which means we will each have our own inflation rate (CPI-YOU). We saw how to disaggregate our spending, illuminating the difference between expenses that are discretionary and non-discretionary, variable and fixed. This process allows us to determine our Retirement Adjusted Spending Amount (RASA), which provides a map for imagining what is likely to change from both a quantity and price perspective.

Next, we looked at ways to limit our outflows by using insurance. We looked at why insurance was created and how it can be used. The important takeaways are that the more likely you are to need it, the more it will cost, and you have to buy it before you know for sure you will need it. While it's tempting to compare insurance to saving and investing, this exercise can miss the point, as insurance exists not to make you rich but to keep you from becoming poor. Quantitatively, we saw that the decision of whether to buy insurance or instead save and invest will depend on factors such as 1) the spread between premiums and benefits, 2) when you need it, and 3) what your money could do instead (rate of return).

The most common expenses we insure against are related to health care, so we looked at health care costs in the form of both major medical and long-term care. We reviewed Medicare, the different options, and the different ways to structure our coverage. We looked at long-term care, what it is, how much it costs, and how to protect ourselves with different kinds of insurance. We compared long-term care to a torpedo—it may miss you and be nothing, but if it hits you, it can be devastating.

Continuing our discussion of things that aren't fun to talk about, we next looked at taxes. The variables that matter are 1) what is taxable, 2) at what rate, and 3) when. The great challenge is that all three of these will change over time.

We then turned the discussion towards inflows. Most of us have outside sources of income that include Social Security, and we looked at how to think about the decision of when to start receiving benefits. Mathematically, the longer you live, the later you should take it, but there are other factors to consider, such as what your other money is invested in and where your income will come from. Similarly, we touched on pensions and, when applicable, how to think about the lump sum versus income stream decision.

If our outside sources of income will not meet our spending needs, we must generate income from our savings. Our savings must be held somewhere and will earn some rate of return. We looked in-depth at the relationship between risk and return. We discussed the problem with the most common measure of risk (volatility), which is the measure of how much the price of something has changed (standard deviation). To earn a higher return, we must take more risk, which again just means more price variability. Price volatility may or may not be that risky; it depends on what the money is for and when we need it. Ultimately, we care about the price that we sell at. If we are not selling, then temporary losses are not a problem. But the more frequently we need to sell, the higher the risk of turning a temporary loss into a permanent one. Volatility when making withdrawals introduces sequence of returns risk, which makes our projections much less reliable.

We then toured the most common tools we use, starting with cash. We also looked at bonds and how they work. We saw how low interest rates are challenging the traditional uses of cash and bonds.

We discussed stocks, how they are valued, what they do over the long run, the importance of your holding period, and how to think about future returns. We also looked at stocks and bonds together and when their correlation works for us and against us.

We then broke off into two tangents, first looking at how to generate income from our investments. The most significant questions to answer are 1) how much I can spend, and 2) how long will it last? There are different ways to answer those questions, with varying levels of certainty. When taking withdrawals from an investment account, the most popular method is to look at what has always worked in the past. This method led to the creation of the 4% Rule. We can also run dynamic simulations using a Monte Carlo simulation. The danger with a Monte Carlo simulation is that the outputs are only as good as the inputs, and if based on the theory of normal distribution, it can underestimate the chance of the extreme outliers that can sink such a strategy. When making withdrawals from an investment account, we have greater upside, but there is always an element of "you never know" since you never know for sure that it will work.

The second tangent was the behavioral side of investing, since the biggest determinant of our success as investors will be how we manage our emotions. The key lesson is that stocks go up over the long run but up and down in the short run. We get in trouble by trying to make stocks be something they aren't—consistent and reliable—and making ourselves do something we can't—predict what they'll do. Almost all of our problems investing in stocks come from trying to get all the gains and avoid all the losses. This desire leads us to try to time the market—selling before crashes and buying back at the bottom. While it's possible to time the market once or twice, it's nearly impossible to do it consistently, and trying usually costs us in the long run.

We then looked at ways to generate income using insurance. We first evaluated annuities. Annuities are a powerful tool as they protect against the risk of running out of money, but they come with tradeoffs and can be seriously misrepresented when sold. We briefly looked at how annuities can be used to grow our money as well, offering a nice tool that fits in between stocks and bonds.

We also looked at life insurance, the powerful tool that has been twisted beyond its original purpose. The biggest problem with life insurance is the use of illustrations and projections. Illustrations are supposed to be used to explain how the policy works, but more often, they are used to sell. As a sales tool, insurance companies have an incentive to illustrate well. When the policy fails to live up to its illustration, strategies built on illustrated values can also fail.

We finished by briefly looking at real estate, specifically at rental income and how to access the equity in our home. For the right person, using real estate to generate rental income can be fantastic, but there are unique risks that make it unsuitable for many investors. As for accessing the equity in our home, there are tools that allow us to access it without selling, but the devil is in the details. Again, as many fortunes have been lost as have been built using real estate.

Finally, we looked at ourselves and how we make decisions. The challenge is that many of the natural tendencies that help us survive lead to less than ideal financial decisions. An industry of financial planners is supposed to help us, but incentive structures within that industry put advice-givers and receivers at odds.

While we covered plenty of technical details, this book is really about making better decisions. If I had to boil down my advice to you, it would be this: Take a breath. Put the spreadsheet down. Give yourself a break. You're not going to make the decision with the best outcome every time, and no one will.

Generally speaking, when it comes to money, people want two things: 1) more of it, and 2) not to lose it. Like having dessert while trying to lose weight, this presents a cruel balance; having more of one jeopardizes the other.

I started this book by comparing the retiree to a sailor stranded at sea. They are both surrounded by the thing they need, but they're unable to trust it. When overwhelmed or faced with uncertainty, we seek confidence. Ironically, this confidence can be the very problem.

That's because confidence comes from certainty in the outcome. When we feel certain, we go all in. We try to maximize. While maximizing is great when things work out, it can lead to catastrophe when it doesn't. We must remember, when we're projecting things like how long we'll live, how much we'll spend, what our investments will do, etc., we can't have certainty, and pretending we can is harmful.

The way to handle this uncertainty isn't to deny it by recklessly storming full steam ahead. It isn't to resist it by trying to outsmart it. It also isn't to be held captive by it by putting all our money in cash and insurance. As you well know by now, the way to handle uncertainty is to embrace it.

We embrace uncertainty by building in redundancies, diversifying, and maintaining optionality. While all three take a little off the top, they are the keys to staying afloat when life doesn't go as planned.

In the end, there are no absolutes. What is right for you may be wrong for others, and vice versa. There are no free lunches. There isn't some magic product, strategy, system, or guru you must follow. Of all the balancing acts we make, how we make decisions will come down to how we answer this question, "Do I want to maximize the outcome if I'm right, or make sure I'm okay if I'm wrong?"

Certainty may be what we crave, but we can't have it. Life isn't predictable, and our financial decisions shouldn't pretend that it is. While that might sound scary, uncertainty is what makes life beautiful.

Embrace it.

ACKNOWLEDGMENTS

One of the great benefits of living in the 21st century is the number of lessons we do not have to discover for ourselves. We are fortunate to have millennia of documented experiences from which to learn.

I am grateful to the following individuals who took the time to chronicle and pass on what they have learned, shortening my own learning curve: Daniel Kahneman, Amos Tversky, Ray Dalio, Nassim Taleb, Richard Thaler, Benoit Mandelbrot, Benjamin Graham, Bill Wilson, Warren Buffett, Charlie Munger, Burton Malkiel, William Bernstein, Howard Marks, Mark Meldrum, the team at Retirement Researcher, Charles Wheelan, Shane Parrish, and Ryan Holiday. Many of their works are listed in the recommended reading.

While writing this, I was struck by the number of seemingly random comments and faces I've encountered over the years that popped into my mind. Whether it was a passing comment or a deeper conversation, the following people had a part in this book, whether they knew it or not. Mike Bemis, Dr. Barry Bryan, Nate Clark, Lorna Donatone, Sarah Gernon-Jones, Dr. Scott Linn, Michael F. Price, Chris Smith, Ryan Stewart, Matt Terry, Dr. Wayne Thomas, Tom and Amy Tipton, Jim Tonniges, Sunny Vanderbeck, and Leah Waldrum.

I must also give a special thanks to Nik Adams, whose question I mentioned in the introduction sparked the conception of this book. Our conversations kept me going.

Thank you to my colleagues at Macro. To Holly Schmidt for painfully proofreading a draft of this book that was eventually completely scrapped. To my mother, Jane, for her confidence, enthusiasm, and encouragement of this project. In a perfect example of asymmetry, her love has been far greater than what my actions deserve. Mothers are truly special.

To my wife, Karlene, you never cease to amaze me. Your attention to detail, focus, and work ethic come from a world with which I am unfamiliar. You are truly inspiring. I know how painful this process was for you. While we butted heads many times, I know you make me a better person and push me to reach my potential each and every day. I am incredibly fortunate to have you in my life.

To our clients, thank you for continuously teaching me something new. I hope you someday learn half as much from me as I have learned from you. I hope this book captures the spirit of what we try to do for you every day.

There also exists a healthy list from whom I've learned what not to do. You, too, have shortened my learning curve and are a constant source of motivation to be and do better.

Above all, there is one person who, without his influence, quite literally and figuratively, this project could have never happened: my friend, colleague, and father, Owen. It feels wrong not to put your name on this book. I feel like I got a head start in life, and I count myself incredibly fortunate to have learned from the example you have set all these years. It takes a special person to tolerate me, and at times, you were the only one who did. You've encouraged me to pursue my questions. While our discussions are often (in)tense, and we certainly don't always agree, I am grateful for your open mind. The older I get, the more I appreciate the sacrifices you made, both personally and professionally. The decision to work together has not been without its bumps, but I would have it no other way. I love you.

ABOUT THE AUTHOR

Taylor Stewart is an investment advisor representative with Macro Wealth Advisors, a Registered Investment Advisor located in the Dallas-Fort Worth metroplex. Taylor grew up in Lincoln, NE, down the street from his future wife, Karlene. Taylor completed his undergraduate studies at the University of Oklahoma, earning a Bachelor of Business Administration in Accounting and Finance, and completed his graduate studies at Southern Methodist University, where he earned a Master of Science in Accounting. Upon graduation, Taylor began his career as an auditor at PricewaterhouseCoopers (PwC), spending just over three years in the financial services practice auditing REITs, pensions, mutual funds, hedge funds, and private equity funds. In the fall of 2016, Taylor decided to follow his heart, leaving PwC to join his father, Owen, at Macro Wealth Advisors.

Outside of work, Taylor is an avid reader and golfer and enjoys spending time with his wife, Karlene, their daughter, Perri, and their dog, Arthur.

An Invitation to Connect

I'd love to hear from you and welcome any and all thoughts, questions, and comments. You can reach me at:

taylor@embracinguncertaintybook.com
www.EmbracingUncertaintyBook.com

About Macro Wealth Advisors

Macro Wealth Advisors is a Registered Investment Advisor (RIA) located in the Dallas-Fort Worth metroplex. Investment advisory services are offered through Macro Wealth Advisors, Inc., an independent registered investment advisory firm. Insurance services are offered through Macro Wealth Concepts, Inc.

Macro prides itself on being 1) fiduciaries, 2) independent, and 3) strategy agnostic. As an independent wealth management firm capable of offering financial plans, investment management, and access to insurance, Macro can help people whether they are looking for a long-term advisory relationship or simply need help making sense of what they have.

RECOMMENDED READING

(Categorizations are my own)

Finance/Investing/Economics/Statistics
The Intelligent Investor by Benjamin Graham
Naked Economics by Charles Wheelan
Naked Statistics by Charles Wheelan
A Random Walk Down Wall Street by Burton Malkiel
The Signal and the Noise by Nate Silver
Mastering the Market Cycle by Howard Marks
The Most Important Thing by Howard Marks
The Flaw of Averages by Sam Savage
How Not to Be Wrong by Jordan Ellenberg

Decision Making/Psychology
Thinking Fast and Slow by Daniel Kahneman
Noise by Daniel Kahneman, Olivier Sibony, and Cass Sunstein
Principles by Ray Dalio
The Paradox of Choice by Barry Schwartz
Why Smart People Make Big Money Mistakes by Gary Belsky and Thomas Gilovich
Nudge by Richard Thaler and Cass Sunstein
The Psychology of Money by Morgan Housel
Influence by Robert Cialdini
Subliminal by Leonard Mlodinow

Philosophy

The Obstacle is the Way by Ryan Holiday
The Great Mental Models by Shane Parrish
Enough by John C. Bogle
The Subtle Art of Not Giving a F*ck by Mark Manson
Everything is F*cked by Mark Manson
The Beginning of Infinity by David Deutsch
The Denial of Death by Ernest Becker

Randomness

Fooled by Randomness by Nassim Nicholas Taleb
The Black Swan by Nassim Nicholas Taleb
Antifragile by Nassim Nicholas Taleb
Skin in the Game by Nassim Nicholas Taleb
The Misbehavior of Markets by Benoit Mandelbrot
The Drunkards Walk by Leonard Mlodinow

History

The Origin of Financial Crises by George Cooper
The Ascent of Money by Niall Ferguson
Americana by Bhu Srinivasan
When Genius Failed by Roger Lowenstein
Against the Gods by Peter Bernstein
A Man for All Markets by Edward O. Thorp
The Man Who Solved the Markets by Gregory Zuckerman

NOTES

Introduction
[1] Tantalus is a character in Greek mythology. His punishment was to stand in a pool of water below a fruit tree with low branches. Whenever he reached up for the fruit, the branches raised just out of his reach. Whenever he bent down to get a drink, the water receded, again just out of his reach.
The name Tantalus became the source of the English word *tantalize*, which essentially means temptation without satisfaction.

[2] Another good example of this concept: Doubling your life savings because you bet on black at the roulette table is a great outcome but is not a great decision.

[3] This distinction between measurable risk and unmeasurable uncertainty was made by Frank Knight in his 1921 book *Risk, Uncertainty, and Profit*

[4] The Serenity Prayer was written by Reinhold Niebuhr in the 1930s. The full first half of the prayer is:

> *Grant me the serenity to*
> *accept the things I cannot change*
> *courage to change the things I can;*
> *and wisdom to know the difference.*

This "prayer" makes for pretty good financial advice as well.

[5] Psychologist and Author Adam Grant calls the desire for clear definitions of right and wrong *binary bias* and has this to say, "No charged issue is so simple to have only two sides." (Parrish, Shane, host. "#112 Adam Grant: Rethinking Your Position" The Knowledge Project, 1 June 2021)

Chapter 1: Groundwork
[1] The technical definition of money is something that is a 1) store of value, 2) unit of account, and 3) medium of exchange.

[2] Modes of transportation that save time cost more to build too, which shows that moving through more space in less time is a costly ambition.

[3] There are many forms of this saying, such as bad is stronger than good. The definition given by Kahneman is, *when directly compared or weighed against each other, losses loom larger than gains.* (Kahneman, Daniel. (2011), *Thinking Fast and Slow.* New York: Farrar, Straus and Giroux.)

[4] This graphic illustrates the concept of Prospect Theory, which is the formal and intentionally ambiguous name for loss aversion. (Kahneman, Danie (2011), *Thinking Fast and Slow.* New York: Farrar, Straus and Giroux.)

[5] A marketing executive once told me, "We sell unhappiness because people will act to fix unhappiness." That's part of why the attitude, "I'll be happy if I…" persists. However you finish that sentence, ask yourself, will you really?

Chapter 3: Forecasting

[1] Jabbi, Bastiaansen, & Keysers, 2008

[2] The book *Noise* makes an intriguing distinction between prediction and judgment. They start by defining judgment as, "measurement in which the instrument is the human mind." (p. 39) They also say, "a matter of judgment is one with some uncertainty about the answer and where we allow for the possibility that reasonable and competent people might disagree." (p. 43) When we make a prediction, however, we "attempt to come close to a true value." (p. 41). They also interestingly point out that a prediction does not have to be about the future. For example, it could be about an existing medical condition that already exists, but is unknown to the predictor. (p. 41) Kahneman, Daniel, Olivier Sibony, and Cass R. Sunstein. (2021), *Noise: A Flaw in Human Judgment.* New York: Little, Brown, Spark.

[3] This quote was taken from the book *Noise.* In regard to unverifiable judgments, "The quality of such judgments can be assessed only by the quality of the thought process that produces them." Kahneman, Daniel, Olivier Sibony, and Cass R. Sunstein. (2021), *Noise: A Flaw in Human Judgment* (p. 362). New York: Little, Brown, Spark.

[4] Deutsch, David. (2011), *The Beginning of Infinity: Explanations that Transform the World.* London: Penguin.

[5] Kahneman, Daniel, Olivier Sibony, and Cass R. Sunstein. (2021), *Noise: A Flaw in Human Judgment* (p. 153). New York: Little, Brown, Spark.

[6] This describes a chaotic system and when relationships are "non-linear," meaning a small change can have a huge effect. Prediction of chaotic systems are much harder. This concept has been popularized as the butterfly effect. Mathematician and meteorologist Edward Lorenz brought this to fame with

the question "Does the flap of a butterfly's wings in Brazil set off a tornado in Texas?"

[7] Taleb, Nassim Nicholas. (2005). *Fooled by Randomness*. New York: Random House.

[8] There are several versions of this story, but I came across the "Baltimore Stockbroker" version in Ellenberg, Jordan. (2014), *How Not to Be Wrong: The Power of Mathematical Thinking* (p. 95-99). New York: Penguin Books.

[9] Mutual fund incubation is a well-known issue, but I again came across it in Ellenberg, Jordan. (2014), *How Not to Be Wrong: The Power of Mathematical Thinking* (p. 97). New York: Penguin Books.

[10] Kahneman, Daniel, Olivier Sibony, and Cass R. Sunstein. (2021) *Noise: A Flaw in Human Judgment* (p. 158). New York: Little, Brown, Spark.

[11] This has to do with processing fluency and how our brain doesn't have to try as hard when the "facts" already align with our beliefs.

[12] This is the logic behind "disproving the null hypothesis." We assume something is true and then prove that it is not.

[13] Taleb, Nassim Nicholas. (2010), *The Black Swan: The Impact of the Highly Improbable*. New York: Random House.

[14] ibid.

[15] ibid.

[16] Taleb, Nassim Nicholas. (2005), *Fooled by Randomness*. New York: Random House.

[17] An insightful look at survivorship bias can be found at: Dimensional. Why Worry About Survivorship Bias? October 12, 2020. https://www.dimensional.com/us-en/insights/why-worry-about-survivorship-bias.

[18] Taleb, Nassim Nicholas. (2010), *The Black Swan: The Impact of the Highly Improbable*. New York: Random House.

[19] While I could not trace the exact origin of this quote, I believe it was inspired by David Deutsch's comments in Deutsch, David. (2011), *The Beginning of Infinity: Explanations That Transform the World*. New York: Penguin Books.

[20] Ellenberg, Jordan. (2014), *How Not to Be Wrong: The Power of Mathematical Thinking* (p. 198). New York: Penguin Books.

[21] Savage, Sam. L. (2012), *The Flaw of Averages*. Hoboken: John Wiley & Sons, Inc.

[22] Damodaran, A. (2021, January 20), *Historical Returns*. Retrieved from NYU Stern: http://pages.stern.nyu.edu/~adamodar/New_Home_Page/datafile/histretSP.html

[23] ibid.

[24] Taleb tells how Danny Kahneman told him, "There are ample empirical findings to the effect that providing someone with a random numerical forecast increases his risk taking, even if the person knows the projections are random." Taleb, Nassim Nicholas. (2012), *Antifragile* (p. 135). New York: Random House.

[25] This is completely anecdotal, but I read a handful of biographies one summer and was amazed by how much of what happened in these great businesses and peoples' lives was not part of the original plan.

[26] Kahneman, Daniel, Olivier Sibony, and Cass R. Sunstein. (2021) *Noise: A Flaw in Human Judgment*. New York: Little, Brown, Spark.

[27] The ability to retrospectively explain things creates the *illusion of predictability*.

[28] Taleb, Nassim Nicholas. (2018), *Skin in the Game*. New York: Random House.

Chapter 4: Longevity

[1] The Health Inequality Project. (2020, May 26). *The Health Inequality Project*. Retrieved from The Health Inequality Project: https://healthinequality.org/

[2] -Chart calculated using data from: https://www.ssa.gov/oact/STATS/table4c6.html
-Idea for this chart based on work by Michael Kitces at Nerds Eye View and can be found at: from https://www.kitces.com/blog/life-expectancy-assumptions-in-retirement-plans-singles-couples-and-survivors/

[3] Based on: Society of Actuaries RP-2014 Mortality Table projected with Mortality Improvement Scale MP-2017 as of 2018. Fidelity. (2020, February 2). *Longevity and retirement*. Retrieved from Fidelity: https://www.fidelity.com/viewpoints/retirement/longevity

Chapter 5: Introduction to Outflows

[1] Blanchett, D. (2013), *Estimating the True Cost of Retirement*. Chicago: Morningstar.

[2] Bernicke, T. (June 2005), Reality Retirement Planning: A New Paradigm for an Old Science. *Journal of Financial Planning*.

[3] Tacchino, K., & Salzman, C. (February 1999), Do Accumulation Models Overstate What's Needed to Retire? *Journal of Financial Planning*, 62-73.

[4] JPMorgan Asset Management. (2020), *Guide to Retirement 2020 Edition*.

[5] U.S. Bureau of Labor Statistics. (2019, September 10), *Consumer*

Expenditure Surveys. Retrieved from U.S. Bureau of Labor Statistics: https://www.bls.gov/cex/tables.htm

Chapter 6: Spending
[1] Blanchett, D. (2013), *Estimating the True Cost of Retirement.* Chicago: Morningstar.

Chapter 7: Inflation
[1] This comment is specific to spending. Inflation will still affect investment and property values, and the effect could be negative or positive depending on your exposure to them.
[2] Investopedia. (2020, April 23), *Consumer Price Index.* Retrieved from Investopedia: https://www.investopedia.com/terms/c/consumerpriceindex.asp
[3] https://usdebtclock.org/

Chapter 8: Insurance
[1] How much insurance companies should charge requires them to find the "goldilocks premium." Not too much they lose business. Not too little they lose money.
[2] While this is a fairly ubiquitous saying, I originally heard it from Roger Cantu of OneAmerica.
[3] After writing this, I came across a very similar description in Meadows, Richard. (2020), Optionality: How to Survive and Thrive in a Volatile World (p. 231). Thales Press. Kindle Edition. Any similarities in content are coincidental.

Chapter 9: Health Care
[1] Genworth. (n.d.), *Cost of Care Survey.* Retrieved from genworth.com: https://www.genworth.com/aging-and-you/finances/cost-of-care.html
[2] Genworth. (n.d.), *Cost of Care Survey.* Retrieved from genworth.com: https://www.genworth.com/aging-and-you/finances/cost-of-care.html
[3] PricewaterhouseCoopers. (2016), *The formal cost of long-term care services: How can society meet a growing need?* Retrieved from https://www.pwc.com/us/en/industries/insurance/library/long-term-care-services.html
[4] -The U.S. Department of Health and Human Services estimates that 69% of retirees will need some level of care.
https://acl.gov/ltc/basic-needs/how-much-care-will-you-need
-PricewaterhouseCoopers stated, "There is more than a 50 percent chance that an individual at age 65 will eventually require some form of formal paid

care over his or her lifetime"
https://www.pwc.com/us/en/insurance/assets/pwc-insurance-cost-of-long-term-care.pdf
-Morningstar stated, "70%: Percentage of people turning age 65 who will need some type of long-term-care services in their lifetimes."
https://www.morningstar.com/articles/1013929/100-must-know-statistics-about-long-term-care-pandemic-edition
-AARP states, "On average, 52 percent of people who turn 65 today will develop a severe disability that will require LTSS at some point.
https://www.aarp.org/content/dam/aarp/ppi/2017-01/Fact%20Sheet%20Long-Term%20Support%20and%20Services.pdf
-An important thing to note about these statistics. they vary on the type and length of care used to determine their estimates. Some mention needing long-term care in general, others mention needing paid-long-term care. The takeaway is this. You are very likely to need some assistance, and you are likely to need some paid assistance.

[5] The *end of history illusion* is the belief that you have experienced significant personal growth and changes in taste up to the present moment, but will not substantially grow or mature in the future. This causes people to have a hard time envisioning how they will change. Author and psychologist Dan Gilbert has done incredible work on this topic.

[6] American Association for Long-Term Care Insurance. (2020), *Long-Term Care Insurance Facts - Statistics*. Retrieved from American Association for Long-Term Care Insurance: https://www.aaltci.org/long-term-care-insurance/learning-center/fast-facts.php

[7] American Council on Aging. (2020, January 20), *Texas Medicaid Income & Asset Limits for Nursing Homes & In-Home Long Term Care*. Retrieved from American Council on Aging: https://www.medicaidplanningassistance.org/medicaid-eligibility-texas/

Chapter 13: Social Security
[1] Social Security Administration. (2020, April), *Updated Baseline for Actuarial Status of the OASI and DI Trust Funds, Reflecting Pandemic and Recession Effects*. Retrieved from Social Security: https://www.ssa.gov/policy/trust-funds-summary.html

[2] Social Security. (n.d.), *Life Expectancy for Social Security*. Retrieved from Social Security: https://www.ssa.gov/history/lifeexpect.html

[3] Social Security. (n.d.), *Life Expectancy for Social Security*. Retrieved from Social Security: https://www.ssa.gov/history/lifeexpect.html

[4] Social Security. (n.d.), *Ratio of Covered Workers to Beneficiaries*. Retrieved from Social Security: https://www.ssa.gov/history/ratios.html

Chapter 16: Risk and Return

[1] Marks, Howard. (2013), *The Most Important Thing Illuminated*. Chichester: Columbia Business School Publishing.

[2] Wicklin, R. (2019, July 22), *Extreme values: What is an extreme value for normally distributed data?* Retrieved from sas: https://blogs.sas.com/content/iml/2019/07/22/extreme-value-normal-data.html

[3] Damodaran, A. (2021, January 20), *Historical Returns*. Retrieved from NYU Stern: http://pages.stern.nyu.edu/~adamodar/New_Home_Page/datafile/histretSP.html

[4] Cooper, George. (2008), *The Origin of Financial Crises*. New York: Random House, Inc.

[5] Meadows, Richard. (2020), Optionality: How to Survive and Thrive in a Volatile World (p. 263). Thales Press. Kindle Edition.

[6] A more accurate distribution model is the power law distribution that follows the concepts of fractal geometry. A fascinating topic, I highly recommend Benoit Mandelbrot's book *The Misbehavior of Markets* to learn more.

[7] Meadows, Richard. (2020), Optionality: How to Survive and Thrive in a Volatile World (p. 279). Thales Press. Kindle Edition.

[8] The finance industry knows this. The most popular measure that differentiates "harmful" volatility from total overall volatility is the *Sortino Ratio*.

[9] Marks, Howard. (2013), *The Most Important Thing Illuminated*. Chichester: Columbia Business School Publishing.

[10] Belvedere, M. J. (2020, February 24), *CNBC*. Retrieved from Warren Buffett's sobering advice: 'Reaching for yield is really stupid' but 'very human': https://www.cnbc.com/2020/02/24/warren-buffett-reaching-for-yield-is-really-stupid-but-very-human.html

Chapter 19: Stocks

[1] Investopedia. (2021, January 9), *Top 10 S&P 500 Stocks by Index Weight*. Retrieved from Investopedia: https://www.investopedia.com/top-10-s-and-p-500-stocks-by-index-weight-4843111

[2] Housel, Morgan. (2020), *The Psychology of Money*. Petersfield: Harriman House.

[3] Malkiel, Burton. (2015), *A Random Walk Down Wall Street*. New York: Norton.

[4] The CAPE ratio was created by Robert Shiller and is popularly referred to as the Shiller PE Ratio

[5] Tresidder, Todd. (2010), *How Much Money Do I Need to Retire?* Financial-Mentor.com.

[6] *Shiller PE Ratio*. (2021, August 30), Retrieved from Multpl.com: https://www.multpl.com/shiller-pe

Chapter 20: Blended Portfolio

[1] This chart was calculated using 3-year rolling year-end returns from the data provided by the source below. Admittedly, this is not the best way to calculate correlations, but it does show how correlations change over time, which is the purpose of the chart.
Damodaran, A. (2021, January 20), *Historical Returns*. Retrieved from NYU Stern: http://pages.stern.nyu.edu/~adamodar/New_Home_Page/datafile/histretSP.html

Chapter 21: Creating Income From Investments

[1] -Withdrawal rates calculated using data from: Damodaran, A. (2021, January 20), *Historical Returns*. Retrieved from NYU Stern: http://pages.stern.nyu.edu/~adamodar/New_Home_Page/datafile/histretSP.html
-Idea for this chart based on work by Michael Kitces at Nerds Eye View and can be found at: https://www.kitces.com/blog/safe-withdrawal-rate-calculator-software-big-picture-timeline-app-reviews/

[2] -Values calculated using data from: Damodaran, A. (2021, January 20), *Historical Returns*. Retrieved from NYU Stern: http://pages.stern.nyu.edu/~adamodar/New_Home_Page/datafile/histretSP.html
-Idea for this chart based on work by Michael Kitces at Nerds Eye View and can be found at: https://www.kitces.com/blog/the-ratcheting-safe-withdrawal-rate-a-more-dominant-version-of-the-4-rule/

[3] -Withdrawal rates calculated from Damodaran, A. (2021, January 20), *Historical Returns*. Retrieved from NYU Stern: http://pages.stern.nyu.edu/~adamodar/New_Home_Page/datafile/histretSP.html
-CAPE Ratio data pulled from: https://www.multpl.com/shiller-pe/table/by-year
-Idea for this chart based on work by Michael Kitces at Nerds Eye View and can be found at: https://www.kitces.com/wp-content/uploads/2014/11/Kitces-Report-May-2008.pdf

[4] https://www.financialplanningassociation.org/article/journal/OCT14-retirement-planning-targeting-safe-withdrawal-rates
[5] https://www.rbcwm-usa.com/resources/file-687839.pdf
[6] S&P Global. (2020, July 23), *S&P 500 Dividend Aristocrats*. Retrieved from S&P Dow Jones Indices: https://www.spglobal.com/spdji/en/indices/strategy/sp-500-dividend-aristocrats/#overview

Chapter 22: Investing in Stocks

[1] Damodaran, A. (2021, January 20), *Historical Returns*. Retrieved from NYU Stern: http://pages.stern.nyu.edu/~adamodar/New_Home_Page/datafile/histretSP.html
[2] Sit, Harry. (2012, October 3), *Does The DALBAR Study Grossly Overstate The Behavior Gap?* Retrieved from Kitces.com:
https://www.kitces.com/blog/does-the-dalbar-study-grossly-overstate-the-behavior-gap-guest-post/
[3] There is one catch to this. With the advent of index funds, any investor can buy the "market" for an incredibly cheap price. So, if a money manager can do better than you, but a money manager can't (consistently) do better than the market (especially net of fees), and you have the ability to buy the market, why wouldn't you just buy the market? (To be clear, this is for the long-term buy and hold growth investor who only wishes to mimic an index of their choosing. If their needs go beyond this, for example, needing to blend allocations between stocks and bonds, rebalance, or make withdrawals, then a professional may be necessary.)

Chapter 23: Annuities

[1] In this example, the drop between life-only and 20-year certain is not significant because the couple is 65 so the insurance company already expects to be paying for 20 years. If the couple was 75, then a 20-year certain annuity would extend how long they are expecting to pay, and the drop in income would be more significant.
[2] Pfau, Wade. (2021), *Retirement Planning Guidebook*. Vienna, Virginia. Retirement Researcher Media.

Chapter 29: Get Out of My (Own) Way!

[1] Thaler, Richard. (2015), *Misbehaving: The Making of Behavioral Economics*. W. W. Norton & Company.
[2] While this list is fairly ubiquitous, I came across it formally organized in a webinar by Dr. Alex Murguia of Retirement Researcher.

[3] (Kahneman, Daniel. (2011), *Thinking Fast and Slow.* New York: Farrar, Straus and Giroux.)

[4] This event happened in May 2021 at NorthPark Center in Dallas, TX. https://dfw.cbslocal.com/2021/05/31/skateboard-fear-active-shooter-dallas-northpark-center-custody/

[5] Fooled by randomness is now a widely used term but was brought to fame in Taleb, Nassim Nicholas. (2005). *Fooled by Randomness.* New York: Random House.

[6] Speaking of science, haven't some of the greatest scientific discoveries in history, like the motions of planets, been a result of observing and recognizing patterns? Absolutely, but remember, the motions of planets are governed by the laws of physics. Unfortunately (actually, probably fortunately) the behavior of humans and when they choose to buy and sell is not as predictable, which means any patterns we identify may just be short-lived coincidences. Isaac Newton, the polymath who also lost a significant amount of money in the South Sea Bubble corroborates this point when he said, "I can calculate the motion of heavenly bodies, but not the madness of people."

[7] Kahneman, Daniel, Olivier Sibony, and Cass R. Sunstein. (2021), *Noise: A Flaw in Human Judgment* (p. 176-187). New York: Little, Brown, Spark.

[8] Kirsten Grind, T. M. (2017, October 25), *The Morningstar Mirage.* Retrieved from Wall Street Journal: https://www.wsj.com/articles/the-morningstar-mirage-1508946687

[9] Daniel Kahneman provided the inspiration for this example. He first made this realization when working with Israeli Air Force pilots.

[10] Housel, Morgan. (2020), *The Psychology of Money* (p. 12). Petersfield: Harriman House.

[11] A lot of fantastic work has been done on this topic. The "original" work on satisficing can be found at: Simon, Herbert. (1956). Rational choice and the structure of the environment. *Psychological Review.* 63(2). 129-138. This concept was also captured in the 2001 paper titled "Doing Better and Feeling Worse" by Sheena Iyengar, Rachael Wells, and Barry Schwartz. Dr. Barry Schwartz's book, *The Paradox of Choice,* provides an excellent tutorial of the differences between being a maximizer or satisficer and the impact of "choice" on our decisions.

[12] https://www.nirandfar.com/illusion-of-control

[13] Gary Belsky, Thomas Gilovich. (2009). *Why Smart People Make Big Money Mistakes and How to Correct Them: Lessons from the Life-Changing Science of Behavioral Economics.* New York: Simon & Schuster.

[14] ibid.

[15] Multiple studies of people dying have found that their biggest regret were

the things they didn't do, like starting a business, taking a vacation, asking that person on a date, etc. In relation to what we're discussing in this chapter however, most people didn't regret "not buying more things."
[16] Housel, Morgan. (2020), *The Psychology of Money*. Petersfield: Harriman House.
[17] Daniel Kahneman, J. L. (1990), Experimental Tests of the Endowment Effect and the Coase Theorem. *Journal of Political Economy*, 1325-1348
[18] Godin, Seth. (2007), *The Dip*. New York: Penguin Books.
[19] To be clear, I am paraphrasing, and this is not a direct quote.
[20] Kahneman, Daniel, Olivier Sibony, and Cass R. Sunstein. (2021), *Noise: A Flaw in Human Judgment* (p. 326-327). New York: Little, Brown, Spark.

Chapter 30: Advisors
[1] September 2020 cover of Financial Planning Magazine. https://www.financial-planning.com/digital-edition/september-2020
[2] Taleb, Nassim Nicholas. (2010), *The Black Swan: The Impact of the Highly Improbable* (p. 369). New York: Random House.
[3] Parrish, Shane. (2020, February), *The Illusory Truth Effect: Why We Believe Fake News, Conspiracy Theories and Propaganda*. Retrieved from Farnam Street: https://fs.blog/2020/02/illusory-truth-effect/
[4] Engelmann JB, Capra CM, Noussair C, Berns GS (2009) Expert Financial Advice Neurobiologically "Offloads" Financial Decision-Making under Risk. PLoS ONE 4(3): e4957. doi:10.1371/journal.pone.0004957
To summarize the research, when making decisions on our own (without advice), the areas of our brain that involve probability weighting is active. When receiving "advice," these areas are inactive, even when advice is bad. This why the term "offloading" is used.
A great article that summarizes these findings and includes an interview with one of the authors of the study, can be found at: https://jasonzweig.com/this-is-your-brain-on-investment-advice/
[5] Martin, Stephen, and Joseph Marks. (2019), *Messengers: Who We Listen To, Who We Don't, and Why*. New York; PublicAffairs.
[6] Parrish, Shane. (2020, March 8), Brain Food No. 359.
[7] Kahneman, Daniel, Olivier Sibony, and Cass R. Sunstein. (2021), *Noise: A Flaw in Human Judgment* (p. 235). New York: Little, Brown, Spark.
[8] The problem becomes systemic (adds to social proof) because of how the compensation structure in the industry works. It is possible for an advisor to earn a "cut" of other advisors' production. As a result, many top producers create selling systems—essentially passing on the methods and practices they used themselves—that other advisors adhere to, which allows the top

producers to build a small army of disciples whose production they can feed off of.

[9] It's important to understand how designations gain value. They gain value when other people think they are valuable. This is obviously the case with J.D. and M.D. But those designations are usually required in order to work. When a designation is not required, people must be convinced that the designation is valuable. A way to convince people something is valuable, is to tell them it is. This is why a designation provider has an incentive to advertise and market their designation.

[10] Kahneman, Daniel, Olivier Sibony, and Cass R. Sunstein. (2021), *Noise: A Flaw in Human Judgment* (p. 369). New York: Little, Brown, Spark.

[11] Kahneman, Daniel, Olivier Sibony, and Cass R. Sunstein. (2021), *Noise: A Flaw in Human Judgment* (p. 228). New York: Little, Brown, Spark.

[12] Jurnecka, R. (2020, January 10), *The '68 Mustang Bullitt Movie Car Just Became the Most Expensive Ford Mustang Ever Sold.* Retrieved from Automobilmag.com: https://www.automobilemag.com/news/original-bullitt-movie-1968-ford-mustang-auction/